CHARLIE & ME
IN VAL-PARADIS

For Hilary & Steve Corless
With fond memories
of our time together
in the Lot
Maureen & Charlie
September 2008

CHARLIE & ME
IN VAL-PARADIS

MAUREEN CASHMAN

SIMON & SCHUSTER
AUSTRALIA   A CBS COMPANY

Charlie & Me in Val-Paradis

First published in Australia in 2008 by

Simon & Schuster Australia Pty Limited
Suite 2, Lower Ground Floor
14-16 Suakin Street
Pymble NSW 2073

A CBS Company

Sydney New York London Toronto

Visit our website at www.simonandschuster.com.au

© Maureen Cashman 2008

National Library of Australia Cataloguing-in-Publication entry

AUTHOR: Cashman, Maureen.

TITLE: Charlie & me in Val-Paradis / Maureen Cashman.

ISBN: 9780731813674 (pbk.)

SUBJECTS: Immigrants – Cultural assimilation – France – Biography.
                  Wildfires – Australian Capital Territory.
                  France, Southern – Biography – Anecdotes.

DEWEY NUMBER: 920.72

Cover and internal design: Xou Creative

Internal illustrations: Walter Deffner courtesy of Sigrid Deffner.

Printed in Australia by Griffin Press

The paper used to produce this book is a natural, recyclable product made from wood grown in sustainable plantation forests. The manufacturing processes conform to the environmental regulations in the country of origin.

10 9 8 7 6 5 4 3 2 1

For the people of Espagnac-Sainte-Eulalie,
past, present and future.

CONTENTS

ACKNOWLEDGEMENTS

Many people gave Charlie and me moral, physical and material support from the beginning to the end of our adventure in Val-Paradis, and later in the process of transforming our story from a mostly personal to a public one. Many figure in the narrative and their importance in our story is obvious. I hesitate to single out individuals; however, I risk naming some, trusting that those I omit will see themselves as naturally included in the larger groups of family, friends and professional people who have contributed to our experience and this book.

For their help in the practicalities of getting to Val-Paradis, staying there and getting back, I thank Florence Beilby, Judy and David Wilson, Rosalind and Alan Macdonald, Gill Gould and Hugh Smith, Fleur and Brian Horan, Sue and Robin Miller, John and Gavan Cashman, Kath and Graeme Ward, Roger Hine, Barry Sreeves and Marlene Hall. I am particularly grateful to the latter for her consistent intuitive practical assistance, including periodically sending me examples of expatriate literature which gave me thought about what I did and didn't want to do in this book.

In addition to their practical help, these and other friends and relations encouraged my efforts to communicate the essence of our experience in Val-Paradis. While they are too many to mention by name, I would nevertheless like to acknowledge the late Naomi Kronenberg who, until March 2004, expressed delight in our adventures while knowing that she wouldn't be able to 'stay' with us until the end.

I thank my fellow expatriates of the Lot for their warm friendship and contribution to our experience, the Kempleys, the Robinsons, Sue Wilson, the van Vliets, the Corlesses, Milou and Eric, and Sigrid Deffner. I am infinitely grateful to the latter for providing her late husband Walter's drawings to illustrate this book. It seems that he and I, though from different backgrounds and lifetimes and never having met one another, have collaborated to express a mutual love of a special place.

For entering into my plans and helping me to achieve them, I thank Martine Benet-Bagreaux, all the other inhabitants of Espagnac-Sainte-Eulalie, Nicole Puel and Line Bresson. For their time, patience and generosity of spirit in sharing some of their stories with me, I again thank Martine, as well as Roger Seigneur, Thierry and Jacotte Dubuisson, Jacqueline Bonzani, Maxim and Antoinette Liauzun, André Pelaprat, Alain and Martine Rochefort, Roger Sudres, Gaby Senac, Solange Cabrignac, Mimi Benet, Rolande Morgues and Georgette Delfour. I also thank the latter for letting me use her late husband's notes on the deliberations of the *conseil municipal* of Espagnac-Sainte-Eulalie from 1839 to 1975.

M. Delfour's notes, Mme Pernet-Lauzur's book on *Espagnac-Sainte-Eulalie* and the *Encyclopédie Bonneton Lot* provided most of the historical background contained in this book. I was also propelled to interesting places and information by those stalwart travel publications, the *Rough Guide to France*, the *Rough Guide to the Dordogne and the Lot*, and the Lonely Planet publications, *France* and *Walking in France*. I found detailed information on villages, towns, natural features and walking circuits from guides and pamphlets produced by the Comité Départmental du Tourisme du Lot, the Communauté de Communes Vallée-Causse and the Parc Naturel des Causses du Quercy.

I have to thank everyone who read and commented on various drafts of this book while it was in progress – Sue Wilson, Sue Spiller, Marlene Hall, Hugh Smith, Gill Gould, Noel Simpson, Florence

Beilby, Sue Farrelly, Pat Lavelle and Keren Lavelle. In the stages of assessment, polishing, finding a publisher, editing and producing it, I thank Dorothy Johnstone, Lois Calvert, Anne Matthews and Janet Hutchinson, as well as the team at Simon and Schuster (Australia), Franscois McHardy, Justine Joffe, Carolyn Walsh, Katherine Burnitt, Karen Young and the team at Xou Creative. Lastly, I would like to thank Jennifer Anderssen-Moll for providing photographs that were adapted for the design.

My heartfelt thanks to all. This book has been a labour of love, in many, many ways.

FREIGHT FRIGHT

It was the correct address, 5, rue du Circle, but the place looked deserted. An empty car park. A row of anonymous buildings with inscrutable doors and windows. Plastic bottles and bags wedged in the angles of a cyclone wire fence at one end of the precinct. Drifts of dirty snow, patterned by two sets of car tracks: one coming in; one going out, as my taxi receded through the blowing sheets of snow in the direction of Terminal One. I pulled the hood of my jacket over my cap and tried to keep calm. Where could he be?

Scanning the buildings again, this time I spied the back end of a truck around a corner. Maybe the driver could help. I left my bags where the taxi driver had put them down in the snow and walked gingerly over the icy roadway to where the truck was, trying to summon the words to enlist the help of an uninvolved *camionneur* in the search for my missing poodle. In French. A wasted effort, because the truck driver seemed to be missing as well.

My throat constricted. How could this have happened? After the months of work and organisation and the help of friends to prepare my house for letting and to find tenants. After the frantic activity of the last weeks and days to pack and store the entire contents – the equipment, tools, hard and soft furniture, books, kitchenware, linen – under some of my friends' houses. After all the visits to the vet for Charlie's microchip, rabies and other vaccinations, and the blood tests. After the business with the animal transport company, the form-filling, making sure we had the right kind of crate for the long journey. After acquiring Irish citizenship and a European passport, thanks to my Irish grandmother, as an insurance against the possibility that Charlie would be able to remain in France but I might not. After long conversations with officials from the Quarantine Service to make sure I understood the requirements for bringing a dog into Australia from France, whenever I decided to return. It didn't matter, the officials explained, that the dog would have gone to France from Australia in the first place.

And now, after all that anxiety, effort and expense, how could I have ended up here, stranded in the godforsaken wasteland surrounding Charles de Gaulle Airport, and Charlie have ended up God knew where? I swallowed hard; I couldn't allow myself to cry.

A thick PVC curtain hung on the side of the building next to the truck. I dragged one edge out far enough to slip inside into a cavernous space, dim and even colder than the car park. I squinted up into the frigid vapours swirling under the roof high overhead. There, suspended from steel beams, were scores of bovine carcasses, monstrous stalactites glowing sickly white, yellow, red and purple in the gloom.

'Well, he doesn't seem to be here, at least,' I muttered to myself grimly. 'Too small.'

Outside, I leaned for a few moments against the side of the building facing the car park, trying to push through the panic that gripped my stomach. Eventually, I made my way back to the spot where my bags sat in the snow. I stood there, gazing at the buildings, wondering what to do next.

'We'll just have to wait,' I said, as if it were Charlie sitting patiently beside me in his usual way, instead of the lifeless bags.

In the distance, planes took off and landed on the runways. Here, the only movement, apart from little flurries of snow across the empty space, was the flapping of a piece of paper attached to one of the doors of a building opposite the car park. After a while, it annoyed me so much, I left the bags again and went over to tear it off.

It was headed *Note au Public*, streaked and torn, the print so faded that it took me even longer to decipher it than the level of my

French usually allowed. I gathered from its terse message that the freight offices for live animal imports had moved to another address two months previously. The new address, *10 rue du F nt me*, was partly obliterated, as was the changed phone number.

One thing was clear: I was in the wrong place. It might have been the Moon.

I heard a soft whirring, and saw a silver BMW slide quietly along the other side of the cyclone wire fence like a space capsule coming into dock. The doors opened and two dark-clad figures, one tall, one short, got out and stood against the fence. I couldn't see their faces, but I knew who they were.

I walked over to the fence, doing my best to smile at seeing them again.

'Thank goodness you're here.'

'What is this place, Maureen?' asked David. 'And what are we doing here?'

Well, I began to explain hoarsely, the freight office address I had been given by the export agency in Canberra was a cold store full of megalithic cadavers. I'd been at the passenger terminal since the plane landed three hours ago, trying to get someone at the said fright, sorry, *freight*, office to answer the phone so I wouldn't have to wait outside in the snow before they opened the office. The man in the luggage office at Terminal One speculated that someone would be at the freight office after 8.30am. If they were, they didn't answer the phone. The luggage man found another number in the airport computer directory, and that number didn't answer either. So I decided to go to rue du Circle anyway and phone Judy and David Wilson to ask them to get out of bed on this miserable Saturday morning, drive to Charles de Gaulle Airport and pick us up. So here we were. But the freight office wasn't. It had moved, apparently. And where was my bloody dog?

'We'll find him,' said Judy calmly, ignoring my hysteria. 'Let's get your luggage over to the car. What's that other address?'

Rue du Fantasme? Fantoche? Fantome? wasn't easy to find, because the new freight arrangements at CDG were still, apparently, fairly fluid, and the road signs were not very informative, but we ended up in the car park of the building next door to the correct one.

Over a little concrete wall, up some steps, into a bright new office. The young woman at the desk handed me Charlie's papers, the very papers I had given the exporter in Canberra thirty or forty hours ago. Charlie must be very near; perhaps just on the other side of that door. As soon as Customs cleared the papers, and I paid the import duty and the other charges, he would be free. Where was the Customs office, *s'il vous plaît, madame*? In rue du Circle. But we'd just been there. The buildings, *madame*, were unoccupied except for the corpses of Jurassic cattle. *Mais non*, there was a temporary office in one of the buildings, the young woman assured me. The normal office was closed because of *une grève*, a strike, by Customs officials. *En fait, madame*, the temporary office in rue du Circle would be open till 11am, and would then close for the weekend.

It was now 10.45am. I was exhausted after the long journey, by lack of sleep, worry about Charlie's welfare and whether he had made it on each of the flights: Canberra to Sydney; Sydney to Singapore; Singapore to Paris. I burst into tears. What did I say as Judy and David hustled me out of the freight office, down the steps, back over the concrete wall and into the car? Who did I not rail against? The export agent in Canberra, who had given me the wrong address; the administration of Charles de Gaulle Airport, whose directory didn't have the phone number of their own live animal freight office; the Customs officials, who were prepared to go on strike on a Saturday morning and leave a little dog in his cage till Monday at the earliest.

David squinted through the misted windscreen and sighed loudly.

Back at rue du Circle, I leapt out of the car and burst through the door where I had found the *Note au Public*, coming to a stop at the foot of a flight of stairs that rose from a small foyer. I stumbled blindly up the steps into a deserted corridor and barged through several sets of swinging doors. At last I saw an open office and inside it a couple of men in jeans: the lovely temporary Customs officers, rubber stamps at the ready. Within seconds I had descended the staircase at this end of the corridor and was back in the car.

The young woman at the freight office in Fantasy, Puppet or Phantom Street appeared to have forgotten my previous remarks and smiled as I paid the duty. *Merci, madame.*

Out the door again, down the steps, up a ramp into the holding bay and there he was, sitting in his blue and white cage, my brave, bleary-eyed boy, too dazed even to pee. I walked him up and down in the snow for a while, but he hung on till he was warm and comfortable in Judy and David's apartment in rue Guersant before voiding his bladder in a luxuriant stream.

'It's OK,' said Judy. 'We were thinking of getting a new carpet anyway.'

SCENE CHANGE

In the blinding snow, I missed the exit from the autoroute. I had to drive almost as far as Cahors before we could turn off onto the main Departmental road that traversed the plateau to the east and would take us closer to our new home. We were already late by several hours, and although I had been in the Midi-Pyrénées region before, and even driven on this road on my previous visit, I wasn't at all sure of how precisely to get to our destination by the little roads that still lay ahead of us. It was less than a week since our arrival in Paris and I was again experiencing something of the same distress. But as we crossed the plateau, the sky cleared and multitudes of glittering stars swirled overhead.

'What a welcome, Charlie,' I murmured, resting my right hand on the wool of his warm sleeping form on the passenger seat.

At last we found the narrow winding road that descended into the valley of the Célé and soon our headlights picked out a sign, *Ancien prieuré*, ancient priory. Here we turned off and nosed across the little stone bridge that led into Espagnac.

In contrast to the sparkling sky above, the village was in complete darkness.

Charlie roused himself and we both peered through the windscreen.

'Well, they haven't waited up for us,' I remarked.

I parked the car on what I guessed to be the *place*, the village square, an area where the road opened out about 100 metres into the village from the bridge. Charlie leaped out as soon as I opened the door and began busily investigating the possibilities of the *place*.

In the feeble light of a street lamp, I negotiated a few snowy steps up to the porch of one of the buildings and found the sign on the door:

MAIRIE D'ESPAGNAC-SAINTE-EULALIE
HEURES D'OUVERTURE
LUNDI   9.00H À 13.00H
               14.00H À 17.00H
JEUDI   14.00H À 17.00H

It was Wednesday. The *mairie*, the municipal office of the village, would be open tomorrow afternoon. The *mairie* owned the apartment I had rented. I had rung on Monday to say that we would be arriving today, but I hadn't anticipated the delay. They had probably given up on us. Meanwhile, where were we to sleep?

I squinted into the darkness. Two narrow lanes disappeared in opposite directions from the high side of the *place*. A third ran round a corner under a tower beside the *mairie*.

'Let's go down here,' I said to Charlie calmly, pretending to be as much on top of the situation as he evidently was.

He followed his nose down the lane, busily branding the walls on either side. These days, a dog never knew if he was just passing through or staying. Best to cover both possibilities.

I stumbled along after him in the dark until, halfway along, I made out a door, a cowbell hanging beside it, and a painted sign attached to the wall on the other side of the door.

MME BONZANI. VISITE DE L'ÉGLISE. SONNEZ FORT.

Charlie sniffed the doorsill, then looked up at me, his pompom vibrating expectantly. I wasn't interested in visiting the church just then; nevertheless I was about to ring the bell loudly, as the sign instructed, when, with a feeling of *déjà-vu*, I saw something white fluttering on the door. I pulled a note off a nail and read it in the light of my torch.

It was addressed to me, Maureen, and signed J. Bonzani.

'It's OK, Charlie. We're in the right place this time. We keep going down here, under this arch. There should be a sign for Les Jardins du Célé. There it is. We go round the corner into a *cour* – that's the courtyard, Charlie, where you'll be able to play – and up some … those … steps. Come on, let's go back and get the car.'

Charlie was very distrustful when it came to getting back in the car after such a short respite. He jumped out again as soon as I parked at the bottom of the steps.

From a landing at the top, a heavy wooden door opened into an entry. A door at the end of each side of the entry and a key in the door on the left.

I glanced again at J. Bonzani's note and breathed, 'That's ours.'

I stood at the threshold. The room was as wide and high as a small refectory. Opposite the doorway was a chimneypiece with a fresco painted on the facade. In the cavernous fireplace was a wood-burning heater. This wasn't lit, but someone had turned on the electric fan heaters on the walls and the lights at both ends of the room, so it was both warm and bright. I felt a flutter of excitement.

While I surveyed the room, Charlie barged straight in and jumped on one of the twin beds at one end and settled down. It had been a long day. He seemed to forget that he hadn't had his dinner. I was as tired as he was, but, while he drowsed on the bed, I spent the next hour trudging up and down the steps between the car and the apartment.

When I had phoned the *mairie* from Paris I had asked what I would be able to buy in the village and what I would need to bring with us. The conversation taxed my vocabulary beyond its limits, but I gathered that I would have to supply my own sheets, pillows, pillowslips, towels and tea towels and that there were no shops in the village. I established that I would need linen for a double bed and two single beds.

So the previous day, Tuesday, I took the *metro* Line One from Porte Maillot to Hôtel de Ville to the big department store, Samaritaine, and returned to the Wilsons' flat laden with huge shopping bags of *draps, oreillers, taies d'oreiller, serviettes* and *torchons* for the household, and Royal Canin *croquettes*, two shiny blue and green dog bowls, and a red bed decorated with terriers, for Charlie. At the FNAC emporium on avenue des Ternes, I bought speakers for the radio-CD player I had picked up duty free in Singapore and a *Harrap's Compact Dictionnaire* to supplement the old French/English dictionary I had used at school.

This morning, just before we left rue Guersant, I bought basic provisions at the little *supermarché*, the supermarket across the road from the Wilsons' flat: eggs, milk, tea, coffee, bread, onions, tins of tomatoes and chick peas, vegetables, pasta, condiments, wine, and several cans of dog food.

Charlie had taken no interest in the shopping expeditions in Paris, preferring to rest cocooned in the warmth of the central heating and the dusky light of the flat, consoling himself with Judy's steak. The weather remained bleak and cold. Whenever I took him out for a 'walk', he lifted his leg on the first suitable doorstep and immediately turned again for 'home'. He came to life temporarily on the Sunday, the day after we arrived, when we went to the Bois de Bologne where he was diverted by a frisky boxer puppy with a rhinestone collar. On the Monday he tolerated another walk through snow along avenue des Ternes and down the rue du Faubourg Saint-Honoré to find the garage where I was to pick up the hire car later in the week to drive here. But generally, he was pained by the slush on the streets of Paris, dismayed by the noise and unpredictability of the traffic and repelled by the fragile-looking poodles with ribbons in their coiffures and yellow-brown stains in the hair under their eyes and tails. He couldn't wait to get out of the joint.

While carrying everything up to the apartment and putting together something simple to eat, I noted other details of the place where we were going to live. Linoleum floor. High ceilings. Stone walls. A long, wooden table and two bench seats. A kitchen area packed with equipment: large fridge, gas rings, electric hotplates, gas oven and griller, bar fridge, washing machine. The gas bottle was empty, I discovered when I tried to cook, and the bar fridge didn't work.

'Oh, well,' I said, 'it'll be good for storing your tinned food in, Charlie.'

At the other end of the main room, the twin beds, a cane sofa, a sideboard, a lamp and a very large television set. In the wall behind the bed Charlie had adopted, a stone arch, which would have opened to a room on the other side, only it was sealed with narrow, rectangular pink bricks.

In the bedroom, a double bed, a bedside table with a lamp on it and a child's wardrobe. In the bathroom, a small cupboard, mirror, plastic shelf and tiny drawers above a washbasin, a toilet, an enormous electric hot water tank and an ancient plastic shower compartment with a hand-held shower rose. My heart sank a little at this; I prefer fixed shower roses, and there was nothing on the water pipes to fix this one on to.

'It won't be as comfortable as our house in Canberra,' I told Charlie, as I emptied the tin of *festin à l'agneau et jardinière de légumes* into one of his new Paris bowls. 'But it has a lot of character. And you'll have the big *cour* downstairs to play in.'

Charlie gobbled up his banquet of lamb and mixed vegetables and went back to the bed, while I sat at the long table like a reclusive monk, with an omelette and a glass of wine, looking at the fresco. It was a design in faded shades of blue, grey, brown, yellow and pink in a border of fruit or flowers or feathers. Within a central circle was a shield divided into sections. Above the shield was a primitive-looking crown with circles drawn on it to represent, I supposed, jewels. In one section of the shield was a rampant lioness poking out her tongue through bared teeth and swishing her tail. Two larger rampant lionesses guarded each side of the shield. The background was a finer, more delicate rendition of the fruit-flower-feather decoration.

Charlie, lying on the bed, framed against the bricked-up arch, watched me through half-closed eyes while I examined the fresco. What would he – what would we both – make of this place? With a twinge of guilt I went over to give him a cuddle and spotted a typewritten notice glued to the side of the chimneypiece:

Cette fresque, témoin du passé, a été restauré récemment.

Elle est fragile, prière de ne pas y toucher. Merci.

'This fresco, witness to the past, has been recently restored,' I translated. 'It's fragile, please don't touch it. It looks like a coat of arms. Whose do you suppose it was, Charlie? Who do you think these lionesses represent? And what could be on the other side of that bricked-up doorway?'

In the morning, when I opened the curtains, sunlight slanted from the left through the tall lattice windows. That meant the windows faced directly south. We would have sunshine all day, I reflected happily, when it wasn't snowing. The apartment was living up to its description in the *Gîtes de France du Lot*, the official guide to holiday accommodation: sunny, one-bedroom, in an ancient priory in a village by a river, with a rating of two *épis*, cornstalks, out of four. Beneath the window was the lane we had driven down to get to the *cour*. On the other side of the lane, a crumbling stone wall, a snowy field, another collapsing wall, the leaden river sliding behind poplars, more fields and the limestone escarpment, ghostly black-blotched white, rimmed with leafless scrubby oak forest.

'It's beautiful, Charlie,' I said, 'you should see it.'

But, of course, he couldn't see it because although the windows reached almost to the ceiling, they started too high off the ground for him to be able to look over the sills, even standing on his hind legs. At our home in Canberra, most of the windows started at the floor, so he could observe everything that went on outside. He also had a dog door there, so he could go out into the back garden whenever he wanted.

'Never mind,' I muttered. 'You'll get used to it.'

In contrast to his attitude in Paris, Charlie was desperate to get outside. While he dashed around the *cour* anointing the stones and bushes and growling with satisfaction at each *coup*, I kept an eye on him from the landing at the top of the steps and took in the view from this side of the building. Directly opposite was a *clocher*, a bell tower with its half-timbered red brick turret, and behind the *clocher* the cut-off church and a ruined wall where the rest of the church must have once been. Beyond the wall, a small cemetery and beyond that, stone houses with towers and pitched roofs, and the escarpment as a backdrop. Way up on the top of the escarpment, an electricity pylon in a sloping meadow: the same meadow from which I had first seen the village of Espagnac. I mentally relived that moment – and I would go back up there with Charlie at the first opportunity.

Charlie started barking at something behind the arches of an arcade on one side of the *cour*. A man walked out, heading for a van that was parked nearby. He squatted on his heels and put out his hand. Barking and squirming forwards by turns, Charlie inched to within patting distance and eventually got the caress he had been angling for. The man looked up at me, smiling.

'*Bonjour.*'

'*Désolée,*' I said. 'He'll bark at you till you pat him.' Anyway, that's what I tried to say. But, anyway, the man seemed to know what was required.

'*Pas de problème. Bienvenue au village.*'

'*Merci beaucoup.*'

Then he climbed into his van and drove off.

We went for a walk around the village which now seemed deserted. All the *volets*, the wooden shutters, on all the windows and doors were shut, although I noticed thin coils of smoke rising from the chimneys of some of the houses.

'Everyone's staying inside,' I remarked to Charlie. 'Too cold for them to be out. Let's go back and fix up our place.'

Charlie had never been impressed by domestic activities and avoided involvement with them. He repaired to the bedroom while I finished unpacking and putting away the basic clothes I'd brought from Australia and the household things I'd bought in Paris. Then I moved the two single beds in the main room against adjacent walls, to make it look less like a makeshift bedroom and more like a living area. Charlie's cage fitted into the angle the beds made: it would serve as a corner table. I connected up the radio-CD player from Singapore and the speakers I'd bought in Paris, and was disappointed that I could only get reception of commercial radio stations. I made mental notes of what I'd need to buy to make the apartment more homely: some cloth to cover the cage; a bit of carpet; a work desk; a reading lamp.

At 2pm we set off up the snowy lane. As we passed under the arch across the lane, I saw that the *volets* of J. Bonzani's windows were still closed. A tarpaulin, slung in the angle made by the wall of the house and the arch, flapped limply, intermittently disclosing empty flowerpots attached to the spokes and rim of a wooden cartwheel. Further up the lane, as we passed under the tower, we heard voices overhead. Charlie strained at his lead, eyes shining, mouth grinning, pompom quivering. Company! He dragged me round the corner and up the steps of the *mairie*. I took a deep breath to suppress the butterflies in my stomach and knocked on the door.

'*C'est ouvert*, it's open.'

The woman at the desk, at the end of a room of gleaming wood and latticed windows, smiled. Behind her, up a couple of steps and through a half-open latticed door, was a little office. This was the room above the arch of the tower, from which we had heard the voices when we were coming up the lane. Two men and a woman were still engaged in conversation and at the same time glancing down at us.

'*Bonjour, madame*,' I said to the woman at the desk, smiling to mask my nervousness. '*Je m'appelle* Maureen Cashman.'

'*Oui*,' she laughed, as if to say, who else would you be? I recognised the warm voice of the woman I'd spoken to on the phone on Monday. Charlie was already dancing beside her on his hind legs, huffing. '*Hé, bonjour, toutou*,' she said to him. '*Comment il s'appelle*, what's his name?'

'*Il s'appelle Charlie*.'

'*Bonjour, Shar-lee*.'

The other woman skipped down the steps into the room, smiling and extending her hand.

The first woman said, '*Madame Cashman – et Shar-lee –* , *je vous présente Madame Bagreaux, maire d'Espagnac-Sainte-Eulali*e.'

Martine Bagreaux, the mayor of the village, was fortyish, pony-tailed, compact in jeans and jumper, her black-rimmed glasses lending her pleasant manner an effect of seriousness. '*Madame Cashman, bienvenue*.'

The two men followed her down from the little office. She introduced them as her colleagues of the *conseil municipal*, the municipal council, *messieurs* Jean-Louis Cabrignac and André Pelaprat. They too shook my hand.

''Ello, Madame Cashman, 'ow are you?' they said, smiling self-consciously at their prowess in English.

'Please call me Maureen,' I said, in French.

Martine explained that she had asked Mme Bonzani to show me to *le petit gîte*, my apartment. The Bonzanis had gone to bed before we arrived, apparently, because they'd planned to leave early in the morning to drive to Normandy. They would return to Espagnac at the end of February.

She turned her attention to Charlie who was dancing around her.

'Did he come with you on your flight?' she wanted to know.

'He came on the same planes,' I explained, 'but not in the cabin with me. He was in a cage in the luggage compartment.'

'*Oh, le pauvre!*' She squatted on her heels and ruffled his ears. 'But he must have been cold and lonely in the luggage compartment.'

'I believe the temperature there is the same as in the cabin,' I said. I didn't add that I'd had the same misgivings, and many more, in the whole business of bringing Charlie to France.

'You gave him something, a tranquilliser?'

I told them, as well as I could, and with occasional help from them, some of the details.

'The vet said it wasn't a good idea. On such a long journey, a tranquilliser would wear off and he'd be disoriented. Also, it's dark in the luggage compartment. The vet said Charlie would probably be asleep most of the time. It was I who needed the tranquilliser.'

They all smiled empathetically.

The morning we left, I continued, the city where Charlie and I lived was ringed by bushfires, the air was full of smoke and 500 houses had burned down during the previous week.

'*Oui*, we saw it on *la télé, les incendies de forêt* at Canberra,' remarked Jean-Louis.

Then the plane to Sydney had been delayed, so that it arrived after the cut-off time for processing and loading live animals on the plane to Singapore.

'*Quelle horreur!*' cried Nicole, the woman at the desk.

But then, from the waiting lounge in Sydney, I saw a utility van dash across the tarmac to the plane with a blue and white cage just like Charlie's on the tray – and almost certainly Charlie's little black nose was poking through the grille at the front. And then the flight attendants on the plane from Singapore to Paris assured me that there were some dogs on board and Charlie was probably one of them. Then, the dreadful morning at Charles de Gaulle and the joyful reunion.

Martine and Nicole were appalled at the suffering Charlie had endured.

Mais, how long had he been in his cage? He had nothing to eat for nearly forty hours? *Hé, mon Dieu! Le pauvre toutou.* Nicole fished in a drawer and produced a sweet biscuit, which Charlie accepted with dainty alacrity before I could intervene.

I noticed on the table that ran the length of the far side of the room a small pile of plastic postal envelopes.

'They arrived for you last week,' said Nicole. 'So we knew you would get here at last.'

There was a pause in the conversation, a question hovering.

'They are some magazines,' I said, 'and some of the research materials for the book I'm writing. I want to start work right away.'

'But of course,' said Martine. 'You are our village writer. We haven't had one for a long time. A writer must write. Now, are you satisfied with your *gîte*? Is there anything you need?'

'Well,' I said. 'Is there a second-hand shop somewhere, where I could buy a desk?'

'No, Maureen, there's no need to buy a desk, we have a spare one here that you can have.'

They had anticipated many of my other needs. Jean-Louis' father, René, would bring me a load of firewood and show me how to light the *poêle*, the wood-burning heater. I must try to use only the *poêle* for heating because the electricity was very expensive. Jean-Louis would ask René to replace the empty gas bottle that evening. Nicole would contact France Telecom about connecting the phone line. Jean-Louis would find me a smaller television. Someone called Boris would be able to tune it. As I already knew, there were no shops in the village, but for bread and meat, Nicole said, the *boulanger*, baker, came in his van on Tuesday and Friday mornings, and the *boucher*, butcher, came on Saturdays. The *bibliobus*, the mobile library, normally came once a month, and Nicole would command them to bring any books I wanted. There were several *supermarchés* in Figeac, closed on Mondays, as well as a *marché* every Saturday.

I had a pleasant memory of the lively *marché* in Figeac as I had been there on my previous visit to the Lot Department. It was full of stalls where you could buy a wide range of fresh food, fruit, vegetables and other produce and specialities of the region.

On that visit I had explored much of the Lot, one of the eight administrative districts that make up the region of the Midi-Pyrénées, the part of France that sweeps north of the border with Spain and runs through the mountains of the Pyrenees.

Cahors was the *préfecture*, the principal city and the administrative centre of the Department, but Figeac, Nicole said, was the closest town to Espagnac, 26 kilometres along the Célé River to the east. Figeac was also the *sous-préfecture*, where many of the administrative functions that were centred in Cahors were also available.

One of my first priorities was to find a bank. I had brought 10,000 euros in travellers' cheques which I wanted to deposit safely as soon as possible, and I wanted to have a bank account so that I could transfer funds from my bank in Australia when necessary.

'And,' I added, 'I'll need to have a cheque book to pay my rent.'

Nicole showed me a map of Figeac and marked on it the location of the bank, Crédit Agricole, and other places of interest such as the *Office de Tourisme* and the *Centre culturel*.

'I'm sorry to take up so much of your time,' I said, 'but there is one other thing. I need to buy a car. The one I drove here from Paris is rented, and I have to deliver it to Albi next week. Is there a second-hand car place you could recommend?'

For once they didn't think they could help. There were second-hand car yards, *mais bon*, they really couldn't recommend them.

'You've said you have to go to Albi?'

'I have Australian friends there; well, actually they're friends of Florence, my French teacher back home. She used to teach them too, before they moved their business to France. I met them when I was here last year.'

'You were here before?'

'Oh, yes, I was in the Lot, but this is the first time I've been to this village.'

'Well, if you are going to Albi, it might be better for you to buy a car there. Albi is much bigger than Figeac.'

This seemed a good idea, and it would solve the problem of getting back to Espagnac once I'd delivered the hire car.

Martine invited me to use the phone in the *mairie* to ring the Macdonalds in Albi, and Alan Macdonald offered to look for a car for me through a contact in the village where he and Ros and their twelve-year-old twins, Callum and Isabelle, lived.

In the course of this conversation, it seemed that all of my difficulties had been or would soon be solved. By the time Charlie and I were back in the apartment and the contents of the postal envelopes were organised ready for use at one end of my table, the butterflies that had accompanied me into the *mairie* had dispersed.

In the evening, Jean-Louis' parents, Solange and René, arrived at my door, he in pullover and overalls, she in flowered smock, cardigan and knitted cap, which she called her *bonnet*, and over her arm a basket of kindling and newspaper. We all nodded, smiled and gestured (Charlie stood on his bed and looked on with interest) as they arranged the paper and kindling in the *poêle* and added some bigger pieces of wood from the pile in the entry. Then René knelt and poked lit scraps of newspaper into the narrow opening at the bottom of the *poêle*. But the *poêle* wouldn't draw the flame, so Solange, shrugging off René's attempts to restrain her, grabbed a hook hanging in the fireplace, pulled the lid off the *poêle*, threw a piece of flaming paper in and dropped the lid back with a clang. There was an encouraging whooshing sound from the *poêle*.

I couldn't understand most of what René said, because he was speaking *patois*, the local dialect. Solange, pronouncing her words slowly, explained that René would bring me a load of wood the next day.

In the morning René's tractor rattled down the lane towing a trailer full of firewood which he stacked against the wall under the arcade in the *cour*. I tried to give him the money, but he said – I gathered – to give it to Solange some time; she looked after the finances, he just did the work.

That evening, Jean-Louis brought a smaller television and put the original one in the *gîte* opposite mine on the other side of the entry. The two *gîtes* were referred to casually as *le petit*, the little one, which was mine, and *le grand*, the big one. I saw, through the open door, that the *grand gîte* was a bit of a mess, with the furniture higgledy-piggledy, extension cords running across the floor and, with the addition of the one from my apartment, two televisions in the middle of the floor. The *petit gîte*, although it had several inclusions that didn't actually work, was neat and spotless, and the *grand gîte* had evidently taken the brunt of the arrangement. I began to understand that, together, the *gîtes* were a work in progress depending on the presence of tenants and their needs, as well as on the constraints on the *mairie*'s budget. I also began to comprehend how much thought had been put into the preparations for our arrival in Espagnac. I seemed to be saying, '*Merci*,' to someone or other all the time.

On the Friday evening, Martine turned up with her sons Boris and Bastien and the spare desk – a metal tubular frame and a wooden top. We assembled it beside the window in the main room and, with a sense of satisfaction, I transferred my papers from the end of the table to the desktop.

'*Très bien*,' I said, smiling at Martine. 'This will do very well.'

'We were very happy that you and Charlie chose to come to our village,' said Martine.

'*En fait*,' I said, 'the choice was made for us.'

Back home, Florence, my French teacher at the Alliance Française, had lent me the *Gîtes de France du Lot*. I found a few places to rent that seemed suitable and wrote to the proprietors. I said that I was a writer and that I wanted a quiet environment in which to work on a book, a garden for my dog and the possibility of an internet connection, and asked about the possibility of a long lease. I received a couple of regretful replies: the accommodation was already booked for the school holidays throughout the year. Most of the proprietors didn't bother to answer.

But then I received an email from Martine saying that an apartment in a restored wing of the ancient priory at Espagnac was available until the end of June, and then again from the end of August. But I would have to move out for July and August because the apartment was already rented for those months. There was a *cour* for my dog.

'It sounded perfect,' I said to Martine now, 'even though I don't know where we'll go for the summer.'

'We will find somewhere for you to stay for the summer,' said Martine, 'maybe not as cheap as here, *mais bon*.'

Boris was a tall, athletic youth of sixteen with the beginning of a furry moustache, a shy smile and a confident manner. Bastien, who was ten, was still a little boy, with Martine's dark hair and eyes and the same sort of black-rimmed glasses and strong lenses she wore. While Boris tuned the television and Charlie did his trick for Bastien – jumping along on his hind legs in pursuit of a piece of cheese – Martine accepted a coffee and asked me about the book I was writing.

'*C'est un roman?*'

Yes, I told her, a novel set mostly in a rural region of Australia, between the two World Wars. From the papers on the desk I extracted a map of the Murray–Darling river system and pointed out the districts and towns in which the first part of my story was to be set.

'The area is about the same as the whole of France,' I told her, moving my finger across the map. 'Last year, as part of the research I did for my book, I made a trip out there and travelled down this river to this town here, where the two rivers meet. Then I travelled back along this other river to this other town, which is also important in my story. The whole trip took three weeks.'

'What's it called, your book?' Martine asked.

'For the moment, I'm calling it *Blue and Brown*, after the colours of the waters in the two rivers, at a time before my story begins. I've read that before white people started using the rivers for farming and transport, the waters of the Murray River were blue, and the pebbles on the bottom were clearly visible. The indigenous people of the region, fishing with spears from canoes, could see the fish swimming around in the water. These days, its waters are nearly as brown as those of the Darling River which gets its colour from the red desert soil it flows through. But in my story, the colours also refer to the personalities of the two main characters.'

'*Bien*, you have done a lot of work already,' Martine said approvingly.

'Not really,' I admitted. 'I've done a lot of research, but the story itself is still in my head. I'm hoping while I'm here to get it out of my head and onto the computer.'

I felt shy to begin with, telling Martine these details. But she listened attentively and I began to relax with her and with the level of my French. I told her that I had been a teacher for many years before I started working on schools policy for the Australian government. Now that I was retired, I was able to spend more time doing what I liked most – writing stories.

Martine told me she worked as mayor of Espagnac-Sainte-Eulalie on Mondays and Thursday afternoons and as secretary of the *mairie* in another village on Tuesdays and Fridays. Before she was elected *maire*, she had been the secretary of the *mairie* of Espagnac-Sainte-Eulalie. Philippe, her husband, worked for the EDF, *Electricité de France*.

'We live here for the whole of summer and all the school holidays and most weekends, but we live in Figeac during the school terms. It's easier for Philippe and me to get to work from Figeac, and for the boys to go to school there. Boris started at the *Lycée Champollion* last autumn. Bastien is still at the *primaire*. They're both learning English.'

Boris, flicking the remote of the television, grimaced at the mention of English.

'He hates it,' Martine said. 'He prefers Spanish.'

'I could help you with your English, if you like, Boris,' I offered.

'Boris wants to live in Espagnac all the time,' said Martine, 'so he can *faire la chasse*, go hunting, whenever he wants. He has just qualified for a hunting licence.'

'Oh,' I said, surprised. It was hard to imagine this mild young man stalking through the woods with a gun.

'Oh, and Maureen,' Martine went on, 'on the first Saturday in March, there is the *repas de chasse*, the hunting dinner in the *salle des fêtes*. We hope you will come.'

'Where is that, the *salle des fêtes*?' I asked.

'It's here,' she said, pointing to the floor. 'Under the *gîtes*. We hold most of the village *repas* there. But don't worry, there aren't many of them.'

I would not in my wildest dreams have imagined that the first social event of my life in France would be a *repas de chasse*. But I accepted the invitation immediately, and not just because of the proximity of the venue.

I asked her about the fresco over the fireplace. She said I should ask Mme Bonzani about it when she returned from Normandy. Mme Bonzani was an expert on the history of the village and, Martine assured me, 'She speaks English very well.'

Martine knew that Canberra was *la capitale* of Australia. But what was its population, she wanted to know. I told her it was about 300,000. It would be very different for me to live here, she suggested. The *commune*, the administrative district of which she was the *maire*, was made up of the two villages, Espagnac and Sainte-Eulalie and a few hamlets. It had a combined population of sixty-seven residents.

But in summer, she said, the population expanded, when the empty houses were let to holiday-makers; or the owners, who lived or worked in Paris or elsewhere in France and Europe, returned for the holidays.

'And, Maureen, we are a multicultural village,' she smiled. 'In summer we have the Kempleys from England, Eric and Milou from

Belgium, and Madame Deffner from Germany. And now, we have *une dame Australienne, et son petit chien.*'

When they were leaving, all three kissed me on both cheeks, and Bastien kissed Charlie on the nose.

As soon as the door closed, Charlie leaped back onto the bed and dashed gleefully from one end of it to the other, grinning.

'OK, OK,' I said, plopping on the bed and catching him in a tight hug. 'Pull yourself together.'

The following evening, we had another visit. Charlie barked, the heavy wooden outer door banged, there was a scuffling in the entry and then a knocking on my door.

'*Bonsoir.*'

'*Bonsoir,*' I replied as a troop of children, filing past me, turned up smiling faces to be kissed. They introduced themselves. Joàn and Eva, Camille and Tanguy, Anaïs.

'Call me Maureen,' I said.

Charlie stopped barking and danced around on his hind legs, by way of escorting the children into our apartment, then went back to observe proceedings from his bed.

There didn't seem to be any particular purpose to their visit. They ranged in age from around four to ten. Eva and Anaïs made their way across the room and sat on each side of Charlie, fondling his ears and swinging their legs as they surveyed the room and stared at me in friendly curiosity. Joàn made a beeline for the computer. Did I have any games?

'I don't know,' I admitted. 'I just use it to write stories.'

Was I writing a book, asked Joàn knowingly. What was it about? Was it a book for children? He loved *'Arry Potteur.* He had read all the *'Arry Potteur* books and was waiting for the next one. He quickly seemed to lose interest in mine.

Apparently the computer was equipped with games, and Joàn was soon engrossed. Camille and Tanguy sat at the table on one of the benches. Camille was keeping away from Charlie because, she explained matter-of-factly, she was frightened of dogs, and proved it by squealing when Charlie jumped down and strolled across the room to his water bowl.

Had I seen the *gros chien*? The children's voices dropped to a whisper and they giggled nervously. The *gros chien* was a big brown Saint Bernard that ambled thoughtfully all day around the village, snuffling loudly, thick ropes of slaver hanging from his mouth.

'It belongs to my grandmother's cousin,' said Anaïs. 'They live in a town in the north, but their apartment isn't big enough for a *gros chien*, and so it has to stay here.'

The children seemed to feel quite at home in our apartment. They accepted juice and biscuits. Eva wanted to give some of her biscuit to Charlie, but I got some cheese from the fridge and showed her how to get Charlie to walk on his hind legs. Everyone wanted to hold the cheese for him, except Camille, who gave an automatic squeak whenever Charlie and the cheese came in her direction. Little Tanguy didn't speak, just smiled a sparkling, delighted smile.

In the course of our conversation, all the children except Anaïs talked too fast for me and barely disguised their amusement at my efforts. Anaïs, seeing my difficulty, began to talk slowly, separating her syllables and providing words for me when I was stumped. By these means, I gathered some details about them.

Anaïs, like Bastien and Boris Bagreaux, went to school in Figeac: her parents worked there. Camille and Joàn attended the Marcilhac-sur-Célé school, Eva the *primaire* at Saint-Sulpice and Tanguy the *maternelle* at Brengues – one school, in three different villages to the west of Espagnac dotted along the Célé River. I opened my Michelin Motoring Atlas on the table and we all leaned over it and located the three villages. The older children were learning English: 'One, two,' recited Camille. 'Jan-oo-ary, Feb-eroo-ary. Red, blue, yel-low.'

Eventually the outside door banged again and there was another knock on my door. It was Jacotte, the mother of Eva and Joàn, in a smeared apron, her face flushed as if she'd had to interrupt her cooking to come and find the children. She kissed me three times.

'I thought they might be here. I hope they didn't disturb you,' she said.

'Not at all,' I assured her. 'It's very nice to meet them. They're welcome to come any time. I could help the older ones with their studies in English and it would be good for me to practise speaking French with them.'

'You are a writer?'

'I intend to write a novel while I'm here.'

'And you are from Australia? It's my dream to be able to go to Australia one day. But it isn't possible, at present. But your dog, it's a *caniche*, a poodle, it's a French dog, *non*?'

No, I said, in spite of his ancestral roots, he had been born in Dubbo, a rural town in Australia.

'But he didn't come to live with me until he was fifteen months old. The people he belonged to moved to the city and he kept running away. The owners didn't want to keep paying to get him out of the dog refuge. He already had his own personality when I got him.'

With difficulty, and with her help, I managed to explain to Jacotte how Charlie and I, in the months after he came to live with me, had gradually come to understand one another. The children looked sceptical, but Jacotte smiled as I tried to explain the process of dog-training.

Jacotte said she would be interested to talk to me about my writing, told Eva and Joàn to come home, bid me *bonne soirée* and kissed me on both cheeks. All the children made low bows, said '*Au revoir, bonne soirée*'. Camille added, 'Goodbye,' in English.

'Well, Charlie,' I said, 'now we have even more friends.'

This time, when the visitors left, he yawned and grinned, then went straight back to the bed and settled down. He was getting used to the social life, apparently.

I began preparing a vegetable curry for my dinner. My tears dripped among the chopped onions but I was smiling as I mentally recited the names of the villagers we had met already: Nicole, Martine, Jean-Louis, André, Solange, René, Jacotte, Joàn, Camille, Eva, Anaïs, Tanguy. Who would have thought in this tiny village there would be so many people interested in us and our welfare?

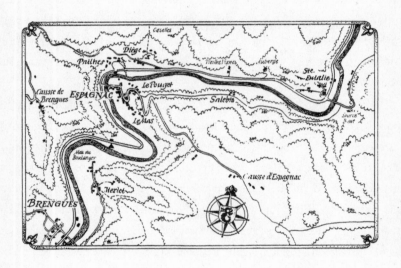

VAL-PARADIS

In the beginning, the people I saw most were Jacotte and her husband Thierry, the man Charlie had barked at in the *cour* that first morning. When Charlie and I set off each morning on our walk, Jacotte, red-cheeked, breath steaming, in woollen hat, thick pullover, track pants, boots and fingerless gloves, might be sitting at a rough wooden table under the arcade, sorting through tubs of potatoes. We would wander across to her, Charlie would put his paws on her lap for a caress and Jacotte and I would exchange kisses and then chat while she went on brushing and sorting.

Later in the morning, we might spot Thierry in a field, banging away with a spade at a clogged harrow behind his tractor. He would interrupt his work and come over. *Il fait beau, aujourd'hui. Il va geler, il va pleuvoir*: it's a nice day, it's going to freeze, it's going to rain. He would point out some aspect of the landscape or the flora and fauna: the buds of the *mimosa du causse*, an animal's tracks, a raptor's nest on the escarpment on the other side of the river, or cloud movements that signalled a change in the weather. From Thierry, I learned some of the terminology of the landscape – *falaise*, for example – which refers to the limestone escarpment that rims the narrow river valleys; and *causses*, the rolling plateaus that separate those deep valleys. Once I came across him mucking out an improvised chicken run beside the track going down past the football field to the river. As we exchanged kisses, he presented me with a warm egg. I held it on my palm, its shell smeared with grass and dirt.

'Thank you, Thierry,' I said, really touched. 'I'll eat it for breakfast tomorrow.'

'*C'est biologique*,' he assured me seriously, 'it's organic. There's no chemical fertiliser in what our chickens eat.'

In the course of our conversations, I learned that Thierry and Jacotte Dubuisson had come to Espagnac from Le Mans in the early 1990s to follow Thierry's dream of organic farming. They ran a business called Les Jardins du Célé. They grew organic fruit and vegetables and raised poultry, which were the basis of the *repas paysan*, country meals that they provided to visitors to the village. Espagnac was on a variant of the Chemin de Saint-Jacques de Compostelle, the pilgrimage route that begins at Le Puy-en-Velay in the Haute-Loire Department, and ends at Compostella in north-west Spain. Many of Thierry and Jacotte's customers were pilgrims on the Chemin, who would rent rooms overnight in the tower beside the *mairie*, and take their evening meal in the Dubuissons' dining room.

When Charlie and I arrived, however, there were few visitors to the village. Sometimes the only life we saw, apart from the raptors wheeling overhead and the voles scuttling across the paths, were Thierry, plying the tractor back and forth across the empty fields, and Jacotte, sorting out the seed potatoes. My heart would lighten when I saw them, and Charlie greeted them like old friends.

Jacotte had strong views about matters of social justice and international politics, in particular the push by the United States and Britain in those early months of 2003 for a United Nations attack on Iraq.

I agreed with her views and confessed my unhappiness that Australia supported that push. 'Many Australians are against a war, but I'm afraid if there is one, we will send soldiers to it, too.'

Jacotte was curious about why I had come to Espagnac: 'Of all the places you could have gone to write your book, why here?'

I explained in my halting way that in the northern autumn of the year before last a group of friends had rented a farmhouse in a hamlet near Marcilhac-sur-Célé. It was like a corner of the Garden of Eden, I told her. The garden of the farmhouse, overflowing with herbs and ripe fruit, merged into a lush meadow that ran down to the Célé River. Our walks took us to the tops of the escarpments over the river. Way below were villages of stone houses and churches, spires and turrets, surrounded by fields of ripe tobacco. In the forests we discovered particular features of the region: *dolmens*, ancient megalithic tombs, and *cazelles*, dome-shaped shepherds' shelters like the discarded stone hats of giants.

'I came back to this part of France partly because I thought the contrast would give me the distance I need to write about Australian scenes. Here, it's so very different from the landscapes I'm writing about. They are mostly arid, desert places, and they have a completely different kind of beauty. The people in my book don't always see the beauty because it's such a harsh environment to live and work in. I also came back because I found the region so interesting the last time and I wanted to explore it more.'

I told her how, on our last day, we walked from Brengues along a track that wound through the village and up to the escarpment high above the river. On the way, we passed under a stone fortification built against the limestone.

'*Le château des Anglais*,' Jacotte nodded.

'Eventually we reached that meadow.' I pointed up to where the pylon was etched against the dove-grey sky.

'*Le Relais*,' she said.

'I first saw Espagnac from up there. But we didn't come down. It was the day before we were to leave Marcilhac, so we didn't have time. We had to drive to Nîmes the next day.'

'You said the garden there at Marcilhac was like *un éden*,' remarked Jacotte, with a pleased smile. 'Do you know the other name for Espagnac? It's called Val-Paradis. You are living in the Vale of Paradise.'

There were days, however, when we met no-one. As on our first morning, the *mairie* was shut, all the *volets* of the village remained closed, Jacotte and Thierry were nowhere to be seen. There seemed to be nothing to distract me from writing my book.

Before coming to France, I had spent more than a year gathering detail on the characters, the settings, the historical perspectives and the incidents I envisaged. I interviewed experts and hobbyists about old train timetables, postal services, Morse code, gold mining, flood years on the Darling River, paddle steamers. While touring the towns and villages along the two rivers, I stayed one night at an old homestead and had a conversation over dinner with a descendant of one of the original grazing families, about his property on the Darling. His ancestors were wealthy squatters of the established Anglican religion; mine were poor Irish Catholic labourers who never fulfilled their dreams of digging a fortune out of the ground or winning it on the horses. The grazier and I discussed likely scenarios for one of the important relationships I envisaged for my story. Later, I interviewed elderly residents of the town of Wentworth about their lives in the 1920s and 1930s and read personal memoirs and books held in the Wentworth library about the old days.

My novel was to follow the progress of the central character from early adolescence to the birth of his first child, a son, just before the outbreak of the Second World War. It would explore the limitations and frustrations of the eldest child of a Catholic family, a sensitive, intelligent, ambitious, dogmatically religious boy. This boy, Arthur, left school early to work in the Post Office so that his brothers and sisters could continue their education and thereby have the opportunity to fulfil their potential. I wanted to show how his personality, experiences and circumstances had set a pattern for his life by his thirtieth birthday, at the outbreak of the war. I wanted to explore the range of experiences, including self-education and work, of a young person in remote postings in communities far from his loved ones, and how the experiences marked him as he reached adulthood. I wanted to describe the loneliness of his early postings in the outback and the ambiguity of his response to the landscapes and circumstances of his life. I also wanted to explore the effects of Irish Catholic dogmatism on my characters' responses to – and decisions about – such things as friendships, liaisons, love, marriage and parenthood. A sub-theme would be how intimate thoughts and feelings, in the kinds of social and religious environments of the story, may or may not be expressed through different modes of communication – such as letters, telegrams, Morse code, physical and non-physical contact.

But when I tried to set to work in my sunny but austere rented *gîte*, the isolation, the cold and my own state of mind combined to numb my purpose. Sitting at the desk by the window that framed the scene outside – the field, the poplars, the river and *falaise* – surrounded by my notes, and with the cursor blinking on the blank computer screen, I felt incapable of the task I had set myself. An ache drifted in the pit of my stomach. I felt frustrated and embarrassed. I was letting down all the people who had given me their time for my research and all the friends who encouraged and believed in me, including, now, it seemed, some of the friends I was making in the village. I was letting myself down, too.

Why couldn't I push through this torpor, 'write' my way through it, as I used to advise my students to do? I knew what I wanted to achieve, but feared that my life experience and my emotional and intellectual gifts were neither broad nor deep enough to give me an entrée into the inner lives of my characters and their circumstances.

I had always loved to write. I must have written hundreds of stories and poems by the time I left school, always with the encouragement of my parents, particularly my father, himself a great storyteller.

My formal education was typical of Sydney archdiocese convent schools in the 1950s and early 1960s: the more or less classical curriculum was embedded in religious observance. Still, I enjoyed learning in the humanities, but found subjects like chemistry and mathematics more mystifying. By dint of the rote learning in which the school specialised, however, I won both a Commonwealth Scholarship and a Teachers' College Scholarship to university. Because it paid a small weekly wage, I accepted the latter.

At Sydney University, I was exposed to new temptations and exciting – and sometimes shocking – revelations about the world beyond the convent and my home. My old school friends pointed out that my upbringing had been stricter and more conforming with Catholicism than theirs. With a thrill of transgression I explored previously banned literature and ideas, but that was as far as my intellectual deviancy went. I soon, however, became involved in the repertory group, the Sydney University Players, which meant several skipped lectures. And I also spent a lot of time writing. Some of my poems, which I submitted under a pseudonym, were published in *Honi Soit*, the student newspaper, but I stopped submitting them when one of the editorial staff challenged me to use my real name.

As a result of this combination of intellectual, emotional and hormonal distractions – and without the nuns to goad me into disciplined study habits – I failed most of my subjects in the first year but eventually graduated with an Honours degree in English followed by a Diploma in Education and a teaching post in a rural town.

I enjoyed teaching and adapted stories into plays and directed student performances on the annual play nights. Through the town's dramatic society I made friends with the other young teachers and bank employees who would normally stay for a few years and then move on if they didn't marry a local. I was one who moved on, to England, where I taught for a short period in London and then for two years in Yorkshire. I continued to write, mostly stories and for my own pleasure.

My writing took a new turn after I came back to Australia in the mid-1970s, while I was establishing and developing my career in education. I completed a Master of Education degree, specialising in curriculum design, and wrote articles and materials for the English Teachers' Association, which ran programs designed to improve English teachers' professional learning and skills.

Then, towards the end of the 1980s, I applied for a job on a project to improve the quality of teaching and learning in Australian schools and got it. Although at first the hours were much greater, the work itself involved nothing like the energy-sapping commitment of teaching. And so, over the next decade, I completed one novel and another was well advanced by the time I retired and began to incubate the ideas for the book that eventually I was calling *Blue and Brown*. I also embarked on a course at the Alliance Française, to refresh my school-girl French. And this led me to think about the possibility of living and writing in France.

I realised there was nothing to stop me from indulging my two great loves of writing and travel. I had no family commitments and no dependents, except Charlie.

So, here we were, in Val-Paradis, where the conditions couldn't have been better for my writerly purpose. Yet I was sitting in front of a blank screen, racked with self-doubt.

Charlie, framed in the bricked-up arch in the wall, lay on the bed with his head between his paws and gazed at me mournfully, occasionally starting up at the sound of distant children's voices and settling down again with a sigh of resignation. The fire in the *poêle* kept going out. This fact, and our shared ennui, drove us out to wander again around the silent village and beyond, in search of kindling.

One of the roads from the high side of the *place* outside the *mairie* climbed the *falaise* and ran along the *causse* between farmhouses and walled fields, continuing as a dirt track into a pine forest. From points along this road, the pale yellow stone and red tile village, the silver-grey river, and the dove-hued *causses* and skies glowed in the transparent air. We would continue through the rocky meadows and the soughing pine forest, or across the *falaise* to a spot above a loop in the river overlooking the two villages, Brengues and Espagnac, bathed in gentle light. In the distance, against the *falaise* on the other side of the river, the stones of the *château des Anglais* shone pale gold.

Another regular walk took us along the Célé past the hamlet of Salabio to a grotto called La Source Bleue, at the bottom of which lay a pool, part of an underground river. In the mornings the road to Salabio was in shadow and snow and ice lay on the verges. Along some stretches of the road the bank fell away steeply from the edge; from others, meadows, a few of them cultivated, the rest overgrown with stunted trees and bushes, rolled gently down to the river. On the other side of the road were rocky overhangs and caves matted with lichens and ferns, interspersed with tracts of dense wood that had overgrown crumbling stone walls separating once-cultivated fields and ruined farmhouses.

Beyond Salabio, the road gave onto a grassy track, then a narrow muddy path through dense woodland, with an almost vertical drop to the river on one side and a steep, sedgy bank on the other. Voles dashed across the path from time to time and birds flitted about in the scrubby trees. Charlie, delirious with excitement, pursued the scents of animals up into the snaggly woods or over the edge of the bank. The first time he disappeared, my heart lurched in fear, but then I saw him, bounding between the trees below, and heard the crash of stones tumbling from the brittle *falaise* as he scrambled back up to the path.

Back in our apartment, with the *poêle* radiating warmth once more and Charlie dozing on the bed, I would settle down to write about where we had been, what we had done and seen. *Blue and Brown* hung like a hoard of paralysed insects in the web of papers on the desk.

SPRING

Tractors churned up and down the fields, through drifts of smoke rising from piles of burning debris. Along the paths, the last hellebores faded into the greening woods. Sweeps of snowdrops segued through purple spikes of grape hyacinths to a carpet of white and yellow daisies. The snaggled branches of the hawthorn trees on the *causse* transformed into clouds of white blossom. Pigeons crashed in and out of the *clocher* of Notre-Dame du Val-Paradis, tripping the bells and exchanging sultry calls. In a sunny meadow by the river grazed a small herd of deer. It was March, the hunting season was almost a memory, and spring was around the corner.

One day, as Charlie and I approached the house where the road to La Source Bleue diverged from the road up to the *causse*, we heard Martine's and Bastien's high voices coming from the other side of the row of bushes that grew along the garden wall. The Bagreaux family was installed for the school holidays. Charlie shot ahead through the open gate into the garden.

I stood at the gate, smiling apologetically, calling him back, while he pranced around Martine and Bastien, and Bastien knelt on the grass to caress him.

'Come in, Maureen!' Martine cried, waving a pair of secateurs.

As I walked down the garden, a tall man carrying a broom emerged from the portico at the back of the house overlooking the river. Instantly, Charlie's tail clamped down, his spine humped and his head turned to look over his shoulder as he skulked back towards the gate.

'But what happened?' Martine asked in alarm.

'It's the broom,' I said. 'He's frightened of brooms.'

'*Pauvre toutou, il est sensible*, he's sensitive,' cooed Martine. 'Philippe, hide the broom!'

The man immediately retreated under the portico and returned to the garden empty-handed. By this time, Charlie was loitering outside the gate, staring up the road with his lower jaw trembling pathetically, casting sidelong glances into the garden to check if he was being observed.

'Maureen, I present to you my husband, Philippe, a very bad man who frightens *Shar-lee* with his broom!'

Philippe bent to kiss me soundly, left cheek, right, left. Then he turned his attention to Charlie. He held out his hands and called him. Martine, Bastien and I also called him, and eventually he ventured back down the garden and nuzzled his nose tentatively into Philippe's open hand. Philippe squatted on his heels and pretended to box Charlie's ears; Charlie snarled in pretend anger. This became their game whenever they saw one another.

Next door, Mme Georgette Delfour had opened her *volets* to the morning sunshine and basked in a chair in her doorway, sighing in the warmth.

Jean-Louis Cabrignac came down the road driving René's tractor. Jean-Louis was home for the school break. It seemed that everyone wound down during the school holidays, even if their work and their lives had nothing to do with schools. Jean-Louis cut the motor and jumped down from the cabin to join the little assembly outside the Bagreaux gate.

Up the road, Gerard Pelaprat was transferring boxes from the boot of his car into his house. He strolled down to say hello to Martine and Philippe and to be introduced to Charlie and me.

'Gerard teaches computer science,' Martine said. 'He'll be able to help you with your internet connection.'

'*Avec plaisir*,' said Gerard.

Martine, Jean-Louis and Gerard started talking business: a meeting of the *conseil municipal* they were planning to have while everyone was back in the village. Charlie and I moved on.

On the dead-end lane that ran past the Senacs', Anaïs's grandparents' house, we passed the *gros chien* coming the other way. Charlie pretended not to notice. The *gros chien*, absorbed by his own cogitations, ignored Charlie.

Further on, we met a woman polishing the windows of a house whose *volets* had been shut every time we passed before. She introduced herself, in English, as Jocelyne Sommie; Espagnac was her husband Pierre's native village; he would soon retire from his job in Paris and they would come to live here permanently. She'd heard I was writing a book. How was it going?

'I write something every day,' I replied vaguely.

What I didn't spell out was that I spent a couple of hours each afternoon at the computer writing about our walks around the village and the people we met. I told myself that I'd get back to the book once Charlie and I were more established here.

The following Saturday, around lunchtime, as Charlie and I returned to the village across the little stone bridge, we saw the butcher's van parked in the road and a small group of people gathered under the awning over the display case. Everyone smiled at us. Two elderly women detached themselves and came to meet us.

'We are Mimi and Rolande,' they said warmly, talking over one another, and kissed me three times each. '*Et bonjour toutou.*' Mimi, the elder, small and dark-haired, began to fuss over Charlie.

'I'm Martine's mother,' she said.

'And I'm Martine's aunt,' said Rolande, her face crinkling in smiles beneath her crop of curly hennaed hair. 'We know who you are, and of course, *le petit Monsieur Shar-lee.*'

In the afternoon, when Charlie and most of the rest of the village were having their customary after-lunch *sieste*, I sat in front of the computer and stared at the screen, trying to think of a way back into my novel whose *volets*, in spite of the coming of spring, remained firmly shut. The environment that I had expected to provide much-needed serenity and writerly solitude was having the opposite effect. It was too quiet, too lonely, and the landscape outside the window was too enticing.

So, when the external door at the top of the steps groaned open, and Charlie jumped off his bed as if bursting through the bricked-up arch and ran to our door, barking, I pushed my chair back, ready to greet whoever was there.

'*Bonjour, toutou! C'est que moi*, it's only me,' came the voice on the other side.

'*Bonjour*, Nicole, would you like a cup of tea?'

Nicole's work included looking after the *gîtes d'étape*, the short-term lodgings in the tower over the *mairie*. With the change of season she had begun preparing the rooms for the holiday visitors and the pilgrims on the Chemin de Saint-Jacques. Sometimes she used the *grand gîte* opposite mine as a workroom.

If what she was doing was transportable, like folding sheets, or sorting out cutlery, she brought it across into our sunny apartment and I helped her with whatever she was doing. She instructed me how to fold fitted sheets the correct way, a skill I had never felt the need of, and which I've never used since. But as we chatted over the *draps*, I also learned more about Nicole herself and about the lives of the *Espagnacois*.

Philippe Bagreaux was *une perle*, a man who does the housework, cooks and looks after the children, and this made it easier for Martine to carry out her responsibilities as mayor. Jean-Louis Cabrignac worked for the *hôtel de ville*, the Town Hall at Brive-la-Gaillarde in the Corrèze Department and lived in a flat in Brive during the week. Christiane, his wife, retired from her job as a dental nurse in Paris at the end of the previous year. Mme Delfour, Solange Cabrignac's sister, had had a dreadful car accident a few years ago and spent a year learning to walk again.

Nicole's husband, who had been seeing his *copine*, his girlfriend, for years, had finally left Nicole last year. It was a relief to her not to bear the humiliation of his infidelity any more, but now that she was on her own, she would have to work till she was sixty-five before she would be able to get a pension.

'Still, now, as a *célibataire*, a single person,' she said smiling widely, 'I can make my own decisions.'

'*Bien sûr*, certainly,' I agreed. 'For instance, I wouldn't have been able to decide to come to live here indefinitely if I had a partner.'

'But you have Charlie.'

'That's different. He didn't have any say in coming here.'

'But he's also content to be here.'

'Yes,' I agreed. 'Just as happy as I am.'

Charlie and I always found a reason to visit the *mairie* when it was open for business. Passing beneath the tower, as soon as he heard voices or movement, Charlie would start tugging at the lead. When I opened the door, he'd bound inside and rush around greeting everyone who happened to be there.

The atmosphere in the *mairie* was a lively combination of serious business and diffuse chatter. Martine in the little office above the archway beneath the tower – her desk overflowing with paperwork, dealing with visiting officials or residents; the door sometimes shut, sometimes not, but opened just to let Charlie in to fawn on her. Nicole on the phone, taking bookings. Jean-Louis, on his day off from work, showing a visitor, a possible property-seeker, the *plan cadastre*, the folio of maps of all the allotments of property in the *commune* of Espagnac and Sainte-Eulalie. People waiting to use the prehistoric photocopier that only Nicole knew how to coax into service. The official business suspended to greet a newcomer to the *mairie* then, after the *comment ça va* and the kissing and idle gossip, resumed.

In a glass-fronted cabinet behind Nicole's desk were a few publications for sale, relating to the village. They included a history of Espagnac-Sainte-Eulalie which had been written by Mme Pernet-Lauzur who some years previously had rented the *presbytère*, the part of the priory adjacent to the church where Camille's family now lived. Her book was written in old-fashioned language that had me rifling the pages of the dictionary even more than usual, but it fired my imaginings of the lives lived here over the centuries, and provided another diversion from *Blue and Brown*.

A few days after Nicole's visit, as we were coming back down the lane from the *mairie*, Charlie stopped short, barking. The Bonzani door was open, and, in the niche between the door and the arch, the tarpaulin had been cast off the wheel of flowerpots. Tubs of seedlings ready for planting were arranged on the table outside the door. Our neighbours had returned from Normandy.

Monsieur, in broad-brimmed hat and overalls, was up a ladder, pruning the roses espaliered on their wall. He gave me a peremptory '*Bonjour, madame,*' and looked askance at Charlie.

Mme Bonzani, short, square, round-faced, in a voluminous dress, apron and wrinkled lisle stockings, appeared at the door with a watering can.

'*Bonjour, madame. Vous êtes bien installée*, you've settled in all right? *Pas trop seule*, not too lonely?'

I replied that, although I *was* rather lonely, I was enjoying life in Espagnac.

''Ere, it's not like living in a city,' warned Mme Bonzani, laughing.

'In the city you can be invisible, but in a village everyone knows everything you do, who comes to visit.'

'I don't think that will worry me,' I replied. 'I have no secrets.'

I said that I particularly liked exploring the ancient towns and villages in the region. 'It's very different from Australia. We don't have any buildings older than 200 years.'

'*Pas de châteaux*, no castles?' She mulled this over. Then, '*Mais votre famille?*' Did I miss my family?

Not badly, I said. Now that I was connected to the internet, I sent and received emails nearly every day. My niece was studying music in Amsterdam and she would probably visit me in the summer, wherever I was then, and so would other family members and some of my friends from Australia at some time or other. Also, I had Australian friends living in a village near Albi and other Australian friends in Paris.

But she was still bemused why anyone would willingly go to live in another country, with a different language, so far from friends and family, on the other side of the world.

I repeated what I had told Jacotte, about the need for distance from the Australian settings of my book. I didn't mention the difficulties I was having with it. I explained that many Australians were dedicated European travellers because they could trace their origins to European countries. *Bien*, did I have French ancestors? No, all my ancestors were Irish. Then why, she insisted, had I come to France and why here, Espagnac?

I told her that I loved French language and literature, culture and history and I liked the idea of living in a village where some people could trace their ancestry back to the Revolution. But it was too hard to explain the impulse to step away from the ordinary existence in which you are well known and try out another self in a different environment, and the exhilaration – the fear and anticipation – involved in moving from the familiar into the unknown. Rather like writing a novel, in fact, except that the excitement there was gradually turning into frustration.

'And you, *madame*, has your family always lived here?'

'*Mais, non!*' she replied, laughing. 'My 'usband and I, we came from Paris. We bought our *maison* through an *agent immobilier*, a real estate agent, without even seeing it. We arrived on a rainy winter's day in 1958 with our five children and a few suitcases.' She burst into a peal of laughter. 'It was a ruin! It 'ad only 'alf a roof! When my 'usband began to restore it, some of the rest of the building, the part where you live now, fell down. It was then, when the chimney collapsed, that the fresco above your fireplace was discovered. *L'ancien maire*, the mayor of that time, it was Madame Delfour's 'usband, 'e 'ad it restored.

'*Ce blason*, that coat-of-arms on your *cheminée*, is of the family of Hébrard and Cardaillac-Saint-Sulpice. But you notice the lions are female, because the 'ead of the priory was a woman from that family. Your room was the *salle des religieuses* – the nuns' room. Our *salon*, the main room in our house, it used to be the *salon* of *la prieure*, the prioress. There used to be a doorway between the two rooms. *La prieure* could go *partout*, everywhere in the priory – every room opened into the next, all around the building. From this little *pont* she could see what everyone was doing in the *jardin*, and keep an eye on the nuns, when they walked along the promenade beside the river.'

She pointed up to the arch that spanned the lane beside her door. 'This lane where we are now is called the Chemin des Dames, the women's walk. Look at the *blason*.' She was still pointing at the arch, and it took me a few minutes to see what it was she wanted me to notice: a chipped and worn relief on the face of the keystone. '*C'est le blason* of the Cardaillac-Brengues family. It was damaged at the time of the Revolution.'

The Bonzanis' house was situated on the western corner of the priory. It had three entrances: one from the Chemin des Dames; one from the cottage garden that lay between their house and the *mairie*, and one in the south-east corner of the *cour*. They owned the *potager*, a walled garden in the south-west corner of the *cour*. They also had a cactus garden on the *pont* that spanned the Chemin des Dames, the little bridge that bore the Cardaillac-Brengues coat-of-arms on the keystone. Mme Bonzani looked after the pot plants around the door and the flowers in the cottage garden, and M. Bonzani did the rest. They always stopped work around 10.30am to sit in the sunshine outside their door and drink tea.

Sometimes, I would pause to chat with them as we set off on a walk; sometimes not, if Charlie was in a mood to harass *monsieur*. Relations between these two, having got off to a bad start, degenerated into a ritual of mutual antagonism. If Charlie was in the *cour* having a pee and M. Bonzani came out on his way to his car or to work in the *potager*, Charlie would invariably bark at him – even more hysterically if I rushed out to the landing and shouted at him to stop. Charlie couldn't understand why M. Bonzani didn't make friends like any normal person. M. Bonzani couldn't tolerate Charlie's barking and feints at attacking his ankles. He glared, shouted, pointed a shaking finger and swung his hoe at Charlie. Charlie braced on his hind paws and bounced on his front paws, barking furiously.

Other times, passing the Bonzanis on their tea break, he behaved as if butter wouldn't melt in his mouth, and, while the humans exchanged pleasantries, he'd sit quietly, grinning at the pot plants and snapping at insects. That is, M. Bonzani uttered a gruff ''*jour, madame*,' and went back to reading the paper, while Mme Bonzani and I chatted. M. Bonzani, I concluded, was naturally diffident, and possibly afraid of dogs, while Mme Bonzani was a dedicated communicator, as inquisitive as she was eager to inform.

'*Votre livre*,' she would say, seizing my arm. 'Your book. 'Ow much you 'af written today? 'Ow many words?'

Not many, I usually had to confess. But, I added, I spent hours reading about the history, the flora and fauna and the geology of the Lot Department and recording our adventures. And so there were days when I didn't try to work on my manuscript at all.

I developed a routine. Will myself out of bed. Throw on my tracksuit. Let Charlie out to run around the *cour*. Tend the fire and hope it hadn't gone out again. Toast for breakfast over Mme Pernet-Lauzur's book or a newspaper or the copy of *Lot Encyclopédie Bonneton* that I'd bought in a bookshop in Figeac. A short walk with Charlie along the *sentier*, the track down past the football field to the river. Write for an hour or two about our walks and what I was learning about our new home. A lunch of soup, bread and cheese with the books again. A long walk along the river or up to the *causse*. Dinner and read or watch television, with Charlie cuddled up beside me.

On Monday mornings I cleaned house. This involved hauling out the ancient industrial vacuum cleaner that lived in a cupboard in the entry. Charlie hated the *aspirateur*. Whenever he saw me wrestling with its tubes and cords and knobs, his tail would adhere to his nether orifice and he would skulk into a corner or wait in the dark in the entry, hoping someone would come and open the door to freedom. He detested it so much that I would take him round to the *mairie* and ask Martine and Nicole to mind him till I'd finished battling with the beast. It was like trying to dance with a Dalek.

When I went to retrieve him, I would be introduced to any stranger as Mme Maureen Cashman, *un écrivain australien*, an Australian writer, who has come to live in Espagnac for – I was surprised to hear this – *un an et demi*, a year and a half, perhaps longer. They would already have met *Shar-lee*, *un chien australien*, *qui n'aime pas l'aspirateur*, an Australian dog who doesn't like the vacuum cleaner. Nicole narrated to *villageois* and visitor alike a version of what I had told Jacotte: how I had first seen the village from *le Relais*, had fallen in love with it, but had not actually set foot here till we arrived that dark and snowy night . . .

Thus, some of my myth and some of my reality entered the story of Espagnac-Sainte-Eulalie, and a little of theirs entered mine.

A SHORT HISTORY

Charlie and I were gradually learning about aspects of people's lives in Espagnac in the present, particularly those that contributed to our comfort and happiness. And although Charlie didn't concern himself with such matters, I began to glean, from conversations with Mme Bonzani, from Mme Pernet-Lauzur's book and from the *Lot Encyclopédie,* more about its rich history

To begin near the beginning, during the ice age, the first inhabitants of the place that became Espagnac-Sainte-Eulalie lived in caves in the limestone *falaise.* They spent the short days roaming the frozen wastes hunting the animals that then lived on the *causses*: horse, ibex, reindeer and bison. In the long nights they painted images of these animals on the cave walls and fashioned weapons and implements from flint and bone.

When the ice age receded the *causses* were gradually covered with oak forests, groves of hazel and wild plum trees, and meadows of juniper, teeming with game and edible plants, a paradise. The people built annexes to their caves from skins and branches, began cultivating crops and domesticating animals, and making more sophisticated weapons, tools and utensils.

Around 5000 years ago, they began constructing the megalithic collective tombs, the *dolmens* that are found all over the region. They began working in leather and metal, and trading and bartering goods with other groups near and far. Eventually, they established armies to protect their trade routes. The Celts arrived from the east, bringing with them the ox-drawn plough. Eventually, the region that now comprises most of the Lot Department became known as Quercy.

The Romans conquered Quercy in 51BC and created the first record of Espagnac, which was named after its founder, Hispanus. The Célé River got its name from the Latin word *celer*, swift. The Roman settlement at Espagnac had villas and workshops, public baths and subterranean sewers.

Around the end of the third century AD, like the rest of the Roman world, the people of Quercy adopted Christianity. When the Franks swept into the region at the beginning of the fifth century, they too became Christians and by the end of the sixth century, most of the rural churches had been established and monasteries founded near major towns like Cahors. There were now agricultural fairs at Figeac and Cajarc and major roads between these centres.

Under the Frankish kings, Roman Gaul disintegrated into a collection of independent feudal states ruled by *seigneurs*. At first the *seigneurs* occupied semi-troglodite strongholds; as their power increased they constructed massive *donjons* and *châteaux*, the ruins of which are dotted, in towns and villages, throughout Quercy. The important clergy, the bishops and abbots, also came from feudal families, so that the authority of the church and the power of the nobility were mutually supportive and profitable. Many monasteries were founded during the next five centuries. In time, the literacy and learning that had characterised the Roman civilisation became the preserve of the monasteries.

The first monastery at Espagnac was founded by Bertrand de Griffeuille, a wandering hermit who, with support from the bishops and the *seigneurs*, founded several monasteries across the south-west of France. The monastery buildings at Espagnac were situated between the river and the watercourse that flows down the *falaise* by the hamlet of Diège. In the winter, the river flooded regularly and the watercourse became a torrent. The monks followed Bertrand's rule, and the rigours of their silent, austere existence and the precarious location of the monastery no doubt contributed to them disbanding after only twenty-four years, in 1160.

Fifty years later, the monastery was revived as a convent for women, a dependency of the Augustinian abbey of La Couronne in Poitou-Charentes, nearly 300 kilometres to the north-west. The new convent had a very different character to its predecessor. All the *professes*, the nuns who took their religious vows at Espagnac, had to be able to trace a noble ancestry on four sides for at least 200 years. The nuns had the right to elect the head of the convent, the *prieure*, but her election had to be endorsed by the Abbot of La Couronne.

Young *professes* brought dowries of land and money. One dowry brought the whole parish of Sainte-Eulalie. Additional donations of land and money came from bourgeois and feudal families of the region. Many *professes* and several of the *prieures* over the next 600 years were daughters of these families. The lands they brought as dowries carried rents from the tenants and, ostensibly, the convent was well able to support itself. The old buildings they occupied, however, were in need of repair and were inundated regularly in winter.

Then one fine day towards the end of the thirteenth century, the convent received a most distinguished guest. Aymeric des Hébrards de Saint-Sulpice had been tutor to the son of the king of Portugal, and had so impressed the royal family that he was appointed bishop of Coïmbra. On a visit home to Quercy to see his relatives, he called in to the convent at Espagnac.

The *prieure* at the time was Aymeric's cousin, Alasie. Naturally she drew Aymeric's attention to the state of the old convent buildings and how vulnerable they were to floods, and while they were chatting, Aymeric conceived an idea. A new convent, that would accommodate one hundred nuns, would testify to his own religious devotion, his status and that of his family. It would be paid for, of course, by his noble and ecclesiastical connections. And, obviously, the *seigneur* of the Hébrards of Saint-Sulpice, the head of his and Alasie's family, would be the Patron. From now on, the Patron would be entitled to enter ten women of the family into the convent. What a *coup*!

The new priory, with its magnificent church, bell-tower and cloisters, was situated further away from the river and the watercourse. It was completed in 1293. Aymeric named it Notre-Dame du Val-Paradis d'Espagnac. Aymeric also gave the nuns a flour mill at Cajarc. When he died three years later, his remains were brought to Espagnac and buried in the church.

As it turned out, however, Aymeric's legacy was a mixed blessing. Noblewomen came from far and wide to be *professes* at the convent, but brought dowries of parishes that were so distant, it was difficult to collect the rents. Soon the money-strapped *prieures* had to resort to asking the nuns' families to pay for their food.

Aymeric's successor as Bishop of Coïmbra, another member of the Hébrard family, was appalled to hear this. He sought advice from the Pope himself. This was during the period when the papal court had left the civic turmoil in Rome for the comparative safety of Avignon in France, and in consequence, there was a succession of French popes.

One of these popes, Jean XXII, had been Bishop of Cahors, and he knew the history of the convent. He ordered the nuns not to admit any more postulants till their number had fallen below sixty. The Patron would pay off the priory's debts and supply the nuns with flour till the next harvest. In return for the Patron's assistance, from now on, the convent would have to admit fifteen girls of the Hébrard family, but, said the Pope, only if there were vacancies.

Over the years, the nuns kept the priory afloat financially, sometimes with difficulty. They had disagreements with successive patrons, who often regarded the convent as a means to relieve themselves of the responsibility of daughters and nieces who, for various reasons, couldn't be married off into other noble families. For instance, when Bertrand II d'Hébrard demanded that the convent take six girls of his family, the nuns protested that they were already over the quota the Pope had set. Besides, they said, Bertrand had kept some of the profits from their mill in Cajarc, and reneged on gifts of wheat that Bishop Raymond had promised them. Also, he hadn't paid any dowry for five of his girls already received into the convent. These local dramas were played out against a backdrop of events that began with the marriage, in the middle of the twelfth century, of Eleanor of Aquitaine to Henry Plantagenet of England. This marriage sparked centuries of conflict between France and England, known as the Hundred Years' War, for possession of Eleanor's vast inheritance and most of the rest of France.

During times of war, the nuns paid off the leaders of various bands of 'English' and 'French' brigands that threatened the safety of the convent. Despite their pragmatism, however, by 1453, when the English finally retreated from France, they had somehow lost their rights to the mill at Cajarc that Aymeric had given them, and most of the beautiful church and magnificent cloister of Notre-Dame du Val-Paradis d'Espagnac had been destroyed. They were not alone in their misfortune. Throughout the region, crops had been destroyed, farms razed, families slaughtered or fallen victim to sporadic outbreaks of plague. Abandoned villages and market towns were in ruins.

Eventually, in the middle of the fifteenth century, the Valois dynasty emerged as the central power of the land, while the other French nobles lost many of their feudal privileges. Quercy was repopulated gradually over the next hundred years and many of the damaged churches, *châteaux* and manors were rebuilt. The nave of the church of Notre-Dame du Val-Paradis and half of the priory were reconstructed: the only parts of Aymeric's creation that remain today. For this work, and to remain financially secure, the convent needed more money.

Raymonde de Bauze was only twenty when she was elected *prieure* in 1518. Like her predecessors, she had difficulty persuading her tenants to pay their rents. Her plight became known to a local man, Galiot de Genouillac, a native of Assier, a town about 15 kilometres north of Espagnac. Galiot had risen to become the King's representative, or *sénéchal*, of the province of Quercy, and his solution was to order his bailiffs to seize the goods of the tenants who wouldn't or couldn't pay their rents to the priory. This is what can happen when you have friends in high places, though it didn't necessarily lead to greater solvency for the convent and certainly would have exacerbated the plight of the poverty-stricken tenants.

Inevitably, the resentment of the old nobility against the Catholic Valois kings erupted into further conflict, known as the Wars of Religion. In their campaign to regain their feudal rights, several of the *seigneurs* of Quercy became Protestant. Armed bands of 'Catholics' and 'Protestants' roamed Quercy, just as the 'English' and the 'French' had done in the preceding centuries. The convent at Espagnac, well practised in dealing with adversity, billeted soldiers of either side from time to time. At times when the conflict got out of hand, most of the nuns returned to their families, and all the *seigneurs*, whether Catholic or Protestant, gave them letters of safe conduct for their journeys. Meanwhile, the priory buildings again fell into disrepair.

By the time peace returned in the seventeenth century, life in Quercy had been transformed. The royal administration improved national infrastructure, such as roads and postal services and navigable rivers. Land under cultivation expanded and new crops and livestock were introduced. Schools and colleges, mostly for boys, were established by reformed or new religious orders like the Jesuits. The town bourgeoisie grew in power and wealth, while rents obtained by the landed nobility gradually eroded.

The royal administration also began to rationalise religious institutions. For example, convents throughout France were required to limit their number of nuns proportional to the resources of the establishments. The convent at Espagnac had managed to survive through centuries of adversity on old principles of patronage and influence, including buying protection; now they had to adapt to and negotiate new economic and social rules.

And so they did. For example, when the Patron, the *marquis* of Saint-Sulpice, wanted the convent to accept one of his illegitimate daughters as a *professe*, the nuns refused and demanded that he pay the cost they had already incurred of keeping and educating her. He took the matter to the Parliament at Toulouse, claiming his old rights as Patron. The nuns defended their position. The Parliament concluded that the *marquis* would be permitted to present his quota of ten girls to the convent, only if there was space for them and he paid a share of their upkeep. Also, girls he presented had to be legitimate offspring.

Then, early in the eighteenth century, for the first time the community accepted a commoner as a postulant. She was Marie Delrieu, daughter of a bourgeois merchant from Villefranche de Rouergue, who paid a substantial dowry, and promised to finance repairs to the buildings and the repurchase of certain lands.

But despite such concessions to modernity, lack of money remained a source of dissension and distress and, finally, humiliation. An old *prieure*, Jeanne de Gontaut de Rousillon, worn out from nearly forty years of trying to make ends meet at Espagnac, resigned in 1721, in favour of her wealthy kinswoman, Françoise du Vivier de Tournefort, a canoness from an abbey in Paris.

This is how it came about. A member of the Vivier de Tournefort family had suggested to the nuns that, if they elected Françoise, the family would donate a large sum of money to the convent. After the election, the nuns, their excitement at the prospect of so much money coming their way tempered with unease about how it was being obtained, consulted the abbot at La Couronne about the situation. The abbot advised them to find out if Françoise knew that her family had approached the convent. If Françoise didn't know anything about it, he advised, then the election wasn't tainted. The nuns were easily able to satisfy themselves on this score; after all, Françoise was still far away in that other abbey in Paris; in fact, she'd never even set foot in Espagnac. With clear consciences, they prepared to receive the new *prieure* and her family's money.

But the Patron formally objected to Françoise's election, and Françoise asked the convent to finance the cost of her defending her case. The nuns were appalled: they hadn't elected a rich woman as their *prieure* only to pay the cost of her court case.

The nuns again consulted the abbot of La Couronne, and this time he proposed that the best thing all round would be for Françoise to resign, which she agreed to do. Perhaps she had thought better of exchanging the environment of her convent in Paris for a run-down priory hundreds of miles away in a place down south that no-one had ever heard of.

Meanwhile, the abbot appointed two assistants to Jeanne to help sort out the finances. In due course, one of these women was elected, and remained *prieure* till 1773. The nuns then elected Anne-Agnès de Lajoinie, the first *prieure* who wasn't from a noble family. She was also the last *prieure* of the convent of Notre-Dame du Val-Paradis. The convent at Espagnac had ridden the tides of the politics of France for nearly six centuries, but it could not withstand the consequences of the French Revolution.

The power struggle between the central government and the noble families, which began with the Wars of Religion in the sixteenth century, now included the bourgeoisie, who had profited during the seventeenth century from the growth of craft industries in France and colonial trade.

In 1789, the Estates-General, representing the three main groups, the nobles, the clergy and the bourgeoisie, with their various vested interests, had been summoned to meet in Paris to discuss taxation. The meeting reached an impasse. The Third Estate, the bourgeoisie, declared itself the National Assembly and some of the lower clergy and minor nobility joined them. The people of Paris expressed their hatred for the royal administration by storming the fortress prison of the Bastille.

The violence in Paris spread across the country. Peasants attacked landowners' *châteaux* and destroyed their title deeds to land. The revolutionary assembly abolished the feudal rights and privileges of the nobility and nationalised church lands.

In 1791, the nuns at Espagnac were ordered by the Revolution to disband the convent and return to their families. The priory buildings were sold to the people of the nearby village of Sainte-Eulalie. All the nuns returned to their families, except the youngest, Sister Marguerite de Meynard, who was twenty-nine years old.

She was imprisoned at Cahors, with two nuns from other convents. She managed to escape in the crowd that had come to town to witness the hearing of the revolutionary Tribunal. One of her companions in the prison was taken to Paris to be guillotined but escaped death when the Terror came to an end on *9 thermidor an II*, the date so named in the revolutionary calendar. On that day, 27 July 1794, Robespierre, who had masterminded the Revolution and decapitated most of his former colleagues, was relieved of his own head.

After the Revolution, there were successive constitutions, which ultimately established the 101 French Departments, and the *commune* as the basic administrative unit of local government. The Lot Department, which comprised most of the ancient Roman province of Quercy, was created in 1790. Under Napoleon 1, the *communes* managed the creation of the first *plans cadastraux*, the survey plans that apportioned all of the land in France, including the lands that had belonged to the religious houses.

During the nineteenth century agriculture in the Lot prospered and by 1850 the population had increased to its historic maximum of nearly 300,000. Traditional mixed farming transformed into a market economy. Navigation of the Lot and road infrastructure improved and the railway arrived at the end of the century. Many new farms were established, and many old churches were reconstructed. The first retail businesses appeared in the villages: *boulangeries*, bakeries, *boucheries*, butchers, and *épiceries*, groceries. By the end of the century nearly every child between five and fifteen went to school. Primary schools opened in almost all *communes*. Children were required to learn in French at school, although they still spoke the Occitan dialect at home.

In 1888, the population of Espagnac-Sainte-Eulalie was 356. It included a miller, a seamstress, a blacksmith, craftsmen, stonemasons and tailors. But the Department had no heavy industry, and with the phylloxera epidemic, an infestation of the vineyards by sap-sucking insects at the end of the nineteenth century, viticulture collapsed. Between 1881 and 1910, nearly 50,000 *lotois* left and many villages and farms fell to ruins. A further 6000 people died or disappeared during the First World War. By 1950, the population was less than 150,000, a depopulation as great as it had been during the Hundred Years' War.

Remembering the massacre of the first war, the politicians of the Lot Department voted to capitulate during the Second World War, but when the Germans actually arrived in 1942, the Department became a bastion of resistance in the south. There were massive reprisals by the Germans, particularly in the Figeac region: 500 massacred and 800 deportees, of whom 200 never returned.

In the early part of the twentieth century, Figeac's main industry was the Ratier metal workshop on the outskirts of town on the Figeac-Cahors road that runs through the Célé valley. During the Occupation, the Germans turned the Ratier plant into a factory making propellers for their bombers. The Resistance destroyed the factory in 1944 and in reprisal, the nearby village of Cambes was razed and 500 men from Figeac and the local villages were sent to concentration and labour camps.

Then, when France was liberated, there were more than a hundred extra-judicial executions of people denounced for collaborating with the Germans.

In the course of the excursions Charlie and I made through the streets of Figeac and in the nearby villages, I would notice modest memorials to victims of the dreadful events of the war. On this corner these Resistance fighters were shot; in this workshop this carpenter's hands were cut off; on a certain day, these children were taken from this school and were never seen again.

The Ratier factory emerged from the ashes of the war to become once more a thriving business, making parts for aircraft and providing employment for the inhabitants of Figeac and the surrounding villages.

Cahors and Figeac have begun to recover with the development of small businesses and industries. The wine industry of the Lot is thriving and agriculture has been modernised. The population has now reached the level of the 1940s, but the demographic has changed. The number of farming enterprises has fallen from 25,000 at the end of the Second World War to 5000 at the turn of the millennium and now *paysans*, the people who make their living from the land, represent less than 20 per cent of the working population.

Espagnac-Sainte-Eulalie was testament to these changes. The land beside the paths on the *causse* and the little roads and tracks connecting the villages and hamlets that made up the *commune* was overgrown by scrubby forest that half-hid ruins of farm cottages and crumbling stone walls that separated once-cultivated fields.

Most of the elderly inhabitants we met were born at home within a 10-kilometre radius of the *mairie*, their middle-aged children and their grandchildren at the hospital at Figeac. The younger ones had gone to Figeac or Cahors, Albi or Brive, Toulouse or even Paris, to work, before themselves returning to retire. Some of the young returned for their annual holidays; some never returned.

Over the last twenty years, Espagnac-Sainte-Eulalie had acquired a few new residents from Paris, Belgium, Holland, England and Germany, who had come on holidays and decided to live there, at least for the summer months. Now, an Australian woman and her poodle had joined the pageant for a while.

From my conversations with Martine, I gathered that the newcomers, whom I looked forward to meeting when they arrived over the coming months, were well integrated into the community.

As for me, after only a few months, I had begun cautiously to feel at home. Charlie seemed to have forgotten his previous existence altogether.

Repas de Chasse

The *salle des fêtes* below my apartment was the venue for *réunions*, meetings, and *repas* of the *commune* and the local *associations*, clubs, and committees. I found myself an involuntary listener at most of them. I would be reading or writing or having lunch or dinner when the first cars would roar down the Chemin des Dames and round into the *cour*. The solid wooden door from the *cour* or the glass and wood door from the Chemin des Dames would crash with each arrival of members of whatever *association* it was this time: *foot* – the football club; *inés ruraux* – old country people, comprising a good proportion of the residents of Espagnac-Sainte-Eulalie and the neighbouring villages; *Chemin de Saint-Jacques* – a few locals and several intellectuals from Figeac; *chasse* – the hunting club; and so on. There would be a clashing of metal on stone as the furniture was set up. Gradually the jovial greetings of the first-comers would become a babble of voices. Then there would be a hush, and the speeches would start.

My apartment was like an echo chamber for the *salle*. The speeches were always long and impassioned and the audience was moved to laughter, interjections and loud applause. At the end of the formal speeches, there would be the hubbub of relaxed conversation over an *apéritif*. The doors would again crash sporadically as people began to leave. The chairs and tables would be collapsed again (bang!) and stacked against the walls (clatter). A few people would remain for an intense post-mortem. Another cork might be pulled. A door would bang. And again. Then silence.

The first *repas de chasse* I went to announced itself several hours before it started with the usual sound effects. Although I could scarcely see or breathe from the smoke that streamed up the chimney of the *salle des fêtes* and down mine, I sat by the *poêle* and read a book till I thought it would be rude to put off going down any longer. I was apprehensive about this, the first social event I attended in the village. How would I manage in the conversations? What if people ignored me? I made my way down to the *cour* and around the corner to the main entrance from the Chemin des Dames. The men sitting at the door taking the money were stocky, with weatherbeaten faces and missing teeth, talking *patois*, clicking their tongues and rolling their 'R's' the way René Cabrignac did.

There was a blazing fire at one end of the *salle des fêtes* near the entrance from the Chemin des Dames, and a bar counter at the other end, opposite the door to the *cour*. Martine was on the fringe of a crowd at the bar. She came over and led me back with her. There was Philippe, smiling, carrying a basket. Kissing me three times. Saying something I didn't understand, even though it didn't have the rumble of *patois*. There also were Boris and Bastien. More kissing. And here were Solange and René, and Jean-Louis and Christiane, and Didier and Pascale and little Manon. And Camille and Tanguy and their parents, Delphine and Cyril, and Anaïs and her parents, Natalie and Pierre. So many names to register all at once. *'Bonsoir Maureen, comment ça va?' 'Très bien, merci.' 'Hé, Maureen, en forme?' 'Oui, très.'* Kiss, kiss, kiss.

'Where is your *couvert*, Maureen?' Philippe asked.

My *couvert*? My place setting – knife, fork, spoon, plate, glass. Philippe had the *couverts* for all the Bagreaux in his basket. Everyone brought their own *couvert* to village *repas*. Martine had mentioned it to me, but I had forgotten.

'Where's *Shar-lee*?' asked Bastien. Evidently, he was expected to come too.

It was no trouble to go 'home' to get both my *couvert* and Charlie, especially as the big wooden door to the *cour*, which was next to my steps, was ajar. When I returned, Bastien took Charlie for a walk around the room, and everyone patted him and said, 'Ça va, Shar-lee, en forme?' Philippe took my *couvert* and set it with theirs on the table nearest the door to the *cour*.

Nearly everyone else was drinking Ricard, a brand of *pastis*, an aniseed-flavoured liquor which turned cloudy white when mixed with water, or *kir*, white wine flavoured with *cassis*, a blackcurrant liqueur. Martine was drinking *vin rouge*. 'That's all I ever drink, for *apéritif*,' she said.

At a certain moment, without any signal that I was aware of, everybody scrambled for their places at the tables and several men, including René and Didier Cabrignac and Boris, entered by the door on the far side of the fireplace carrying boards the size of stable doors.

The men carrying the boards were members of the *Société de la Chasse de Brengues-Espagnac-Sainte-Eulalie*, the hunting club of the two communities. Two men carried each board, and on each board were steaming tureens of soup, which they deposited smartly on the tables, with only a little splashing. Meanwhile, one man made his way around the room dropping handfuls of thick slices of *pain de campagne* at the end of each table. The wine bottles were already in place.

Jean-Louis had a flyer with the menu. *Potage vermicelle*, vermicelli soup. The *gibier*, the game we were going to eat, was *chevreuil*, venison. *Pommes de terre à la reine*, potatoes. *Salade*. *Cabécou*, little round goat's cheeses. *Dessert*. *Vin à discrétion*.

'Do you hunt?' I asked.

'*Pas moi*,' he replied, laughing at the idea.

It turned out that nobody at our table was interested in hunting, not even the *cuisinier* from the *Hôtel-Restaurant Le Romantique de Brengues*, who had cooked the *chevreuil* we were about to eat. Martine and Philippe couldn't explain why Boris wanted to be a *chasseur*. He didn't get it from them. Martine said Boris wanted a *chien de chasse*, a hunting dog, but who was going to look after it? They wouldn't be able to keep it at Figeac. Gerard Pelaprat suggested Boris could borrow Charlie. At the sound of his name, Charlie, sitting on the bench next to Bastien and watching the soup, looked around quizzically.

À propos de Charlie, I mentioned that I'd been looking for a good *pension*, boarding kennels, for when I made trips where I couldn't take him along. I'd looked at a place in a village near Albi, where I'd gone to deliver the car I'd hired in Paris and, with Alan Macdonald's help, to buy my second-hand Ford Fiesta. But Albi was so far away. Martine asked how much the *pension* cost. When I told her, she said that, for six euros a day, during the holidays, Boris could look after Charlie, take him for walks, *et ainsi de suite*. She held out her hand, miming Boris holding Charlie's lead. I was elated by this offer, but said Boris wasn't allowed to take him hunting.

Before the soup was removed, Martine insisted on initiating me in the *lotois* tradition called *le chabròt*. She grasped a bottle and poured a little wine into the soup at the bottom of my bowl.

'*Il faut que tu boives*, you have to drink it!' she cried, rapping on the table.

So I lifted the bowl nervously and drank the mixture of lukewarm wine and soup, while everyone sang, beating time on the table:

Quò's lo chabròt que reviscòla	The *chabròt* bucks you up
Quò's lo pus grand dels medecins	It's the greatest medicine
Vos encanta la garganhòla	It delights the throat
E bota la crèba a bocins.	And puts a cold to flight.

Of course, I didn't know the words of the *chabròt* song then, and wouldn't have been able to translate them from Occitan into French or English, even if I did. Just as I didn't know, but learned in the course of that evening, that *vin à discrétion* doesn't mean a discreet, but rather an *unlimited* amount of wine.

Over the bony pieces of venison that were served in a sauce after the soup, Christiane Cabrignac offered to lend me her *canapé-lit*, a sofa bed that she had brought from Paris when she retired and came to live in their house in Espagnac. The *canapé-lit* would be useful when visitors came. Ditto *un four électrique*, an electric oven, because my gas oven, I'd discovered, didn't work, even with the full bottle of gas René had brought. Martine said we would make room for the *canapé-lit* by moving one of the single beds to the *grand gîte*.

The bones were followed by meat in more sauce with potatoes, then salad and little rounds of soft *cabécou*, goat's cheese, and an iced custard slice for dessert. There seemed to be a general view that the custard slice was a disappointment, and it was necessary to take away the taste with *eau de vie*, also called *prune*. This was a clear plum brandy, about 95 per cent proof, in an unmarked bottle produced stealthily from under the table. Under its mellow influence, I said it was the best I'd ever tasted, and asked where could I get some, but my question fell on deaf ears.

The conversation wasn't all about me. At that stage, Charlie's and my own physical needs were about all I could manage to talk about reasonably successfully. This was a group of friends, some of whom had gone to school together. They had common interests that had nothing to do with me and spoke a kind of communal language that wasn't anything like the formal French I'd learned at school. Martine would say (in French), 'Talk properly, Philippe. Maureen can't understand when you talk like that.' Much of the conversation I didn't follow at all, there was much that I missed, and much that I misinterpreted.

For example, between the *cabécou* and the custard slice, I noticed that a pool of water had formed under Philippe's chair, and shortly afterwards, Philippe's head, which had been resting heavily on his hand, slipped and crashed onto the table, narrowly missing the custard. Nobody looked surprised or solicitous; in fact, nobody took any notice at all, which I thought was very discreet, very French, and

I tried to be as nonchalant as the rest. I made a mental connection with the *vin à discrétion* and the *prune*.

(The next day, passing by the Bagreaux house, I saw Martine in the garden and asked how Philippe was. She said his ankle was much better, thanks. The facts were these: Philippe had sprained his ankle. Before coming to the *repas*, he had taken a strong dose of painkillers and Martine had wrapped his ankle in ice. The painkillers combined with one glass of wine had knocked him out. The ice had melted onto the floor. Everybody at the *repas* had known this, except me. *C'est tout.*)

And so, there were long periods when I simply relaxed in the atmosphere of eating, drinking, talking and laughing, picking up on things occasionally, asking and answering questions. From time to time one or more of my companions would interrupt the flow of repartee and attend exclusively to me. It must have been like looking after a rather slow but pleasant child.

Still, borne along on the *eau de vie*, I floated into deep conversation with Didier and René about hunting. In Australia, I had been practically vegetarian. I realised not long after arriving at Espagnac that vegetarianism was not a popular practice there, and that if I was going to have a social life, I would have to become a carnivore, at least in public.

Perhaps because they were such enthusiastic hunters, Didier and René didn't pick up on my qualms about eating meat or the practice of hunting. Perhaps they didn't care. Certainly, buoyed by the *eau de vie*, we washed fairly steadily over the language bar. Sometimes they broke off from speaking earnestly to me, to have a little clarifying argument about something between themselves. For example, there was a discussion about the closing date of the *bécasse*, woodcock, season, and the flight path of the *palombe*, wood pigeon, which migrates between northern Europe and southern Spain.

'There's a corridor through the Dordogne and the Pyrenees,' said Didier. René appeared to disagree. '*Oui,*' Didier continued, '*mais,* in the past, the passage was closer to the Pays-Basque.' René again. 'It depends on the weather,' Didier compromised.

Whenever René said anything, I would nod away while he was talking and then turn to Didier for the translation. Didier had black, curly hair, flashing eyes and high colour in his cheeks. When he spoke, he leaned forward so that his forehead was only inches away from mine.

'There are two kinds of hunting dogs,' he murmured, '*le chien courant* and *le chien d'arrêt. Chiens courants*: you have the griffon, the beagle, the Gascon. *Chiens d'arrêt*: the spaniel, the set-taire.'

Absorbed in Didier's exposition, I didn't manage to pick up the essential difference between these dogs as far as their uses in hunting go, but basically one sort runs and the other sort stops. I said I thought poodles were hunting dogs too, but my remark hung for one second, before we all let it drop, with a light laugh. Philippe Bagreaux mumbled unconsciously.

'Your dog is very beautiful,' I said to Didier. 'What's his name?'

'Tenor,' replied Didier. 'He's a Gascon.'

'Oh, *un chien courant*,' I said, to show I'd been listening.

Tenor lived in an enclosure in a corner of the Cabrignac yard, between the chicken run and the road. He had a white chest with pink skin showing beneath the hair, high black head, brown flapping ears, and dark honey-coloured eyes with pinprick pupils. Unlike Charlie's, his eyes never gave me the impression that we could ever understand each other. Now that the hunting season was over, Didier's dog spent all day in his enclosure, with only Solange's chickens and Manon's pet rabbit for company. Occasionally he would howl in desperation at his situation, and the mournful sound reverberated through the valley. If he woke up and saw Charlie and me passing on the road he would jump up and splay his forelegs and big soft pads and nails against the wire of his run, emitting deep-throated whimpers. Charlie paid him little attention, except to pee perfunctorily against his wall. I would be torn between walking on quickly so as not to get his hopes up, or stopping and talking to him. René, cutting and stacking firewood in the yard nearby would shout '*Tais-toi, imbecile*, shut up, you idiot!'

René launched into a long explanation, illustrating what he was saying by moving the wine bottle and the cutlery around the table.

'The way hunting is organised for *gibier*, wild game,' Didier translated, 'is called *chasse en battue*. We meet at daybreak at an agreed spot and then disperse, with the dogs on leashes scenting where the animals have been. Then we rendezvous to share a snack – *pot au feu, charcuterie* and a little glass of red wine – and discuss our tactics. Where the *piqueurs* will take the dogs to flush out the animals and where the *tireurs* will wait with their guns for the beasts to emerge from the woods.'

René offered more *eau de vie*.

'*Mais*,' Didier continued with a laugh, '*gibier* don't always go where you expect them to. Then you have to stop everything and listen for where the animals and the dogs have gone and catch them up with the vehicles. If it's too late in the day, or if the dogs go beyond the limit and into the *Chasses gardées*, the private game reserves, you telephone the others on your *portable*, your mobile phone, and stop altogether. If the dogs get lost, you return without them and find them next day.'

'Do you sometimes spend a day without killing anything?' I asked hopefully.

'*Mais oui*,' Didier replied, smiling. 'We often return empty-handed. It's not an exact science – the aim is to get the animals moving – hear it,' he cupped a hand around an ear; 'do it,' he clapped his hands. Philippe started in his sleep and snorted.

Now we were all sitting back in our chairs. My eyes were closing in spite of myself.

'I started going out with my father and grandfather when I was eight or nine years old, learning the secrets of the terrain and animals,' said Didier.

'Back then,' he translated for René, 'we didn't have vehicles or *portables*. People could go out whenever they wanted to with a dog for an hour every day and shoot a rabbit or a hare for the *repas*, but now you have to stick to the season.'

I made a mental note for the future: the middle of September to the end of the first week in January, Saturday to Monday, and Wednesday. I would have to keep Charlie on a lead on hunting days – if we were still here in Espagnac after the summer, of course.

'Nowadays, there are so many rules and regulations. Too many townspeople who don't know traditional methods get permits and are dangerous unless restrictions are placed on them. And now of course, with the *putain* European Union ...'

I raised my eyebrows. I'd already gathered that, in general, the further you were from Paris, the less you were likely to think well of the EU, with all its regulations and standardisations of what you can grow and produce.

'*Les écologistes,*' said Didier, smiling sardonically, 'don't speak the same language as hunters. We know more about the *falaise* than *les intellos*, the eggheads in Paris or Brussels.'

Meanwhile, the dance music continued: tango, *java*, a kind of waltz, *paso doblé*, rock, and regional French and Spanish step dances. Everybody danced, except the men at the bar and the little boys who whizzed around chasing one another outside in the frost in the *cour*. The little girls danced with natural rhythm, especially Anaïs, who told me she learned '*ip-'op* at a dance studio in Figeac, and shimmied with delight in herself. Martine was whisked off whenever the music was rock'n'roll, dancing lightly, confidently. Slim, elegant Christiane danced a smiling, subtle, self-contained, easy twist. Although I'd never regarded myself as a natural dancer, I danced with the *cuisinier* from Brengues, before he too repaired to the bar. Some of the women and girls did a simple line dance they called the Languedoc Rock. A hard core of people, including Martine, were still dancing when, staggering with fatigue, I took Charlie home around 2.30am. Bastien was asleep, sprawled across Philippe, who was recumbent in a chair. We slipped out the door behind them into the frosty air of the *cour*.

Back at 'home', I read in bed for a while, then turned out the lamp and lay awake, listening to the sound of the drum-driven rock below, thinking about the hunting gene. Its apotheosis millennia ago in cave dwellers armed with primitive flint spears, then the hunter-gatherers with their bows and arrows, and now René, Didier, Boris and the weatherbeaten old men of the *Société de Chasse* with their guns and their mobile phones – no longer a means of survival, but of enjoyment and identity. How it had missed Jean-Louis, but hit his brother Didier, missed Philippe, but hit his son Boris. It certainly missed me.

I yawned. Charlie, I mused, had found a bit of a talent for hunting since we'd been here, scampering up and down the *falaise* on the scent of the deer and *sanglier* that inhabited the woods we walked through every day. But it was hard to say if he was a *chien courant* or a *chien d'arrêt*. He had a bit of both in him. He was only a self-educated amateur, after all.

Around 4am the music stopped; soon afterwards the door below slammed shut for the last time and silence fell on the priory.

FIGURES IN LANDSCAPES

❖

I was still trying, from time to time, to confront my difficulties with the technical and psychological dimensions of *Blue and Brown*. I made several attempts to write specific crucial scenes, thinking that in time I would be able to link them together somehow, but I wasn't confident.

It was much easier to yield to the wishes of Charlie, lying on the bed with his eyes fixed on the rival computer, his nose between his paws, the embodiment of ennui. As soon as I pushed back the chair, he jumped down and pranced around the room in an exhibition of joy that would have looked like satire if he wasn't actually a dog for whom it seemed every event, no matter how often repeated, is experienced anew.

I had bought a book describing several walking circuits of the Lot Department. Charlie and I explored all of them between the neighbouring villages, and sometimes we went further afield, to hamlets up on the *causse* or over the other side into the valley of the Lot.

At Marcilhac-sur-Célé, we poked around the collapsed walls and broken columns of the Benedictine abbey of Saint-Pierre, destroyed, like the priory at Espagnac, during the Hundred Years' War. We traversed the windswept *sentier* along the edge of the *causse* between Marcilhac and Saint-Sulpice, still a semi-troglodyte village, where the houses are built against the *falaise* and cabbages grow in the thin soil of rocky sloping gardens.

In Neanderthal times, only flapping animal skins and branches separated the caves from the elements. In the modern dwellings, solid windows and doors had been fitted into the external apertures. The rooms were furnished with electric stoves and wood-burning *poêles*, tables and chairs, beds, televisions and computers. Little white satellite dishes mushroomed on the outhouse roofs.

At the high edge of Saint-Sulpice, where the road became a narrow, vertiginous track up the *falaise*, reared the stark ruin of the medieval donjon of the Hébrards. From here, generations of *seigneurs* had surveyed the valley and the *falaise* on the other side of the Célé. They prepared for battle against would-be usurpers. They trained their sons and nephews to defend the lands they had taken by force or acquired as dowries, perhaps also with force involved. They negotiated their daughters' marriages to the aged scions of other noble families, more than once, as the successive husbands died in battle or old age, or the girls and women in childbirth or of plague. They ensured by reward or terror the loyalty of their soldiers, concubines and household servants, the obedience of their wives and children, and the toil of the serfs who laboured on their lands. They nominated the sons and nephews who would become powerful bishops or abbots, and the daughters and nieces who could become *prieures* of compliant religious houses.

I tried to imagine what went on in the girls' minds, at this distance in time, history and culture. Perhaps the daughters and nieces who entered the convent at Espagnac breathed a sigh of relief to escape marriage with old men, strangers, idiots or brutes. Some girls perhaps thought wistfully of physical and domestic pleasures they would never enjoy with real or imaginary lovers. Or, perhaps, they gratefully embraced a future in which they would receive an education and might wield some authority in this life, in the certainty that they were saving their souls for the celestial pleasures of the next. Perhaps, having no choice, they simply accepted the life that others ordained for them.

One warm spring day, our walk brought us to the portal of the twelfth century fortified church in the village of Saint-Pierre Toirac, on the far side of the *causse* overlooking the River Lot.

In the past, in times of peril – from the English, or during raids by brigands or Huguenot forces during the Wars of Religion – the villagers could ascend into the square tower and stay there until the danger passed.

I was hesitating at the door, looking for something to tie Charlie up to, when a voice from the darkness of the portal said, '*Venez, madame, venez.* Come in, come in.' I gestured towards Charlie. '*Venez, madame, votre chien, aussi.* This church is for dogs as well as for people.'

We stepped down into the cool gloom. The old man who had spoken was holding a pencil torch in one hand. With the other he took me by the elbow and led me into the dim church.

'*Regardez, madame,*' he whispered. I looked up to where the thin red ray of his torch traced the delicate lines of barrel vaulting, double arches, carved stone capitals. Then he gently pressed my arm to turn me to face one of the tiny side chapels, where a single candle illuminated the statue on the altar there.

'Saint-Roch,' he said.

A wild-looking pilgrim leaning on his staff, raising the hem of his ragged garment to disclose a wound above his knee; on his foot, a golden sandal, and at his side a little dog wearing a golden collar. The old man looked from me to Charlie and back to me, beaming delightedly.

'The patron saint of dogs – and their owners,' he explained, bending to pat Charlie, who helped by standing on his hind legs and resting his forepaws lightly on the man's knee. 'Also of painful knees. Would you like to hear his story?'

I nodded, smiling. We sat down on a bench against the wall. Charlie sat back on the flagstone and looked up at the old man while he spoke.

'Roch was born into a wealthy family. He had *une tache de naissance*, a birthmark, in the form of a cross, over his heart. As a child, he took pity on the poor, the homeless and the sick. When he was only twenty years old, he renounced the privileges of wealth and gave everything he had to the poor.

'He set out on a pilgrimage to Rome and when he arrived at the holy city, he found many people were suffering from the plague. He cured many of them, using the sign of the cross. But of course, eventually he himself fell ill. The sore above his knee is a plague sore.

'When Roch caught the plague, he didn't want to trouble anyone, so he hid away in a hovel to die. A little dog found him in the hovel, and every day came to visit him and brought him bread. The dog came from a villa nearby. The owner noticed the dog trotting off every day with *un petit pain* in his mouth, and one day he followed the dog and discovered Roch in the hovel on his estate, close to death. He told his servants to bring Roch back to his villa and there, he nursed him back to health.

'When he recovered, Roch thanked the rich man and bade him farewell. God had called him back to France. The faithful little dog came with him. This was during the war with the English.

'When Roch arrived, nobody recognised him as the fine young nobleman who had departed years before. They took him for an English spy and threw him into prison. Still, the little dog didn't leave him, but stayed by his side. In prison, Roch wouldn't tell anyone who he was. Instead, he helped the other prisoners, and after a few years he died there. It was then, when they were preparing him for burial, that the *tache de naissance* – and his true identity – were revealed.'

The old man must have seen the question in my eyes, and concluded: 'As for the little dog, *madame*, we don't know what happened to him. *De toute façon*, at any rate, I'm sure that dogs are permitted in heaven, and the little dog of Saint-Roch is there.'

He bent down to pat Charlie again. '*Hé, mon petit, pourquoi pas,* why not?'

The old man, in his pleasure in storytelling, reminded me of my father, whose stories provided some of the background to *Blue and Brown*. My father's only departure from strict Catholic dogma was his conviction that some dogs have souls, and they will be reunited with their owners in Paradise. I pictured him, asleep on some billowing cloud, glasses askew, a textbook having fallen from his hand, with the gentle old golden cocker spaniel, Abbie and the roan, Twit, who was given to sudden bursts of pointless anger, lounging beside him.

During these long walks, just Charlie and I in the landscape, my mind played idly with our experiences in the village and the history of the region, and how I would write about them later. I also mulled over the problems of my novel. And sometimes an encounter, such as the one with the old man in the church at Saint-Pierre Toirac, aroused memories and thoughts that resonated through my dilemma over *Blue and Brown*.

My father had had the greatest influence of anyone on my life. When he died in 1979, my grief was deep and complex. He was very proud of me but while he was alive I felt that I wasn't free to express certain thoughts, ideas and situations in stories and poems because he would be scandalised if he ever read them. His firm commitment to Catholic dogma and belief, his integrity, intransigence and capacity for moral outrage had great power over me.

My mother had a more tranquil temperament and showed her love for her children unconditionally. She suffered from kidney disease, and in her terminal illness came to live with me. My school was very understanding during the weeks leading up to her death and I was able to spend a lot of time quietly at home with her in front of the fire, preparing materials for my classes, while she read and dozed. She died in July 1987 and my sorrow at her passing was straightforward and immense.

Sometimes, roaming along the windswept *causse*, I longed for the kind of human companionship I'd had with my mother, and my thoughts and memories would arouse silent tears. If an involuntary noise escaped my throat, Charlie, distracted from his adventures in the undergrowth by the sounds of human distress, came running for reassurance.

Occasionally, in the middle of a week when the *mairie* was closed, we would forsake the silent villages and ancient *sentiers* that connected them and drive the 26 kilometres along the river to Figeac.

I had read the legend that the town developed around an abbey that was founded in the eleventh century by an abbot called Anastase. Anastase already had a monastery, but it was dilapidated because of repeated flooding. He roamed the region, hoping to find a better spot for a new one. On one of his excursions, he climbed a hill and saw below a sunny valley that would be perfect for a new monastery. But he had no money to build it.

He returned often to the sunny valley, imagining how wonderful it would be to found a monastery there. One day, he spied a dove caught in a poacher's trap. Gently, he released the dove from the trap and threw it into the air. But, instead of flying away, the dove hovered nearby. Anastase was astonished when the dove spoke to him.

'You have saved my life. What can I do for you in return?'

'I don't think you can help me, little dove. I want to build a monastery in this beautiful valley, but I don't have any money. I need a rich sponsor, but where will I find one?'

'I have an idea!' cooed the dove. 'The King will be in Quercy soon. If you can get him to come to this valley, I'll look after the rest.'

And it flew up into the sky.

When the court came to Quercy, Anastase made sure the King and his retinue came to the sunny valley.

'There's going to be a miracle, Your Majesty!' Anastase promised the King.

'Really? What fun! What should I be looking for, Anastase?'

'Um,' Anastase hedged, looking at the sky, 'look up there.'

To everyone's amazement, from far to the east, a great white cloud approached. As it came nearer and nearer, they saw that the cloud consisted of thousands of white doves. Suddenly one of the doves broke away from the flock, flew down into the valley and placed a laurel branch on the ground.

'Why,' exclaimed Anastase excitedly, 'the dove has placed the laurel branch on the exact spot where I want to build a new monastery! But,' he continued, looking sideways at the King, 'I don't have the means to build it.'

'You shall have your monastery. *Fiat là* – it shall be built there!'

And that's how the monastery was founded and the town got its original Occitan name, now Figeac.

Charlie and I both loved Figeac – Charlie immersed mostly in the smells, and I mostly in the sights. We would stroll beside the Célé and explore the narrow streets and *places* redolent with centuries of human and animal habitation. The stones of the pavements and foundations of the medieval buildings, the mounded earth around the ancient plane trees, the friendly pedestrians and the different shops we patronised gave Charlie much to store in his own little hard drive of a brain, to be opened up again next time we came. I loved the tall, half-timbered brick houses decorated with little turrets, carved lintels, glinting dormer windows, ironwork and open lofts where geraniums flowered in pots and bed sheets fluttered in the breeze. Many of the old houses were derelict, but many had notices on them advising that restoration work was in progress. The streets were full of people walking purposefully with shopping bags and baskets over their arms, or greeting one another, kissing, laughing and stopping to chat. The town had a relaxed, optimistic air.

We usually stopped by the Place des Écritures, hidden away in the heart of town, paved with a sculpted replica of the Rosetta Stone. The Rosetta Stone was 'discovered' by a French soldier in 1799 during Napoleon's occupation of Egypt, but, to the annoyance of the French, not to mention the Egyptians, somehow found its way into the British Museum in London and has stayed there ever since. Jean-François Champollion, who was born in Figeac in 1790, became a scholar of ancient civilisations. Using illustrations of the three kinds of writing carved into the Stone – Greek, demotic Egyptian, and ancient Egyptian hieroglyphics – he translated the hieroglyphics. He was able to show that the three texts contained the same information, and thus cracked the code.

I would rest on a plinth in the shady colonnade surrounding the replica of the Stone, and Charlie would wander across the ancient symbols as if they were ordinary cracks in the paving. Charlie was less moved than I was by the atmosphere of the Place des Écritures, but I always managed to get him back into the street before he could demonstrate his disregard in the usual way.

I would buy a few things at the health food shop or the electrical shop – the pretext for the 50-kilometre round trip – browse in the bookshop, buy an English newspaper, then settle at one of the tables in the main *place*, Place Carnot, and order a coffee. Place Carnot, a spacious raised area surrounded by stone steps and covered by a roof supported by columns, was the hub of the Saturday *marché*. Mid-week, it was filled with tables and chairs of the cafés and bars tucked into the corners of the *place*. The waiters, when they brought out the coffee, always brought out a bowl of water for Charlie too.

Then we would go home and I would add the excursion to the notes I was making about the scenes, stories and events of our lives, which grew into the monthly reports I had begun sending back to our friends in Australia. This activity gave me an idea and revived my enthusiasm for my novel: narratives that my characters would devise for one another, using various means of transmission, to breach the physical distances between them. Of course, there was a major difference between what I was doing and what my characters could do. With modern technology it was much easier to communicate over even greater distance and longer physical separation, and easier to refine and modify the experiences, thoughts and feelings to be expressed.

APRIL

We had now lived in Espagnac for over two months. One morning as we passed, Mme Bonzani was snipping sorrel in the *potager*. She stood up, gripping her scissors firmly, and looked me in the eye.

'My 'usband,' she said, ''e doesn't think you're writing a book at all.'

'He's partly right,' I admitted. 'I've written three beginnings and it isn't working.'

'What is it about?' she inquired.

I gave her the general outline that by now I could easily rattle off in French.

She leaned towards me with a curious smile. '*Yu 'af red dee Ton Budz?*'

I turned this over in my head, trying to translate it. My what?

'*Ton Budz!*' she repeated impatiently. '*Coline Mac Cullosh!*'

'Oh!' I said, as the penny dropped. No, I hadn't read *The Thorn Birds*. I hadn't read anything of Colleen McCullough's.

She adored Colleen McCullough. She had commanded the *bibliobus* to bring her *anozzer* book by Colleen McCullough every time it came to Espagnac. From her imaginative leap from my description of my book to the *oeuvre* of Colleen McCullough, I gathered that mine could very well be, in her view, *de trop*.

'But,' I added, 'I do write for one or two hours every day – about the villages here and the people, our walks, the landscape, and I email what I write to my friends ...'

Now, in April, there were blossoms and flowers and new life everywhere. Along the *sentiers*, convolvulus, daisies, periwinkles, primroses, cowslips, wallflowers, harebells, honesty – all those 'English' flowers we used to sing songs about in the antipodean schools of my childhood without having a clue what they were. Gardens came alive with pink and white fruit-tree blossom, forsythia, tulips in fantastic colours and patterns, irises, camellias.

A few weeks after the '*ton budz*' conversation with Mme Bonzani, there was another *repas* in the *salle des fêtes*. This one was organised and prepared by the *Association des amis d'Espagnac-Sainte-Eulalie*, the friends of Espagnac-Sainte-Eulalie, of which Didier Cabrignac was president. The *repas* was called *poule farcie* – literally, stuffed chicken. Soup, *salade composée* – lettuce, eggs and smoked duck breast, the *poule farcie* – chicken and stuffing with big yellow potatoes, *cabécou*, *tarte aux poires* – pear tart, and *vin à discretion*.

Nearly everyone from the two villages was there, including the children and some very old people. It was like a big family get-together. The children took it in turns to promenade Charlie around the room, while the adults stood in loose groups or installed themselves at tables and drank their *apéritifs* of choice. Mine, I had decided, was *kir*.

Jocelyne introduced me to her husband Pierre, who had now retired from his job in Paris and returned to Espagnac to live. In his retirement, Pierre was taking on the role of *animateur* in the village, a kind of all-purpose master of ceremonies. He had a huge library of dance music for different kinds of function. Tonight it was *musette* – accordion music: waltzes, polkas, *paso doblés*.

Martine introduced me to Martine and Alain Rochefort. I recognised them as the couple I often saw in a white van, tending to the sheep in the meadows around the village, who smiled and waved as Charlie and I passed by. This time, they both kissed me.

I had remembered to bring my *couvert*, and one for Nicole. She had been working in the tower that Saturday, getting the *gîtes* ready for the pilgrims on the Chemin de Saint-Jacques de Compostelle. When the moment arrived to be seated, we found ourselves at a table with Rolande and Mimi and a hale old man who, like them, lived at Diège, and whose identity I knew, as he did mine. Rolande introduced us formally.

'*Monsieur Roger Sudres, je vous présente Mme Maureen Cashman.*'

'*Oui, je sais,*' he said, with a sheepish smile. 'I know.'

'I wrote to you from Australia, when I first thought of coming to stay here,' I said, 'asking about your *gîte* at Diège. I found it in the *Gîtes de France du Lot.*'

'*Oui, je sais,*' he repeated. 'I never answered. *Dommage*, what a pity!'

While we ate, I asked the older people about aspects of their lives here in the past. Mimi and Rolande's father had worked in a bank at Villefranche de Rouergue before the family moved to their farm alongside the road at Diège. After the war, Mimi had married Georges Benet, who, like M. Sudres, and later Rolande, had gone to primary school in the former salon of the priory, which was now the dining room of Les Jardins du Célé. Georges had later won a scholarship to be educated in a seminary, training for the priesthood, but changed his mind when he met Mimi soon after his graduation from high school. Meanwhile, Roger had spent the last years of the war, when he was in his twenties, as a forced labourer in a Volkswagen factory in Germany and had never married.

'All the good ones were taken when I got back,' he said, with a broad smile of resignation.

I thought that, if I had the opportunity after I had got to know them better, and my French had improved enough, I would ask them for more detail, to supplement with personal stories what I already knew in general terms from my reading about the village and the region.

Almost as soon as the long *repas* was finished, Rolande drove Mimi and M. Sudres to their respective homes at Diège, and then came back to dance. As at the *repas de chasse*, all the adults who could stand up unaided, and all the little girls, danced, while the little boys chased one another around the *cour*.

Nicole, Charlie and I slept in one of the *gîtes d'étape* in the tower, so that I wouldn't have to wait till everyone went home before I could get to sleep; and so that Nicole wouldn't have to drive back to Figeac.

'Have you noticed, Maureen,' yawned Nicole, 'how many old bachelors there are in the Lot?'

'No, I haven't,' I laughed. 'Why are there so many?'

'They had to stay and look after the farm and their parents when *they* got old. Now these old men have a lot of land, but they're too old to farm it themselves, and farming isn't profitable anymore.'

One morning towards the end of the month I opened the curtains to find the Senacs' field on the other side of the wall occupied by quiet ewes, their newborn lambs racing and butting one another, long tails shivering and twitching. Along the road to Figeac, calves and foals chased one another up and down the meadows.

Walking through a village or hamlet, we would hear a continuous shuffling noise, and see an adult or a child on a bicycle, followed by a little flock of ewes and lambs on their way from the *bergerie*, the sheepfold on the *causse*, to the lush green spring pastures. I would put Charlie on his lead and we would wait beside the lane while the sheep danced past. Charlie looked from the sheep to me, alert, making the little huffing noise that said he was interested, bemused, and he might have a go if he wasn't on the lead.

Not long after, one Saturday evening Charlie and I were going for a stroll before dusk, when, passing the church, we heard a voice inside and I realised that there was a Mass going on in Notre-Dame du Val-Paradis. I had never been in the church, and as far as I knew, it was opened only when Mme Bonzani took visitors in on her guided tours.

I took Charlie home and went back. I let myself in the door and stepped quietly down into the musty space. Inside, there was soft electric lighting and candles burning on the altar table. The priest was in the middle of the sermon, addressed to the two other people there, Solange Cabrignac and Rolande. I slipped between rows of the child-size wood-and-rush chairs at the back of the nave and glanced around discreetly.

I had read in Mme Pernet-Lauzur's book that the apse and the choir had been built in the fourteenth century. The modern, plain altar table was set up in the choir because an eighteenth century altarpiece, consisting of ornate gilded wooden panels and twisted columns and statuettes of saints and a ponderous painting of the Assumption, took up most of the apse. The altarpiece partly obscured the five perpendicular windows of the apse rising to a graceful vaulted ceiling. One of the windows, the one behind the altar, which faced onto the road outside, was bricked-up.

The cosy little nave where I was standing was the only part of the original church that had survived the Hundred Years' War. To my left, near the entrance, was another baroque touch, a red marble baptismal font in a filigree iron frame, too solid for the space it occupied. Around the walls were nineteenth century paintings depicting the Stations of the Cross, the oil paint so darkened by time and smoke from candles and incense that the Stations were indistinguishable. The captions beneath them were in both French and Spanish. I tried to visualise the simple beauty of the medieval structures without the eighteenth century excesses that cluttered the original high and light spaces. It would have been wonderful in Raymonde de Bauze's time.

As soon as he had given the final blessing, the priest departed, without waiting for the two euros Solange had collected – one from Rolande, and one from herself; in my haste to get back to the church, I'd neglected to bring any money. While Solange and Rolande tidied up and put away the Mass things, I went up the step into the apse and looked at the effigies in the niches beside the altar. On one side, his faithful dog at his feet, lay Hughes de Cardaillac, *seigneur* of Brengues and Montbrun, who died in 1345, and on the other, his wife, Bernarde of Trian. Back in the nave, in a dim niche, was the effigy of the Bishop of Coïmbre, Aymeric d'Hébrard himself.

'*La toumbo del Beat.*' Solange pronounced the Occitan words carved above the niche. 'It means the tomb of the Blessed One.'

The following afternoon I answered the knock on my door to find Rolande, smiling shyly, suggesting we go for a walk up the track to the *causse* above Diège. Rolande and Mimi lived in adjoining houses on the Figeac-Cahors road, on a sharp corner where a steep minor road cut up from the valley to the *causse*. From this road branched off the lane that straggled up the hill between the old dwellings of the hamlet of Diège. Further down the hill was the watercourse beside which Bernard de Griffeuille had founded the original monastery.

The hamlet of Diège had half a dozen houses still standing and as many permanent residents. In a bend in the lane was a disused communal oven that had been used to bake the bread of families that had once filled the dwellings that were now, mostly, holiday houses of absentee owners.

Rolande parked her car at the end of the lane and we set off up the stony hunters' track. It was a warm day.

'We must watch for *serpents*,' Rolande said. 'I hate *serpents*!'

'Are the snakes here dangerous?' I asked.

'No, but I hate them,' replied Rolande, shuddering. 'I hate them as much as the *vipères*.'

I called Charlie, who was padding ahead. It hadn't occurred to me that there might be snakes and adders in Val-Paradis.

Rolande strode along staunchly beside me, but after a while stopped, exclaiming, when she could get her breath, '*Tes longues jambes*, your long legs!' I was so used to marching around with just Charlie, I had to remember to slow down if I was walking with other people.

As we walked, she told me a little about herself. She had lived in Diège for most of her life, had gone to school at Espagnac and had seen many changes in her lifetime. She had two married daughters. One lived in the Aveyron Department and the other at Figeac. Her husband had deserted the family when the youngest daughter was still at school.

Under the brow of the hill were three *cazelles*, stone shepherds' shelters, two of them crumbling in places, but the third was in good shape, with a fireplace, an oven and a stone bench around the wall. Inside this one there was even a stack of wooden gates that had once been used for sheepfolds. The fields all around were overgrown with bushes and vines.

'It's a long time since there were sheep here,' said Rolande.

She led on, clambering up a blackberry-covered slope and over a barbed-wire fence into a field of lucerne. Charlie and I followed. 'The farmer lets us cut across his field. We always come up to the *causse* that way, since we were children.'

Over the field we went and joined another track running beside a pasture full of the local black-eared, black-eyed sheep.

'*Benny-Ben!*' Rolande called to the sheep, '*Benny-Ben!*'

The sheep aimed their gorgeous dark eyes at us and flapped their soft black ears. Charlie stared back, huffing, curious.

I asked Rolande about the Mass the previous evening.

'I didn't think the church was used anymore,' I said.

'*Si!*' she said. 'There are Masses every weekend in different villages of the parish. It was our turn this weekend, but everyone forgot it was on. The priest isn't *sympa*, nice. He says Mass and takes off without even waiting for the collection.'

'It must be a hard life for priests here nowadays, having to travel around to say Mass for tiny congregations,' I said. 'It used to be like that in the early days in Australia.'

But Rolande was unmoved. She told me about *l'ancien curé*, the priest they had had in the past, how he used to organise excursions and pilgrimages for the faithful of the six or seven village churches he was responsible for. 'We went to Lourdes, Fatima, everywhere. This one does the weddings and the funerals, the baptisms, that's all.'

When we got back to her house, she asked me in for a cider, pausing on the way to whistle to the bright little red and black orioles in a cage on her porch. On the wall of her cool parlour was a large studio photograph of a young blonde man with the same transparent and innocent smile as hers. As we drank the cider and she slipped a biscuit under the table to Charlie, she saw me looking at the photograph.

'*C'est mon fils*, that's my son,' she said and gestured towards the window. 'He was killed on the road just there. He came down the hill on his motorbike into a car.' She told the story without any self-pity or recrimination, with dry-eyed stoicism.

When Charlie and I were leaving, I hugged her.

A few days after the walk with Rolande, Charlie became lethargic and stopped eating. I knew the signs, and made him stand on the end of my long table, where the sun slanted in the window, to feel him all over for ticks. I soon found one firmly entrenched in his scalp. I was surprised because I'd treated him with a tick control agent only a fortnight before.

Everyone had some advice.

Thierry asked about the colour of his urine. Was it *foncé*, dark? *Bien*, he was getting rid of the poison. '*Il va guérir*, he'll get better.'

Martine said to go to the pharmacist at Figeac and get tablets for the piroplasmosis, the infection of the blood carried by ticks.

Mme Bonzani was shocked when I said I'd just pulled the tick out with tweezers.

'First, you must make 'er *paralysée*, paralysed. If you don't make 'er *paralysée*, she won't let go.' She bent her knees and curled her body up into the shape of a gigantic tick. She formed her hand into an imitation of the tick's head and fastened it on my arm, digging her index and middle fingers into my flesh. ''Er 'ead will not come out.'

It was no good telling her I had already got the whole tick out; she was on a roll.

'You must send 'er to sleep with *éther*. You 'ave *éther*?'

Of course I didn't have any ether.

'You must put *beaucoup d'éther*, much *éther* on some *coton*, and put the *coton* on 'er for the longest time possible, until she goes to sleep.' She closed her eyes and put her head on one side, then she opened one eye to check if I was paying attention, closed it again and opened the other one.

We went to Figeac and got a bottle of ether and a bag of cotton balls for next time, and a course of penicillin for now, and Charlie recovered.

The smell of the ether wafting from the cupboard in the bathroom where I stored the bottle lingered in the nuns' room for months.

There was a run of days alternately 'blue' and 'grey', and after the rain there appeared hundreds of fat cream-coloured snails dragging their yellow-brown shells along the *sentiers*, followed by dozens of human collectors with baskets on their arms, gradually filling with the hapless gastropods.

I asked Nicole what they did with them.

'First,' she said, 'we put them in a mesh cage for around fifteen days without any food, to purge them. Then we rub each individual snail with a mixture of rock salt and vinegar it to make it dribble copiously. Then we immerse the snails in a big pot of boiling water for five minutes. When they are cool enough to handle, we pull the bodies out of the shells and clean the shells thoroughly. Then we boil the snails again in a *court-bouillon* for an hour. We prepare a sauce of melted butter, garlic, parsley, nutmeg and country ham. We replace the snails in their shells, pour the sauce over and serve.'

'Thank you, Nicole,' said I, sinking into a chair, as blanched as a snail. 'But I have a question. Is it necessary to return each snail to its own original shell, or doesn't it matter?'

Not long afterwards, Nicole asked if I would like to join her and her daughter and son-in-law, Christel and Frédéric, and their little daughter Maeva, *chez* Jacotte and Thierry for a 'wild food' *repas*.

The dining room was at the front of the house, part of the priory building that faced the road that ran through Espagnac.

'In the time of the nuns, it was the *grand parloir*, the parlour,' Thierry said as he ushered us in. 'Afterwards, it was the village schoolroom.'

I looked around the big square room: lattice windows, polished wooden floorboards, huge chimneypiece decorated with a late medieval painting of a lute player. A couple of music stands, supporting old reproductions of medieval music sheets. In this room over centuries the *prieures* received bishops and bourgeois donors and argued with the patrons. Here, Monsieur Delrieu had paid the *prieure* Jeanne de Gontaut de Roussillon the price of admission of his daughter Marie to the community of *professes*. Martine's father, Roger Sudres and Rolande had also gone to primary school here.

For *apéritif* we had *beignets aux orties*, nettle leaves dipped in salty flour and deep-fried. They were like light chips with a delicate flavour. The soup was made from *fanes*, turnip tops. Then a rice and mushroom mould with preserved figs in the middle, followed by slices of lamb, cut from a leg.

'The sheep here are called *caussenade du Lot*, and also *mouton à lunettes*, because they look as if they are wearing sunglasses,' said Thierry. 'These sheep are immune to piroplasmosis.'

'So if Charlie was a real lamb, instead of a pretend one,' I said, 'he wouldn't have got sick.'

'*Exact*,' said Thierry.

After the lamb, a salad of lettuce and walnuts, and three kinds of *brebis*, sheep's cheese. The dessert was a *myrtille*, wild bilberry, tart. And *prune*.

At the end of the month, as a way of showing my appreciation of everything they had done for Charlie and me so far, I invited Martine and Philippe, Jean-Louis and Christiane and Nicole for an *apéritif*. I served some of the fine fare I had begun to buy as a matter of course on my Saturday trips to the *marché* and *supermarché* at Figeac: *kir*, of course, *saucisson*, thick sausage, *saucisse*, thin sausage, paté, *Roquefort*, olives and *cornichons*, little gherkins. When they arrived, Jean-Louis and Philippe carried in a cabinet that nobody wanted, for me to use as a bookcase. We put it behind my desk by the window and when I moved my radio-CD player to sit on top of it, I found that I could now tune it to France Musique, the classical music station with no advertisements, and I was very happy.

SALADE QUERCYNOISE

Shortly after my drinks evening Nicole invited me to spend a Saturday in Figeac with her. We would go to the *marché* in the morning, have lunch, and after lunch we were going to load the prunings of her fruit trees into a skip she had hired.

The *marché* occupied several of the *places* and streets of the town. Place Carnot was crammed with stalls where *producteurs*, the producers, sold their vegetables and fruit, cheeses, poultry, seedlings, breads and cakes, hams and sausages, blood puddings and patés, juices, jams, honeys and wines.

The three of us wandered through the cobbled streets from *place* to *place*, past stalls where the vendors, in clouds of aromatic steam, cooked *beignets aux pommes*, apple fritters, *aligot*, a viscous mixture of mashed potato and melted cheese, and delicious-smelling Spanish paella. The open *places* were crowded with stalls and vans selling meat, nuts, olives, marinated vegetables, and fish that flipped around in buckets of water until the customers pointed at the ones they wanted and the *poissonnier*, the fishmonger, pulled them out and knocked them on the head.

Charlie kept his little body between us, out of the way of the battery of moving feet. Nicole gave me a running commentary on which stalls had the best apples, the best lettuces, chickens, *et ainsi de suite*. We stopped at a van displaying specimens of poultry I'd never seen in quite that way before. There were whole chickens and ducks with lolling heads, veiled eyes and rigid feet; trays of necks and feet; *magret*, preserved duck fillets; carcasses, stripped of meat, for making stock; *gésiers*, preserved duck gizzards; hearts; livers.

Nicole bought a *magret*, some *gésiers* and a small *foie gras* – literally, fatty liver, which I had read came from geese that were force-fed till they couldn't stand up. She said she was going to make a traditional *salade quercynoise* for our lunch. I tried to absolve myself in advance for what this involved; the population of France would not be moved from their partiality for *foie gras* if I disappointed and insulted a friend who wanted to introduce me to its delights.

Back at Nicole's house, she unlocked the door to her *cave*, her cellar. It was lined with wine racks full of dark, dusty bottles.

'Not long before he went to live with his *copine*,' she said, 'my husband and I bottled 100 litres of Nuits Saint-Georges. I drink very little, myself, but when I bought him out of the house, I kept the wine.' She laughed grimly. '*Tant pis pour lui*, too bad for him! *Et tant mieux pour nous*, all the better for us. We are going to have some with our *salade quercynoise*.'

While Nicole was preparing the *salade* – lettuce, *échalote* – small sweet onions, *gésiers* fried in a little duck fat, sliced *magret*, slices of *foie gras* fried briefly in a very hot pan, walnuts – I recounted to her Sarah Turnbull's story in her book, *Almost French*.

'She served pasta as the main course at a dinner party. One of the guests took her aside and said that was *pas comme il faut*, not done.'

'Ha!' Nicole snorted. 'Maybe it's like that in Paris. Here, we have a saying: it's better to eat an omelette with a friend than *foie gras* with an enemy. *Mais*,' she gestured to me to be seated, 'today we are making an exception, because we are friends, Maureen.'

We started with a glass of sweet Pineau des Charentes, '*pour digérer*, for the digestion', and raw baby radishes dipped in salt and eaten with fresh buttered bread. Then Nicole dressed the *salade* with a few drops of red wine vinegar and fat from the *gésiers* and poured little glasses of the rich red Burgundy wine.

'*À ta santé*, Maureen!'

'*À ta santé*, Nicole!'

She watched me take my first bite of *foie gras*.

'It's really delicious,' I said sincerely.

She laughed with pleasure. '*Bon appétit, toutou,*' she said, slipping Charlie a *gésier*. 'How do you say *bon appétit* in English?'

'*Bon appétit,*' I said. 'It's the same as the French. We don't have our own word for it.'

Nicole looked smug. '*Et comment dire caniche en anglais?* How do you say *caniche* in English?'

'Poodle.'

'Poo-doll,' she experimented, her lips pursed, as French speakers do. The French 'l' sound is formed just behind the teeth, not on the palate, like the English 'l' is with words like poodle. 'Pood-ul. Pood-le.' Nicole rolled her eyes.

To finish, we each had a slice of *Roquefort*, the delicious blue sheeps' cheese.

'The flavour comes from a special *champignon*, a fungus that grows only in the rocks around the village of Roquefort-sur-Soulzon, where the cheese is made,' said Nicole, holding a piece up for Charlie, who was pirouetting from one of us to the other in anticipation, like a true Pavlovian.

Saint-Roch, I thought, smiling, as the aroma of the Nuits Saint-Georges filtered in spurts of contentment directly into my brain, *dogs in heaven, a talking dove, a fungus-flavoured cheese, what a culture.*

After a concluding little *digestif*, we didn't make much headway with the prunings. '*Tant pis!*' said Nicole, making a little exploding sound with her lips.

VISITORS

Between bouts of social activity, in general I lived a solitary, reflective life – reading, writing, eating simply, talking seldom and then mostly about day-to-day matters, listening much. Although I experienced spells of loneliness, my circumstances allowed me to give rein to aspects of my personality I liked, such as my interest in and ability to empathise with other people, my love of sharing stories and ideas, and my sense of humour. My life in Espagnac was much less cluttered and complex than it had been in Canberra. This, I realised, made redundant or at least suppressed some of the aspects of my personality I didn't like, such as worrying about what people thought of me, and occasional lapses into alienation and resentment. In my monthly reports which I emailed to friends in Australia, I could choose what to include, for example Charlie's and my involvement in the social life of the village, and what to leave out, such as my many linguistic gaffes and feelings of frustration and loneliness, and this gave me a tone of authority and confidence about the image I was projecting.

As for my neighbours in Espagnac, for them, I felt, there was a certain mystique to my existence here. Although my particular purpose for coming was losing its initial clarity, I was gradually taking on an identity that I liked and I thought they quite liked it too. I was the *écrivain australien,* immersing herself, within the limits of her language and her foreignness, in the life of the village and clearly delighted to be there.

In my attempts to write my novel, in the long walks by day, and in the long quiet evenings and nights, I spent many hours mulling over my feelings about the country where I was born, educated, had taught and contributed to curriculum innovations in schools.

I respected my work colleagues and admired my friends, but I felt that the qualities I found in them – their thoughtfulness, tolerance and caring about other people – were not as prevalent among the rest of the population as I once believed they were.

I loved Australian literature, art and some of its music. Sitting by my window in the nuns' room, I could close my eyes and call to mind various Australian landscapes, and the flora and fauna, as easily as I could see the fields and *falaises* outside. But I remained troubled by much of what had happened in the 200 years or so since European settlement – not just in terms of cultural insensitivities and bad farming and environmental practices, but also by my country's involvements in various international conflicts.

The day the war in Iraq began – 20 March 2003 – Charlie and I were a long way from Espagnac, exploring Najac, a little town in the Aveyron Department dominated by a ruined fortified castle and keep on a high cliff overlooking the deep valley of the Aveyron River. I thought about the parallels between the long-forgotten warriors who had fought countless battles over the silver and copper once mined in the area, and the situation in the Middle East now, which was also partly based on the world's desire for a precious resource. I bought an English newspaper and sat at one of the tables outside a café in the wide main street to read about the invasion. 'BRING IT ON!' exclaimed the headline hysterically. The proprietor of the café, who brought my coffee, saw my tears of chagrin and returned with a bowl of water for Charlie and some tissues for me.

In emails from Australia, I read the same concerns as I had – a sense of helplessness, embarrassment and shame about what was happening within the national psyche.

I reflected sometimes in the lonely evenings that these thoughts would have been hard to bear on my own, without the comfort of Mozart and Mahler on France Musique and the contented minimalist music of Charlie's snoring on the bed.

My first English-speaking visitors, apart from Judy and David's occasional weekend visits from Paris, were friends from Birmingham, Mary, John and Fiona. Mary was the 87-year-old mother of one of my friends in Australia, and John and Fiona were Mary's next door neighbours, who treated her like *their* mother. Mary was clinically blind and stooped with age, but as strong and wilful as she had reputedly been all her life. I had last seen them all at the wedding of one of Mary's grandsons in Canberra a month before I came to France.

Despite my often bleak thoughts and the loneliness, I found that visitors disrupted the tenor of my life at Espagnac more than they would have done back home. I responded to the disturbance to my quiet life and my role in the village ambiguously. I enjoyed being able to discuss in English what was going on in the rest of the world, however worrisome, to catch up on the gossip, to try to describe Charlie's and my extraordinary ordinary life in Espagnac. Another part of me, however, was uneasy at being extracted, albeit temporarily, from my niche in the village. At speaking English in the presence of my neighbours about things so remote from the daily round of Espagnac, they could really have occurred in another universe. At dealing with visitors' views about 'the French' or their questions about 'what the French are like, really'.

One day Mary, John, Fiona, Charlie and I drove to the railway station at Figeac and took the train to Najac. The plan, when we arrived, was to phone a taxi to drive us from the station, which is in a gorge of the river, 2 kilometres up to the crag where the village and the castle perch.

We were the only passengers to alight. The platform was deserted, except for our little group and the station attendant. He waved his flag and blew his whistle, the train whirred off and then he too disappeared into his little office. Mary and Fiona waited on a seat on the platform while John and I looked around outside for a phone booth. There was no phone booth, no other building, nobody.

The station attendant was sitting at a desk in his office, enveloped in clouds of cigarette smoke.

'*Excusez-moi, monsieur,*' I said, '*désolée de vous déranger,* sorry to disturb you, but we need to find a taxi to take us up to the town.'

He looked sceptical, and made that puffing noise with his lips that meant, 'Hmm, I don't know about this.' He drew deeply on his cigarette. '*Un taxi,*' he said slowly, as if trying to remember what that was.

'Here's a number.' I showed him my guidebook and pointed out the phone number of the taxi service. He took the guidebook out of my hands, picked up the phone on his desk and called the number.

We waited and waited. Eventually someone answered the phone and the attendant spoke rapidly for a minute, then fell silent again. After another long wait, he rapped out, '*Merci,*' and put the phone down. 'They can't locate a driver,' he said matter-of-factly.

He pushed his chair back and stood up and we both went out onto the platform. He flicked his cigarette onto the railway line. He sized us up: John and Fiona, an able-bodied young couple; me, an able-bodied woman of a certain age; Charlie, a poodle; and Mary.

He turned back into the office, checked the electronic board behind his desk, picked up the phone again, told somebody something, locked the office, herded us out to the station car park and into the only car there, and drove us up the steep winding road to the village.

As soon as he deposited us outside the town wall and drove off again with a cursory wave of his hand out the window, we made our way to the tourist office and I asked if they would organise transport for our train back to Figeac at 6.30pm. I told them about the problem with the taxi service, that they couldn't locate a driver. The woman in the tourist office rang another number and had a long conversation with the person at the other end.

'It's difficult,' she explained, 'there are several *internements* on today, but if you will be outside the tourist office at 5.30pm, they will be able to help you.'

I explained to the others that our predicament had something to do with a large number of burials taking place that day. We could only speculate as to our slot in the *internement* schedule. 'I hope they're not counting on me,' said Mary.

Our transport at the end of the day turned out to be a combined ambulance, hearse and taxi that came from the flower shop and undertakers' at the village of La Fouillade. Despite the rigours of his calling, and his busy schedule, the driver was very affable and let Charlie surf with his front paws on the console all the way down to the station.

'He'd make a good driver,' he laughed, as Charlie leaned into the corners.

In the train on the way back, there was a seat between mine and the window, and Charlie jumped up on it. There were some other people in the carriage, some *randonneurs*, hikers, wearing boots and carrying walking sticks and backpacks. I looked at them anxiously to see their reaction to the poodle sitting by the window. They smiled with amusement.

'Oh, he wants to see outside,' said one woman, who came over to pat Charlie. 'What's his name?'

Charlie stayed on the window seat, giving little gasps of wonder and contentment all the way.

The following evening, we were passing a little terrace behind the wall beside the communal kitchen of the *gîtes d'étape* and heard voices. Some *randonneurs* were having a picnic at the table there. Charlie, with his usual interest in such occasions, disappeared into the terrace through a gap in the wall.

'*Est-ce que c'est Shar-lee?*' cried the *randonneurs*. 'Is that you, Charlie? *Bonsoir, Shar-lee, tu veux du fromage,* would you like some cheese?'

During the visit of the Birmingham Three, Charlie had his first French *toilettage*, at *Toutou chic*, a salon in Figeac. He had a number four cut all over, except for a little extra hair on his head and ears and tail.

'Was he good?' I asked Sylvie, the groomer. 'He's sometimes a little *méchant* with me.'

It was another one of those linguistic confusions, I learned later when I told Martine about it. '*Méchant*' means 'naughty' when applied to a child, but it means 'vicious' when describing an animal.

'*Méchant!*' Sylvie repeated, opening her eyes wide with disbelief. '*Shar-lee? Non, non, Maureen, il était a-dorable!*' She shook her head, hard, once, as if to affirm that she had never come across a dog as *a-dorable* as the one that was at that moment struggling to escape her ardent embrace and the rain of her kisses on his coiffure. *Jamais*, never.

AU REVOIR

By May the oaks on the *cause* and the poplars along the river had put on their leaves, and as the month progressed, from my window a sea of changing shades of green undulated under the blue-grey sky. Cuckoos called all day from the woods, and the baby blackbirds in the nest on the ruined buttress on the other side of the Bonzanis' *pont* had learned to fly and sing. A gang of swallows had joined the pigeons in the *cour*, ripple-darting between the *falaise* on the far side of the river and the *clocher* of Notre-Dame du Val-Paradis.

The Senacs' meadow beyond the wall of the Chemin des Dames was first studded with yellow dandelions, then with white pinwheels, and finally with tall rippling grass. Some mornings I opened my curtains to find the meadow occupied by beautiful sleek horses, rolling in and cropping the lush grass. The riders had spent the night in the *gîtes d'étape* in the tower, and would now be having breakfast *chez* Thierry and Jacotte. There was also the odd donkey, carrying the load for the pilgrims.

The *sentiers* through the woods were still strewn with buttercups and daisies, honeysuckle, convolvulus, campanula and little delicate white and yellow groundcovers and blue buttons, as well as thousands of blue and pink orchids and pink clover flowers. Poppies began to splash the green with orange-red.

One day, Eva Dubuisson guided me up a stony track off the road that climbs up the *falaise* to the Causse d'Espagnac, to a meadow teeming with wild narcissi, small white skirts, each with a little yellow bell in the centre. We picked as many as we could carry, and the narcotic scent of them filled my apartment and temporarily overcame the smell of Charlie's ether.

In the middle of the month, Espagnac's *Anglais*, Terry and Anne Kempley, who spent the warmer months at Espagnac, and the winter in England, returned to the house and *grange* they had bought as a ruin twenty years previously. In the weeks before their arrival, the village was abuzz with excitement, and several people came to tell me they were coming.

'You'll have someone to speak English with,' said Solange.

I couldn't tell if the delight in her face was for me or for the village, for *les Kempleys* were obviously well liked and were evidently particular friends with Solange and René.

When I met them, I understood why. Charlie and I were crossing the bridge when we spied them in their garden below the road, so we stopped to introduce ourselves. They were gracious and friendly and invited us for an *apéritif* that evening. They clearly loved the place and the people as much as I was growing to do. They showed me photos of their house and the *grange* where animals were kept in the past, as they were when they had bought them: the crumbling roofs and walls of the house; the piles of straw and manure on the floor of the *grange*. They had transformed the buildings into the beautiful turreted structures I always admired from the landing at the top of the steps outside my *gîte*. The interiors they restored to retain the simple beauty of a French country house. They had added a swimming pool beside the *grange*.

They were the first of the summer influx of owners of the houses that had been shut up ever since Charlie and I arrived.

Florence, who had been Judy's and my French teacher at the Alliance Française in Canberra, had come to France to visit her daughter, who was living in Paris. She also wanted to revisit her friends and relatives in Poitou-Charentes on the Atlantic coast, north and west of our region, the Midi-Pyrénées. Towards the end of May, Florence, Judy and I took the opportunity to do a three-day walk in the Loire-et-Cher Department. They took the train from Paris, and I drove from Espagnac, and collected them at the station at Vendôme. At the end of the walk, Judy returned to Paris, and Florence and I wended our way in my little Ford back to the Midi-Pyrénées through the Pays de la Loire, Poitou-Charentes and Aquitaine.

Meanwhile, Charlie stayed with Terry and Anne, who in two weeks had become his great friends, and with whom he achieved a certain cultural cachet. They took him with them to an art exhibition in Figeac, and a photo of him (on the floor, near somebody's feet) appeared in the regional section of *La Dépêche du Midi*, the newspaper of the whole of the Midi-Pyrénées. *'Un caniche cultivé'*, read the caption.

Florence and I rested for a day or two at Espagnac, then, with Charlie back on board, continued south to the Languedoc-Roussillon region, where Florence, Judy and David and several other Australians had bought a house together the previous year in a village near the town of Béziers. We made excursions to the tourist towns and grey beaches strung along the Mediterranean, sampling *moules frites* – mussels and chips – and swimming in the tideless sea. Charlie tried to make friends with the poodle that spent most of its time sitting on the counter of the *Bar-Tabac* in the village, but the poodle and the poodle's owner were nervous about this foreign contact, even though the other poodle's name was, mysteriously, Skippy.

At the end of that week of relaxation and desultory exploration in the warm south, we began our return to Espagnac, making a wide detour to Aix-en-Provence and Avignon and other towns that, frankly, were more interesting for the people than for the poodle. He was unimpressed by the Palais des Papes and he peed on the Pont du Gard. The tinned food I fed him while we were travelling gave him diarrhoea. We spent our last night away from home at a *chambre d'hôte* perched high above a gorge in the Cévennes. My bed was adorned with an enormous stuffed lion. Normally Charlie was distrustful of stuffed animals, or perhaps their state aroused in him vague forebodings. Anyway, normally, he barked at them. This time he climbed on the bed and curled himself into a ball against the lion's belly, closed his eyes and gently snored.

'Welcome back!' cried Martine, when I took Charlie round to the *mairie* the Monday after our return from the south. '*Et toi aussi, monsieur Shar-lee!*'

'Charlie didn't enjoy it as much as I did,' I said. 'He prefers village life to travelling.'

I told her all about where we had been and what we had seen.

'*Bien sûr,*' she said, 'You should take advantage of your time here, to see other parts of France.'

'After all,' I said, 'the world isn't waiting for my book.'

'*Bien sûr.* After summer, you can settle down to work.' She eyed me questioningly. 'You're going to come back to Espagnac?'

'I'd like that very much.'

'*Et toi, toutou?* You want to spend the month of July *chez nous* at Espagnac?'

Charlie danced around on his hind legs, grinning.

He had become more a part of the landscape than I.

I was going to spend the month of July with a friend who lived on the Mani Peninsula in the Peloponnese, and Charlie was going to stay *chez* Bagreaux. Then, when I returned to France, we would spend the month of August in the village of Grèzes, in a converted barn owned by the parents of Pascale Cabrignac, and my niece Penny would join us from Amsterdam.

'While you're away, you can leave all your things in the *grenier,*' said Martine.

During our absence in Loire-et-Cher and Languedoc-Roussillon, work had begun on the construction of a wooden staircase in the entry between my apartment and the *grand gîte* opposite. The staircase led to the *grenier,* the attic that extended to the end of the building overlooking the Bonzanis' *potager.* Eventually, the *grenier* would be converted into two more *gîtes,* but not, Martine assured me, in my time as tenant, nor indeed in her time as mayor.

One day when Charlie and I were out and about we met a woman with a walking stick in the Chemin des Dames, coming down towards the *cour.* With a vivacious smile she introduced herself, in English.

'Sigrid Deffner. I would like to invite you to dine at my house on Saturday night. Your dog, too. But you can visit me at any time before and after that.'

I knew who she was and where she lived. Mimi and Rolande, her friends of many summers spent in Espagnac, had been looking forward to her return from her home in Osnabruck in Germany where she spent the winter months. Charlie and I often passed her Hansel-and-Gretel cottage when we took the steep path up to the *causse.*

That afternoon as we passed the house on our way back, she was sitting at a wooden table in her little garden working on some crochet. She beckoned me to come in the open gate and she showed us around the stone cottage. I kept Charlie on the lead to stop him from dashing around in his usual fashion, exploring every nook and cranny of premises new to him.

The ground floor was an open area with a kitchen at one end, a big fireplace at the other end and a long table in the middle. She pointed out the niche in the wall that was used in the past as a sink for washing. A hole in one of the far corners allowed the water to drain outside the house. A staircase led up to a small bathroom and two small bedrooms with gabled windows. She told me that the cottage, like the Kempleys' house and *grange,* had been a ruin when she and her husband, Walter, bought it. Not long after they had finished restoring it, in 1989, Walter died.

We went back to the garden with a pot of *tilleul*, tea made from the blossoms of the lime tree near her house and we fell naturally into conversation. Sigrid's English, it turned out, was as good as her French, and although we agreed that it would be better for us to practise speaking French together, it was easy to lapse into English, so our conversation was a mixture of both.

Over time, in the course of many pleasant hours in her garden, I gathered something of hers and Walter's story.

During the Second World War Sigrid was a schoolgirl in Osnabruck, 70 per cent of which was destroyed by bombs. Her family's apartment was destroyed and they had to start again from scratch. There was not enough food until 1949. She met Walter in February 1950 and they married in July 1951.

Walter had not completed his apprenticeship as a compositor in his father's little printing business when he was conscripted into the German army. He was taken prisoner-of-war in 1944 in Normandy when he was twenty-one years old. He was transported to a prisoner-of-war camp in the United States and the following year to England where he had to work in a steel factory until December 1947. His younger brother had died near Vienna in 1945, a few days before the end of the war.

When Sigrid and Walter married, much of Osnabruck was still rubble and they lived in one room of Walter's parents' flat, where their first son was born two years later. It wasn't until the end of the 1950s, and they had two more sons, that they had a flat of their own, the same flat that Sigrid lived in now.

'But,' she said, smiling, 'it was a very different time and everybody was happy to have survived this terrible war.'

They first came to Espagnac in 1971. They had been canoeing on the Lot and were looking for a quiet place to camp for the last few days. The municipal camping ground at Brengues had just opened and while they were staying there they visited Espagnac. They bought the ruined barn in 1981 and spent their holidays restoring it.

Sigrid showed me a little book of sketches and descriptions of Espagnac that Walter had made in the summer of 1987, two years before he died. She translated the words he had written at the front: 'This summer we intended to write a lot of letters to our friends, relations and sons. But the summer passed too fast with a lot of work and activities. But now you have them in another form.'

'He did with his drawings what you are doing when you write about our village,' she said.

The dinner that Saturday night, the first of many, with Mimi, Rolande and Terry (Anne had gone to England), was in Sigrid's little walled garden, by moonlight with soft electric lighting slanting into the garden through the French windows.

A few weeks later I gave my first dinner party for Sigrid, Mimi and Rolande. The menu: melon and ham; *pintade*, a guinea fowl that I bought from Martine Rochefort, with cabbage and apple and green beans; salad; cheeses; *tarte normande*, apple tart. It was too hot to stay inside the nuns' room. I set the table under the walnut tree in the *cour*, and we ate by candle- and moon-light. Eva, dressed in a traditional peasant costume, hung out of Jacotte's kitchen window in the warm dark and wished us *bon appétit*.

And now it was June, and, as I knew from the beginning, the nuns' room had long ago been let to others for the following two months.

That summer of 2003 was one of the hottest and driest on record. It was accompanied by nationwide strikes, protesting against the government's changes to working hours and superannuation entitlements, which disrupted transport, health and education services.

It also brought an invasion of flies. Jocelyne Sommie gave me some fly papers which I hung at various places in the apartment, and within days sticky black gobbets of fly jam were dripping off them onto the floor.

On Saturday evenings that summer Terry Kempley and I offered English lessons. Our students ranged in age from five (Manon Cabrignac) to over seventy (Solange and René, Rolande), and in experience from none at all (Manon, Solange, René, Rolande, Christiane), to current primary school (Camille, Bastien, Anaïs), to high school some time ago (Martine, Jean-Louis, Didier, Pascale, Anaïs' parents Natalie and Pierre). René said that if he didn't learn anything in the first *séance*, he wouldn't return, and he didn't. Boris Bagreaux never appeared. We divided the class up into beginners, whom Terry took, and the adults who had studied English at school.

I took this group. They would tell me the situations in which they thought they might need English. Pascale was an anaesthetist at the hospital in Figeac, so she wanted to be able to talk about medical matters. Pascale and Didier, Natalie and Pierre sometimes went on holidays to anglophone countries, so they wanted to talk about 'olidays and shopping. I would invent a scenario and provide vocabulary and phrase lists. They would divide into two groups and compose a little script, which they would perform for one another. The performances usually involved torture and extreme violence such as tooth-pulling and plane hijacking.

Towards the end of June the annual village clean-up day was held. I worked on the banks of the Célé, raking up and piling the branches and weeds the men chopped down with their power tools. Afterwards there was a *repas* that started after 10pm. It was so hot that we carried the long tables out from under the arcade into the courtyard and ate under the stars.

All the permanent *villageois* I knew were there, and so were the summer residents I'd met: Terry and Anne from England, Sigrid from Germany, and France and Lucien from Paris, who owned a house in Diège. And a new couple, whom Martine introduced as '*nos belges*, our Belgians', Milou and Eric, bronze-skinned from their winter on the Costa del Sol: Milou, straight blonde hair; Eric, a mane of black swept-back hair; both beaming.

'Hel-lo,' said Milou, in English. 'We know all about you. We've been looking forward to meeting you.'

'And now I have to go away,' I replied.

In the midst of all these new and newer friends, I felt sad, and not just because I was leaving Charlie for a month.

'But you will return,' said Martine. '*Nous garderons Shar-lee en otage*, we will keep Charlie hostage.'

On the morning before I took the train to Paris, on my way to Greece, I delivered Charlie and a month's supply of his food to the Bagreaux. At the doorsill of their kitchen, he cast a backward glance at me, gave a little uncertain shake of his pompom, then trotted inside.

GRAND RETOUR

Paris is subdivided into twenty administrative districts, called *arrondissements*. They spiral clockwise from the first *arrondissement*, which surrounds the Jardins des Tuileries and the Musée du Louvre, beside the Seine. If you walk straight up the Avenue des Champs Élysées from the Jardins des Tuileries you arrive at Place Charles de Gaulle-Étoile, the grand star-shaped intersection with the Arc de Triomphe in the middle. Just north of here, in a little street in the seventeenth *arrondissement*, was the Wilsons' flat. The last time I had been there was when Charlie and I first arrived, with the incident of the freight office still raw and unnerving and the city shrouded in sleet and snow.

That was January, and now, on my return from Greece, it was the beginning of August, when shops close arbitrarily, Parisians desert the sweltering city to go on holidays, and even though the tourist season is at its height, services are cut or changed *without warning*.

From Judy and David's, there are two fairly direct ways of getting to the Gare d'Austerlitz, from where the trains to Figeac depart. The shortest way is via the *métro* Line 1 from Porte Maillot to Bastille, then Line 5 to Gare d'Austerlitz. The other way is via the RER – *Réseau express régional*, the regional express rail network – directly from Porte Maillot to Gare d'Austerlitz. I decided to take the RER, so that I wouldn't have to cart my luggage between *métro* lines. I gave myself, I thought, enough time.

But, among the spate of summertime *fermetures exceptionnelles* – 'extraordinary' closures – the RER terminated at Invalides, leaving me twenty minutes to find another way to Gare d'Austerlitz. It was too far to walk. A station attendant proposed a bus.

The bus was waiting around the corner. By the time I arrived with my little backpack and wheeling my suitcase, so was a sea of other people, tourists surging towards Musée d'Orsay, Notre-Dame de Paris and beyond. Each wave rippling onto the bus stopped beside the driver to ask, in a form of English, where they should get off.

'We wanna goda Noder Dayme,' shouted a man, apparently the Incredible Hulk's twin brother, as he lurched up the steps ahead of a woman and two children, also of superhero proportions, each member of the family lugging a suitcase big enough to contain several changes of green muscle-suits.

'Does this bus go anywhere near Noder Dame?' Mrs Hulk shouted even louder, to make sure the driver understood. 'Ask him where we godda gedoff, Hank.'

I leaned forward from my haven between the perspex shield behind the driver and the side of the bus. 'I'll tell you where to get off,' I promised earnestly. 'Just move into the aisle.'

The bus arrived at Austerlitz with one minute to spare. I climbed over the Hulklings sulking on their suitcases and leaped out of the bus. I raced blindly through the concourse, with no time to focus on the information boards, where the changing letters and numbers, giving the destinations and departure times of trains standing in many of the nineteen platforms, tumbled and rattled as I ran past. I counted on seeing 'Brive-la-Gaillarde', where I had to change trains, on one of the platform entrances.

There was a whistle from a train revving in the last platform. The platform guard helped me up the steps, pushed my bag in after me and slammed the door shut. The train began to move.

The guard on the train smiled, wagged his hand from the wrist and made the puffing sound French people use to express a range of strong emotions or observations, in this case, 'That was close!'

'Is this the train for Brive?' I asked. Though there wasn't much I could do about it now if it *wasn't* my train.

'Bien sûr, madame.'

Train passengers in France are responsible for having their tickets stamped in one of the machines dotted around the stations, to ensure that the ticket is used only once. I hadn't had time to *composter* my ticket.

'*Pas de problème*,' said the guard, who had a little machine for dealing with people like me. He passed my ticket through it. '*Voilà, madame!*'

Passengers are also responsible for making sure that they are in the correct carriage. Parts of the train would uncouple at Limoges and go on to other destinations. Bouncing from side to side, lugging my case across the couplings, wrestling with the electronic doors, pushing past groups of people chatting in the corridors, it took an hour to negotiate the thirty carriages before I found my carriage and seat. Some of the carriages I passed through seemed to be air-conditioned, some not. Someone else was in my seat, so I took someone else's seat and so on. A guard came through and said there were some vacant seats in a carriage where the air-conditioning was working. Some people preferred to remain where they were, lying in the aisles, where a stream of air, a degree or two lower than the furnace-like atmosphere above them, swept along the floor.

Thus passed the five hours before the train arrived at Brive-la-Gaillarde. From there, what was left of the main train would go on to Cahors, and passengers for villages and towns between Brive and Rodez, capital of the Aveyron Department, would change to a regional train.

When the train drew into the station at Brive, a single small diesel-driven carriage was waiting at the platform on the other side of the tracks. Some of the passengers opened the doors on the railway line side, threw their bags down, jumped after them, clambered up the side of the little carriage and bundled themselves in. By the time I had hauled my bag down the steps, through the underpass and up onto the other platform, the carriage, whirring like a model railway, was stuffed to the gunwales.

We who were left on the platform formed a crowd around the station attendant, evidently a stand-in for Jacques Tati's film character 'Mon Oncle', hoping he had a solution to the problem. He drew reflectively on his pipe and wagged a finger to indicate subtle changes in his thoughts on the matter. There were a lot of '*Oui, mais*'s' and '*Parce que*'s', but nothing concrete until another attendant came along and said that there was a bus outside to take passengers going to Rodez. This news spread through the carriage and some of the people struggled out of the seats, aisles, luggage racks and so on and onto the platform. Meanwhile, 'Mon Oncle' strode purposefully out to the bus to try to negotiate a stop at Figeac too. He came running back along the platform shouting that the bus would go to Rodez or Figeac, but not both. So it went along the carriage that the Figeac people had to get off. Then there was a jam at the doors as the cunning *Rodezois* tried to worm their way back on between the departing *Figeacois*. The other attendant was sent back out to the bus to clarify which destination the bus was actually going to go to and some of the *Figeacois* tried to get back in the carriage. I kept saying I was going to Assier, which is the station before Figeac, and eventually a space was found for me just inside the door, on top of someone's bag. The other attendant returned saying that the bus would now go to *both* Figeac *and* Rodez and I had to get out of the carriage again while the *Rodezois* who owned the bag I was sitting on removed it and got off again. About twenty minutes later, with everyone who was left on the brink of asphyxiation, the little carriage gave a grunt and took off.

'*C'est un chien de campagne*,' said Martine, with a sheepish smile, once Charlie had stopped flipping around and sat down in front of us, grinning from ear to ear. He certainly looked different from the dog I had left: matted curls, dirty feet, twigs in his ears – and something else about his ears; what was it?

'Philippe couldn't get the burrs out of his ears, so he cut his hair off.'

Philippe had cut Charlie's wool straight across the bottom of his ears, so he looked like the young Prince Valiant, instead of the mature Louis XIV, the royal personage he normally resembled, especially after a visit to Sylvie at *Toutou chic*.

Philippe came out of the house and saw Martine and me inspecting Charlie. He smiled proudly at his handiwork, Charlie jumped up to greet him and Philippe clouted him around the head; Charlie growled fiercely.

'You're a country dog now, *Shar-lee*,' he said. '*C'est bien, ça.*'

The Parisians who had rented the nuns' room were there for another three weeks. Meanwhile, Charlie and I took up residence in a barn just outside the village of Grèzes, on the road that cuts up from the valley of the Célé onto the *causse*. The barn belonged to Marie and Claude Pocot, Pascale Cabrignac's parents, who had a house in Figeac and a holiday house across the road from our barn. They were in residence in their holiday house, and as soon as we arrived, they invited Charlie and me over for an *apéritif*. It was about eleven o'clock in the morning. We sat at a table outside the house in the shade of a walnut tree festooned with overflowing flytraps, eating cheese biscuits and *cornichons* and drinking whisky on the rocks. Then Marie proudly showed me through her house, which had also previously been a barn, bigger than ours, and which they had converted: kitchen, bathroom and sitting room on the ground floor; bedrooms in the loft.

'This is Manon's room when she stays with us,' said Marie, as we bent to enter a little attic room, full of bright pictures and bed covers and stuffed animals. Charlie barked at the stuffed animals, so we descended again to the garden, where Claude had poured another whisky.

Our barn had thick stone walls, a low roof, double wooden doors covering the entire entry, and wooden *volets* on the windows. Inside,

Marie and Claude had furnished a chimney corner with a table and armchairs, and installed a curtained bed over the former manger in the corner diagonally opposite. In the area between were a long dining table and dresser, a settee and a bar. All the cups and glasses on the shelves of the bar had the name of the drink they could be used for: Pernod, Dubonnet, *pastis*, whisky, Irish coffee, and so on. Two steps descended to an annexe, consisting of a galley kitchen, bedroom and a bathroom. In the kitchen was a fridge, a dishwasher, a gas stove with a lid, a sink and some shelves overhead.

'At Christmas,' Marie said, 'the whole family comes here for the *repas*: Pascale and Didier and Manon, my other daughter and son-in-law and their little ones, my son who has the bar-café La Cazelle at Figeac. We close the door and light the fire and the candles and we feast all day.'

It was hard to imagine Christmas now. It was too hot to walk after eight in the morning or before eight in the evening. Around six each morning Charlie and I would slip outside and set off along one of the dry-walled *sentiers* that crisscrossed the *causse* through the oak forests. Many of the trees had already put on autumn browns and russets. Though the beginning of autumn was weeks away, the *sentiers* were thick with leaves, too desiccated and exhausted to cling on to their branches any longer. The village *potagers*, so carefully tended since the beginning of spring, were hard and weedy now that water restrictions were in place.

At that hour, only the clinking bells of sheep in copses beside the lanes punctuated the morning quiet. Treading on leaves, we startled deer and rabbits grazing in the *sentiers*. The deer flew ahead, dislodged a little avalanche of stones from a break in the wall, then shied off through the trees, their bounding arcs cutting through the slanting green-gold light. Once, in a graded lane, a flock of sheep fell in behind us. Charlie was disconcerted by the clopping and breathing at our heels. He kept looking over his shoulder, then up at me as if to ask, 'What do they want?' At the end of the lane a gate opened into a walled field. Charlie and I stepped aside nimbly while the sheep trotted on into the field. Then we turned and padded away.

It was lovely to see our new 'old friends' again. Apart from Martine and Philippe, the first *Espagnacois* I saw was Jean-Louis Cabrignac. I had driven down into the valley to Marcilhac-sur-Célé, to get some bread at the *boulanger*. He had ridden over from Espagnac on his bicycle for the same purpose, and also to buy fresh goat's milk from a farmer there.

'*Hé*, Maureen,' he exclaimed when he saw me coming out of the shop. He leaned across his bicycle to exchange the usual number of kisses. 'Welcome back! *Et toi, Shar-lee,* you're pleased to see your mistress again?'

Our barn was on the road the *Espagnacois* would take to go up to the villages on the *causse*. Once or twice a day a car or bicycle on its way to Livernon or Assier would pull up on the other side of the low wall separating the barn from the road. I would hear the ordinary news of the village – the problems with the water supply in Espagnac, how the Parisians parked their cars wherever they wanted in the *place* outside the *mairie*. The visitor would hear our news – how we had been followed by a flock of sheep, how Charlie had jumped the wall to chase a bicycle.

'*Non, non, Shar-lee,* that's naughty,' the visitor would admonish. 'You'll be run over. They drive fast along this road. You have to be careful of him, Maureen.'

Some mornings I would drive down to the valley and park in the *cour* of the priory. Charlie and I would stroll around the village, stopping to chat to Sigrid drinking coffee in her garden, Solange collecting eggs in her hen yard, Mme Delfour resting in her cool parlour behind the half-closed shutters of her French windows.

As we passed the Bagreaux house, Charlie would push through the gate and bound down the garden to see if Philippe could come out and play.

The searing summer worked itself into a succession of spectacular *orages*, storms. By evening every day enormous black thunderheads were roiling over the *causse* and colliding in vivid shafts of lightning, which were followed by deafening thunder that reverberated against the *falaises* and rumbled along the valley.

On one such evening, an English violinist gave a concert in the church at Espagnac, part of the summer entertainment organised by the *Amis d'Espagnac-Sainte-Eulalie*. I drove down from Grèzes to hear the concert, and also to support the *Amis*. I said that I might not be able to stay till the end of the concert because I had to meet the train at Assier at 10.30pm. My niece, Penny, was about to commence studies at the Conservatoire in Amsterdam. While waiting for the faculty to regroup after the summer, she was going to spend a few weeks with me.

The church, for once, was packed. The whole village as well as the summer crowd seemed to be there, fanning themselves in the heat. The violinist, even if he had considered the likely tastes of his audience, evidently disregarded them. His sweat flying around the church like holy water from the aspergillum of a zealous *curé*, he played a repertoire that was as dissonant as the atmospherics outside.

The members of the audience wriggled on their little rush chairs. Rolande squirmed beside me. 'I don't like the violin,' she confided in a loud whisper. 'I prefer the accordion.'

At ten o'clock, the violinist showed no sign of giving in. I whispered to Rolande that I had to leave.

'*Je comprends*,' she stage-whispered back sincerely, 'I understand.'

Charlie was waiting in the car. To the clash and grumble of thunder we drove up the winding road to the *causse*. The modest beams of our little pewter-coloured car preceded us through the dark countryside, while lightning danced around the sky, rimming the purple clouds with brilliant silver and spotlighting out of the blackness here a copse, there wind-tortured branches, here a house, there a line of telegraph poles. Exhilarating but also frightening, even though the lightning would be more likely to strike the trees and poles than the little Ford scuttling across the *causse*. It was a relief to park at last in the lee of the station and sit under an awning on the platform, watching the spectacle outside.

Charlie, as usual, was unfazed by the pyrotechnics. Where other dogs would cringe and tremble at the sound of thunder and furious wind, he became alert, looking around at each thunderclap and shaft of lightning, huffing and puffing in excitement as we waited on the platform. But even he tired in the end. At eleven, the train still hadn't arrived, and the station office remained locked. A man's *portable* rang and he relayed the news: a tree had fallen across the line and the train would be stopped till it was removed. Then everyone else pulled out their *portables* and rang the other passengers, to say they were going home to await developments.

I didn't have a *portable*. I read all the notices on the windows of the station office, then we went for a walk around the car park and I read all the notices on the outside walls of the station. One of these announced a public meeting to protest against plans to close the station at Assier. That would be a shame, I thought. It would mean that the people who lived in villages around Figeac would have to drive 20 kilometres or more to catch or meet a train.

We walked around the village in the dark. Charlie was startled by the behaviour of a tuft of grass: he was just about to pee on it, when it started to edge away. Forgetting to pee, he lowered his leg slowly, and followed the hedgehog in little starts until it disappeared into the undergrowth.

We returned to the platform and sat on the bench under the awning again. I kept an eye on the red light 100 metres along the line, where the track traversed the road by which we had driven into the village. If it turned green, it would mean the train was coming, and the gates across the road would come down. It remained red. I yawned and rubbed my eyes, which were sore from tiredness and the strain of watching the psychedelic storm. Charlie slept on under the seat.

Around midnight, a few cars proceeded along the road outside the station and stopped, lights dimmed. Then another car sped up and stopped abruptly, the door slammed, and the station attendant, putting on his cap, strode onto the platform, unlocked the office door and disappeared inside. Bells rang, the green light came on, and the gates ground down across the road. The headlights of the train beamed out of the cutting and glinted along the tracks.

Penny was exhausted. She had been travelling for nearly twenty-four hours, nearly as long as it would take to fly from Australia.

'God, I'm starving,' came her muffled voice through my hair as we embraced. 'I shared my food with this French girl and she gave me some of her water. The trains were packed. Nobody knew where their seats were. The air-conditioning wasn't working. We all lay on the floor trying to get a bit of air.'

'I know, I know,' I said.

THE HORROR AT LES HALLES

For some reason, in the course of the month Penny and I spent at Grèzes, the number of visitors increased from one or two a week to several each day. The *boulangers* and little *supermarchés* at Livernon and Assier must have profited from the business that was thus diverted from Figeac. Penny was in the bloom of young womanhood: tall, slim, athletic, optimistic, decisive and showing, in her direct smile and appreciative exclamations, delight in everything she saw and experienced. The only foreign language she had studied was Japanese, but she communicated much through her expressive body language and candid blue eyes. It must have surprised the *Espagnacois* that the niece of the homely *maman de Shar-lee* should turn out to be such a stunner.

'*Magnifique*!' said the men, when they were introduced to her.

She was embraced enthusiastically by everyone who stopped by, and we enjoyed many long and convivial *apéritifs* with our Espagnac friends, at their homes down in the valley as well as *chez nous* on the *causse*.

We had missed some of the traditional summer activities, such as the *marché fermier* – farmers' market, and the *brocante* – the second-hand market, both of which had been held in the priory *cour*.

The *méchoui*, pronounced 'mesh-wee', was also supposed to happen in the *cour*, but due to the threat of *orages*, the venue was changed to a long covered, open-sided shed beside the road at Brengues.

'What's a *méchoui*?' I asked, when Martine and Philippe, passing by our barn, stopped to remind us about it.

'It's one of our traditional *repas*,' said Martine, vaguely.

The shed at Brengues wasn't the romantic setting of the priory *cour*. Close by was a field designated as the car park, swirling with dust as the cars nosed around it. Inside, among the crowded tables set out in geometric patterns beneath the corrugated iron roof, the heat seemed even more oppressive. At the end of the shed furthest from the car park a stage had been set up, and an *animateur* was playing a bracket of accordion music. Naked electric light bulbs were fixed at intervals along the back wall under the roofline, and dimly glowing bug zappers were attached to the tops of the poles along the open side of the shed.

By the time we arrived, everyone seemed to have claimed their places at the tables. I spied Milou and Eric and Jocelyne and Pierre at a table near the open side of the shed. Although the table was already full, they beckoned us over. Another chair was squeezed in for me, and Penny sat on Milou and Eric's esky. The others at the table were all relatives of Jocelyne's from Paris.

One was a young man with a five o'clock shadow, dressed in dark jeans and shirt. His hot-looking clothes matched his smouldering expression, which lightened when he looked down the table and noticed Penny perched on the esky.

'This is my son, Gilou,' said Jocelyne. 'He's been visiting his cousins in Brittany. It's cold there. He didn't realise it would be so hot here, and he hasn't brought the right clothes.'

My dictionary said that *méchoui* was a Moroccan dish of spit-roasted lamb, but it was for some reason one of the traditional *repas* of the *commune* of Espagnac-Sainte-Eulalie. The first course was *soupe au fromage*, a thick melange of bread and runny cheese. Penny thought it was very funny that the soup had to be eaten with a knife and fork, and set the mood for the evening by laughing so hard she fell off the esky. The *soupe* was followed by *melon au muscat*, half a melon each, with enough muscat in the hollow to compensate for the dryness of the *soupe*. Then *agneau de Quercy*, lamb, not spit-roasted but grilled, *flageolets*, beans, *Rocamadour*, little round goat's cheeses, *pâtisserie*, in this case chocolate eclairs, and *café*. The wine, as ever, was *à discrétion*.

Penny practised her Dutch with Eric and Milou and exchanged linguistic jokes with them including one with a punchline about what the Norwegian language sounds like – vomiting, apparently. Jocelyne suggested to Gilou that he sit next to Penny to practise his English. Gilou had wanted to practise English from the moment Penny arrived. He appeared more relaxed as the evening wore on and his brooding glower gave way to sweet, fleeting smiles. A clown in a harlequin suit took the stage, but he was so far away at the other end of the shed we couldn't see him, and the microphone distorted his jokes into meaningless roaring and mumbling. After the clown, the recorded accordion music was replaced by a real button accordionist, a local boy who was introduced excitedly by the *animateur* as the junior champion of the world. Eric wanted reassurance that we all loved him. Pierre said he adored Eric and kissed him on both cheeks. A buck's party with an inflated naked woman turned up and a table was set out for them outside near the car park, where they did rude things with the inflated woman and sang lewd, drunken songs. In spite of the conflict between the musical offerings of the accordionist and the buck's party, Pierre tried to teach Penny some of the local dances. They stepped around in the dust outside the shed, while thousands of moths immolated themselves in the sickly glow of the bug zappers overhead and fell to the ground in reeking spirals of smoke.

A few days later, Gilou came to our barn for afternoon tea. He was dressed in the same dark clothes he had worn to the *repas*. This time, he didn't look brooding so much as serious and slightly distraught.

'I drove past several times but I couldn't see where the gate was.' He was dripping with perspiration, and his five o'clock shadow was now a moist stubble.

Gilou's English was really quite good. He was very polite and wouldn't eat anything. Once he was sitting in the relative cool of the dim chimney nook with a cold drink, he began to unwind. At first, he and I did most of the talking, half in French and half in English, and Penny ate a plum.

In Paris, he was a trainee in a screen and sound laboratory where he worked on the days when he wasn't attending classes at the *Polytechnique*. He didn't like living in Paris, didn't like living in France. There were too many restrictions, too many rules. He wanted to travel. He had been to Amsterdam; there was much greater liberty in the *Pays-Bas* than *here*.

Penny, who now lived in the *Pays-Bas*, smiled and nodded sympathetically.

'But I don't find living in France very restrictive at all,' I said. 'In Australia, we seem to have many more rules and people are always ready to tick you off if you don't follow them. Here, people are more tolerant of other people's behaviour. And if they think the rules are stupid, they just ignore them.'

Gilou was not convinced. Of course, his situation was very different from Penny's or mine. We were both doing what we wanted to do, and everything for us was fresh and new. He hung on Penny's descriptions of the apartment she shared with another Australian girl above the Best Thai Restaurant on Elandsgracht, with the little canals at each end, and the wonky bicycle she got around on, that she had inherited from the previous tenant.

The conversation between them progressed to music and singers that I knew nothing about and eventually settled on what Gilou really preferred to do in life, which was composing and singing his own songs. His guitar was in his car.

'Would you like to bring it in?' I said.

He did, and played and sang several songs, most of which were his own compositions, in intense torrents of words and anguished chords. Charlie jumped down from the settee and came over to see if anything was wrong. Gilou, perspiring like an English violinist, broke off from time to time to apologise for the huskiness of his voice and accept a glass of water.

'This song,' he said eventually, 'is a poem my friend wrote and I set it to music. I didn't write it, my friend wrote it. I liked the poem, because it was so true-to-life. It's about a boy who returns to Paris after the summer and can't stop thinking about the girl he met on holiday.'

'God,' said Penny as we stood at the gate at the end of the garden waving him goodbye. 'I don't need any complications in my life right now.'

'He seems a nice young man,' I said. 'A bit intense, though.'

'It's your fault. If you hadn't had so much wine at the *méchoui* you wouldn't have invited him.'

'Did I invite him? I thought it was you.'

'I think,' she said, 'it's a good thing I'm going back to Amsterdam next week.'

Charlie's cheerful and accepting personality had served him well in Espagnac so far. He made friends with almost every human he met in the *commune* and beyond, and expected and received caresses from their hands and tidbits from their tables. He hardly concerned himself with the other dogs of the *commune* – Tenor confined in Solange's chicken run; Java, Odette's little deaf terrier that spent all day locked in a garage, barking compulsively, while Odette was at work; and the nameless, wandering Saint Bernard whose owners lived in the north. Charlie usually acknowledged them only by a cursory pee on their respective walls as he passed by. And the two Rochefort border collies, which we saw in the distance from time to time, were too busy working with the sheep to be bothered with an unemployed poodle.

He normally didn't anticipate dangers. Where they lurked or loomed – a *serpent* in the grass, an electric storm on the *causse*, a car speeding past our barn – he either didn't notice them or, as with his tick-sickness in the spring, forgot about them as soon as the hazard passed. Occasionally he mistook an object for a threat, such as M. Bonzani's hat, or a pile of rocks, and he would give a low, uncertain growl, or bark to make them go away. This was his least successful attribute. M. Bonzani only shouted back, and the pile of rocks refused to budge, so Charlie had to run backwards and forwards on one side of it to distract it, then creep past before the rocks could work out what he was up to. But generally, he behaved as if he had nothing to worry about.

One mercifully cool morning, Penny, Charlie and I walked the Brengues-Espagnac circuit. Bright butterflies, like shapes punched in a painted stage set to disclose the azure sky beyond, fluttered ahead of us along the path. I wanted Penny to see the views of the two villages from the escarpments on each side of the Célé and the ancient man-made springs and fountains below the Château de Brengues.

'The family lorded it over the *causse* and the valley in that loop of the river for nearly 1000 years,' I said. 'The peasants threw the *seigneur* out during the 1789 Revolution. But he wasn't murdered, like so many of the aristocracy at that time. I think they appreciated all these cisterns he had constructed so they didn't have to cart water up the *falaise* from the river.'

We rested by a mossy pond the *seigneur* had created, where red carp slipped through green water among white water lilies. Huge moths, the size of hummingbirds, hovered over the bushes on whizzing wings, dipping their long red proboscises into the flowers. Charlie lapped the water desultorily and splashed through the sodden weed.

'This is so strange,' Penny said. 'I can't believe we're sitting in the middle of where all that drama happened. But it's like that everywhere in Europe – all the towns and cities where famous events happened, where great artists and writers and composers lived and worked. In Amsterdam, the museums! And if I had the money I'd be able to go to a different concert every night at the Konzertgebau. Australia will seem very tame after this.'

'Well,' I said, 'Espagnac isn't Amsterdam, but I feel the same. There just seems to be so much more to discover and appreciate here, more depth to life. It's the length and the richness of the history, I suppose, even though a lot of it is pretty gruesome.'

'Australian history is all gruesome,' said Penny. 'The convicts, the way Aboriginal people have been treated. What we do with refugees.'

'Well, not all. Some of it is pretty optimistic.'

I reminded her of the way Australia had welcomed people from all over the world who'd gone there to escape various kinds of gruesomeness in their own countries. And how as a consequence we now had a thriving multicultural community that would be more difficult to achieve in France. And that along the way we'd produced some great authors and artists and musicians.

'I suppose a big difference,' I added, 'is that European and other old cultures are well-developed, whereas ours is still a work in progress.'

Descending by the rocky track back to Espagnac, we passed the Rocheforts' house in the hamlet of Pailles. It was after one o'clock, and Alain and Martine's van was parked beside the house. They were home for the midday *repas*, the main meal of their long working day. I took the opportunity to call in and ask Martine if she had any eggs to sell. I unlatched the gate to their front garden and knocked on the door. Penny and Charlie waited in the lane.

Alain was sitting at the table in the dim parlour, with a big bowl of *pot au feu*, a half-eaten lump of *pain de campagne* and a glass of red wine before him. Martine's serviette was lying next to her meal, which she had broken off to answer the door. The two dogs, Oualou and Tam, came to the door with her, and Martine held Tam's collar, to stop her going outside.

Although they were in the middle of their lunch, Martine waved aside my apologies and went down the steps to her cellar for the eggs, while I sat at the end of the table, declined Alain's offer of a glass of wine and caressed Oualou's silky head. When Martine returned, they all came to see me out. As soon as the door opened, Oualou shot out to the lane and bit Charlie ferociously on his side. Charlie and Penny both screamed in fright. Penny picked Charlie up and took him off down the lane, while Martine and Alain, mortified, sent Oualou and Tam back inside the house. Charlie, though safe in Penny's arms, went on screaming in protest.

'He'll be all right.' I tried to assure them that he was, after all, a bit of a drama queen. '*C'est un chien un peu comédien.*'

But when I joined Penny and Charlie, her hand holding his side was covered in his blood.

This was the first time it occurred to him that there were perils in Val-Paradis.

Before we had set off I had parked the car in the village, near the Bagreaux house. Even though we had walked to Brengues and back and despite his injury, Charlie raced down the road and into the garden, where the family was just finishing their lunch.

'*Hé, Monsieur Shar-lee,*' said Martine, 'you'll soon be back with us in the village, eh?' Then she noticed the blood on his side. '*Mon Dieu.* What happened?'

'Oualou bit him,' I explained. 'I think she thought he was a stray lamb.'

Philippe went into the house and came out with antiseptic lotion. He sloshed it on the wound and pulled Charlie's ears to cheer him up.

'We *loved* looking after him while you were in Greece,' Martine said. 'We will be happy to look after him *any time* because we all *love* him.'

'But why is he so frightened of the broom?' asked Philippe. 'Did someone hit him with a broom when he was small?'

'I don't know,' I confessed. 'I didn't get him until he was fifteen months old. He was born in a rural town in New South Wales, so he really is a *chien de campagne* originally. He's come a long way since then. The family I got him from brought him to Canberra. They didn't have enough time for him. They had a *montgolfière*, a hot-air balloon, and they used to spend their weekends flying in their balloon. Even when they were at home, he wasn't allowed in the house. He ran away and they had to pay to get him out of the dog pound. So the husband of the family advertised him on the internet at work and I downloaded him. I got him for a hundred dollars.'

'*C'est un chien virtuel, alors*, so he's a virtual dog!' exclaimed Martine, laughing.

Philippe was looking at Charlie with new respect.

The next morning Penny, Charlie and I drove into Figeac to buy a few things at the Casino, the little *supermarché* on Place Carnot, where the Saturday *marché* was held under the covered area of the *place*, called Les Halles. I came out of the Casino to find Penny chatting in English with a Frenchwoman who had a German shepherd dog on a lead. The conversation continued, and the woman asked me why I had come to this part of France.

'I came here on holiday with some friends,' I said. 'I thought it was so beautiful, and the people so friendly, that when I decided to come to France to live for a while, this is where I wanted to be. I didn't want to live in a city.'

She agreed that it was a very beautiful part of France and that big cities are not pleasant places to live. She had moved to Figeac from Paris some years before. She said she had always lived in Paris, but that it began to be unlivable some fifteen years ago – the population, the traffic, the pollution, the tourists. She agreed that the people of the Lot were very friendly, but she thought they were narrow in outlook.

Our conversation was suddenly interrupted by Charlie, who was screaming again. We were all horrified to find that the woman's dog had Charlie's head in its mouth. The woman hauled on her dog's lead, trying to pull it away. The German shepherd's jaws locked tight. I took Charlie's lead from Penny's hand, but didn't want to risk dragging on it. The woman began beating the German shepherd on the head with her hands, and at last it let go. A small crowd had gathered. The woman dragged her dog off a few metres and continued hitting it.

'I'm so sorry,' she repeated, between blows, while various members of the crowd aired their opinions on the incident.

Someone said the dogs should have been on shorter leads. Some people wanted to know if *le pauvre petit chien* was all right. Someone came out of a shop and shouted at the woman – perhaps telling her to stop hitting the dog, or perhaps to take the dog away. At any rate, she and the German shepherd disappeared while Penny and I, with shaking hands, examined Charlie for damage. Though he continued to whimper and tremble, we couldn't see much physical harm. We thought it was fortunate that the flap of his ear had been in the way of his jugular vein. Feeling weak, we walked up to the top of the town where we had parked the car outside the wall.

Back at the barn, on the doorsill we found a bottle of wine for me and a bouquet of flowers with a little poem in English for Penny. Although the poem didn't make much semantic sense it was charged with feeling. We didn't know whether to laugh or cry. The gifts were touching and a little embarrassing but at that moment both of us felt completely overloaded emotionally.

Penny put the flowers in a jug and I started to bathe the spot where blood was beginning to seep through the wool under Charlie's jaw. Then I saw more blood above his ear. The flesh had been torn in both places.

'We need to get him to a vet,' said Penny.

We returned to Figeac. Docteur Delmas, the vet, said Charlie would need stitches and would have to stay at the clinic overnight.

Penny and I both felt sick. But we had already bought tickets for the train to Toulouse the following day. On our way back to Grèzes, we diverted to Espagnac, where the Bagreaux were just about to start their evening meal. They were almost as upset as we were at poor Charlie's plight and we all had a glass of wine.

'Go to Toulouse tomorrow,' said Philippe. 'I'll telephone Docteur Delmas in the morning and find out when to pick Charlie up and get all the information. I'll look after him till you return in the evening.'

When we came to get him the following evening he had stitches above his ear and in his neck, a bandage round his neck and a wide plastic collar to stop him scratching at the wounds. He looked like a cross between an Elizabethan courtier and the Pope at Easter time. He kept misjudging the space around him and bumping into things so I took the collar off, and he obliged by not scratching.

After the horror at Les Halles, he added another technique to his repertoire for enjoying the pleasures and avoiding the perils of life: screaming for help *before* disaster could strike.

The summer tenants of the nuns' room departed a few days early, so Charlie and I, with Penny, were able to move back to the *gîte*. We were just in time for the culmination of the holiday season: the village fête, which was held on the last Sunday in August.

In the preceding week, the *cour* was transformed. A marquee, which would serve as the *buvette*, the bar, was set up in the corner closest to the Chemin des Dames. A truck scraped its way under the tower and between the walls of the Chemin des Dames to deposit a load of trestles, tabletops and benches at the entrance to the *cour*. Didier and a team of helpers strung coloured flags overhead between the arcade and the walls of the *cour*. On the Saturday afternoon the men set up an outdoors dance floor.

The night before the fête, Penny accepted Gilou's invitation to dinner and I lay awake till my mind shut down of its own accord.

'We went to a little restaurant in Cajarc,' she said in answer to my questions in the morning. 'I just ordered a salad, because he probably doesn't have much money. We talked about his work and where he lives in Paris. He lives in an upstairs flat in an apartment block in one of the suburbs with his father and his dog. The dog's pretty old. You needn't have worried about anything happening to me, because we had only one glass of wine each, and he doesn't drive nearly as fast as you do.'

Then she went down, whistling, to the *commune* kitchen under the *foyer rural*, to help Milou and the other women of the *Amis d'Espagnac-Sainte-Eulalie* with cutting up the melons and the bread for the *repas*, and putting together the *couverts*, the plastic place settings that everyone would receive in exchange for their ten euros.

The day began with a Mass in Notre-Dame du Val-Paradis. The congregation was bigger than the usual two or three people and included the parents and godparents of some children, most of whom were old enough to walk to the red marble baptismal font to be baptised, and for whom the Mass appeared to be a novelty. Martine was also there in her official capacity and Bastien had accompanied her in a show of loyalty. After the Mass the *curé* disappeared promptly as usual. When everyone had been kissed by everyone else, the *villageois* followed Martine and M. Roger Sudres, the village war veteran, who was carrying a bouquet of flowers, up the road to the *mairie*. M. Sudres placed the bouquet under the plaque commemorating the men of the *commune* slain in the two world wars. Martine asked for a minute's silence. When she thought the minute was up, she called out to Pierre Sommie, who was inside the *mairie* ready to start the music. Nothing happened. There was another minute's silence because the leads to the loudspeaker on the landing outside the *mairie* weren't connected. There was some shuffling and '*merdes*' from behind the plants on the landing, then a sudden burst of the Dead March followed by La Marseillaise. Then everyone went home for lunch.

Around two o'clock several men and boys, and a few women, drifted down the Chemin des Dames and into the *cour* carrying cases of *boules*, steel balls, to practise for the big *pétanque* competition. I had vague hopes of being able to join a team, and Gilou coached me courteously for a while. But as more and more competitors swaggered into the *cour* and started to practise, chaffing one another and cheering and jeering as their *boules* smacked and scattered, I understood that no team would want a dilettante like me and that Charlie and I would make excellent spectators. Penny was tired and would have a long journey back to Amsterdam the next day, so she stayed in the nuns' room, resting.

Charlie and I sat on the wall at the bottom of my steps, where we had a view of the whole field. The competition was conducted as a round robin, and during each round, the players whose turn was still to come organised practice games with one another alongside the official games. This meant that there were about forty games going on at any time, and *boules* flying everywhere like cannonballs. The 'guns' were squinting, crouching and leaning from side to side to ascertain the lie of the land, before bowling or pitching or tossing their *boules* to scatter the others and get their own *boule* closest to the 'piglet', the little wooden ball called the *cochonnet*. This was the point of the game, what every one of the hundred or so players was striving for.

At the end of the first round a crowd converged on the *buvette* to buy drinks before the next round. I could see Eric was manning the bar by himself, so I took Charlie up to the apartment where Penny was still asleep and, dodging the ammunition, went to help him.

Pétanque is a thirsty game and the drinking needs of *pétanque* players are diverse and immediate. In no time I learned the names of everything the bar stocked: Coca (Coca-Cola), Oasis or Bunga or Orangina (fizzy orange), *demi* (medium glass of beer), *pression* (large glass of beer), *panache* (shandy), Perrier (Perrier), Ice Tea (iced tea). Several people tried their English out on me: ''Ello, Madame Maureen. 'Ow are you?' and I tried my bar technique out on them. '*Que-vou-lez-vous, m'-sieur?*' 'A-Co-ca, please.' Boris Bagreaux saw how I was pulling the beer, so he came round into the marquee to show me how to do it properly. The financial part of working in the *buvette* was easy, because every drink cost one euro and fifty *centimes*. Boris's team had already been eliminated, so he stayed to help, as did other defeated players as the afternoon wore on into evening, and the atmosphere became as convivial behind the bar as it was outside. Terry Kempley bought me a *pression* as my *pourboire*, my tip.

In the evening, different drinks became available for *apéro* – *sangria*, *kir*, Ricard.

The *pétanque* competition was won by a team from Figeac. There were prizes for the winners and runners-up of every round, and all the prizes were bottles of wine. Many very small children, some of whom had been baptised with holy water that morning, were wandering round with bottles of wine tucked under their arms.

It was perfect weather for the *repas* in the evening. As soon as the prize giving was over, the *amis* assembled twenty or thirty ten-person trestle tables beneath the coloured flags and lights. Didier hung a ham from Thierry and Jacotte's window above the arcade. Penny sat with Gilou's family and I sat with Rolande, Sigrid, Milou and Eric, France and Lucien. It was Milou's job to sell the entries for the competition to guess how high off the ground the ham was. The prize for guessing was the ham itself. I helped her. We went to every table, selling three guesses at a go. Because this happened during the *repas*, Milou and I didn't have much to eat, but I met a great many people, who all seemed to think they knew me. There was dancing between and during courses and after the last course. To get from one side of the *cour* to the other, while we were selling the tickets, we had to pass across the dance platform, and each time we did a little *faux* tap-dance to let people know we were coming. I didn't feel at all inhibited about this, as I might have done in the past. All the carpenters and builders took a long time to make their guesses, and wanted to know whether the distance was measured from the top of the ham or the bottom. In the end the ham was won by France Dabout.

When the music was *musette*, accordion music, Rolande and one of her old school friends, Geneviève from Brengues, danced together, a brisk, straight-legged waltz that was second nature, as if they were joined by invisible strings at hip, knee and ankle, left to right, right to left, back and forth. Rolande told me she used to dance a lot with her husband, before he ran off with *la factrice*, the postwoman.

'And you're still dancing,' I said.

'*Et tant pis pour lui!*' she grinned. Too bad for him.

Everybody danced the Languedoc Rock. The finale was the boat 'dance': everyone who was agile enough sat on the floor with their legs around the person in front and followed the movements of the lead person, waving their arms, ducking their heads, pitching from side to side and so on.

'Be careful, Terry,' said Anne Kempley. 'Remember your hip replacement.'

Around one o'clock, as the party was breaking up, I went up to join Charlie in bed, but didn't sleep. Eventually I heard Penny come in. She slammed the door and paced backwards and forwards across the apartment, hair streaming, eyes wide, like the alert and alarmed lionesses frozen in the fresco behind her.

'He wants me to go and live with him in Paris. I've known him for only two weeks. Totally unrealistic.'

'What did you say?'

'I said no as nicely as I could. He was really upset. But God, what does he expect?'

'The French are more impetuous than we Anglo-Celts,' I said. 'Some of them. I suppose.'

After Penny went back to Amsterdam, there was some curiosity among the *villageois* about the outcome of the young people's romance. I thought the best way to settle the matter was to speak to Martine, who would make sure the received version got around.

'She isn't really interested in romantic attachments at the moment. She's in Europe to study. She wants to develop her musicianship. She thought it was just a holiday thing. She didn't realise it would get so serious.'

'*Ça peut arriver*,' said Martine, 'well, it does happen, sometimes, but Penny and Gilou, yes, they are both serious, but they have very different lives.'

Long after the curiosity over the Penny-and-Gilou idyll had been put to rest, in the course of one of our conversations at the *mairie* I asked Martine how she and Philippe had first met.

'I was a housemistress in a boarding school near Figeac. Philippe's parents lived in a village 10 kilometres away. He used to come down from Paris to visit them. We met at a dance, and *tac*! We fell in love.'

CANNED LITERATURE

When Charlie and I returned to the nuns' room that August, I was delighted to find that some of the renovations for the two *gîtes*, that the *conseil municipal* had planned before we arrived, had been accomplished. In the *petit*, there was a new gas stove top, electric oven, double sink and workbench. My happiness, however, was tempered by the facts that there were no storage shelves under the new bench, one of the old cupboards had disappeared and the doors of the remaining cupboard hung loose. I had to resign myself to living out of cartons for the time being. Also, the curtains had been taken down, washed and re-hung, but in the process some of the hooks had broken and had not been replaced, so the curtains drooped like *coquilles Saint-Jacques*. M. Roger Sudres' niece, Odette, who was a member of the *conseil municipal*, had been assigned to make a little curtain to draw across the space under the workbench, but she had met a sheep farmer from a neighbouring village at a dance …

'Odette has bought the material for the kitchens in the *gîtes*,' Nicole told me. 'Oh, Maureen, the pattern is pretty. Odette has very good taste.'

'Maybe *I* could make the curtains,' I suggested, although I hadn't touched a sewing machine in years.

But no, Nicole said, Odette wanted to make the curtains herself. She had a special technique.

I asked Martine if I could at least paint the cupboards. She agreed, but I would have to wait till Jean-Louis bought the paint.

Before I went to Greece, the main reasons for my being discontented from time to time came from frustration with the inadequacy of my French, the lack of progress on *Blue and Brown*, and sporadic loneliness. Now, with winter coming on again, I looked around the apartment at the cold stone walls and the grey squares of linoleum on the hard cold sloping floor, and sighed. The light bulbs in the square brown glass lampshade screwed to the ceiling over the kitchen blew with monotonous regularity and were too high for me to replace them. Each time, I had to wait till a Wednesday when Christophe, the *homme à tout faire*, the *commune* handyman, came to mow the grass in the *cour*.

Christophe was nearly 2 metres tall, but even so, he and I had to carry the table across the room and put a chair on it so that he could reach the light. I handed the screwdriver up to him so he could detach the lampshade. While he was there, I asked him if it was possible to retrieve the cupboard which had been taken up to the *grenier* in the course of the renovations. I'd noticed it when I was bringing down all the things Martine had let me store there while I was away.

'*Pour toi, Maureen*,' he said, '*tout est possible*, for you, everything is possible.'

Before long the cupboard was back on the wall and he'd fixed the drooping doors of the other cupboard for good measure. I was learning my way around the system.

I asked Martine to let me buy new hooks for the window curtains. I went to Figeac and bought one packet, as instructed, and borrowed René Cabrignac's ladder to attach the hooks. The ladder wasn't quite high enough to do this comfortably, but high enough to discover that several of the curtain rings were missing. Nicole explained that she had been obliged to use them for the curtains in the *grand gîte*. Nicole said the job would have to wait till I had bought new rings and hooks. I could see where that was leading. With as much authority as I could muster, I said I'd borrow them from the *grand gîte* and buy new ones to replace them later. I was pretty pleased with myself that I had managed to take control of the situation. But as I stood on the ladder with my mouth full of hooks and my fingers festooned with curtain rings, I saw that, to get the rings on the curtain rod, the brackets holding the rod would have to be unplugged from the wall.

Fortunately Jean-Louis was in the *grand gîte*, installing the supports for the little rod for the curtain under the kitchen bench, in anticipation of Odette producing the curtains for the two *gîtes*, and he unplugged the brackets for me. At last the window curtains were hanging properly. Well, almost: Jean-Louis couldn't quite reach the far corner of the rod, and nor could I, so one end of the top of one of the curtains, its hook dangling an inch or two below the corresponding ring, stuck out at a teasing angle.

Soon after, Eric and Milou, France and Lucien and Jocelyne and Pierre came to dinner: tomato soup, rabbit hotpot, salad and cheese, oranges and walnuts in wine.

The guests brought presents, as usual. France and Lucien brought a cyclamen in a pot. Jocelyne and Pierre brought a long narrow vase filled with jellified red-dyed paraffin with a wick through the centre. When lit, it cast a satanic glow over the surfaces of the wine glasses and cutlery on the table, as well as all our faces. The lionesses in the fresco over the fireplace stuck out their tongues and swished their tails ferociously.

The previous time Eric came for dinner, he brought a big lime-green and white umbrella, stamped with the logo of the Belgian Metal Workers' union, *Metaal*, one of the affiliates of the Christian Workers' Union syndicate of which Eric used to be the secretary. This time he and Milou brought two bottles of Belgian *witbier*, a tin of Milou's home-made venison paté, fig and wine jam she had made to go with the paté, home-made grape jam and a crumpled little book, about 6 centimetres by 9, written in Polish in miniscule print.

'We used to smuggle them into Poland packed in cans of *cassoulet*,' Eric explained, responding to my puzzled look.

'Madness,' said Milou, shaking her head. 'You could have been shot.'

'Yes,' Eric agreed complacently, 'but I was younger then. It was a lot of fun.'

In the 1980s, Eric told me, he organised a program of aid from *Metaal* to the Solidarity movement in Poland. Over a period of ten years, he made more than twenty trips in trucks to Poland, delivering money, food and banned literature, which was hidden in secret compartments of cans of food.

'The French and Belgian governments gave me documents and letters of reference to Polish bishops and government officials. I kept all the letters and cards from families we helped, and all the press cuttings from Belgium. I've got three photo albums of them. I'll bring them over to you tomorrow. I've got photos of me with Lech Walesa and me with the Pope. The Pope, he invited me to the Vatican and gave me a medal.'

Half in French and half in English I told the joke about the two Australians – let's call them Eric and Dave – who go on their first trip to Europe. Eric keeps getting lost. He gets lost in the Vatican palace on Easter Sunday, just before the Pope is due to come out on his balcony and bless the crowd in Saint Peter's square. Somehow Eric manages to follow the Pope out onto the balcony, and Dave, waiting in the crowd below, nudges his neighbour and asks, 'Hey, who's that guy up there with Eric?'

'*Oui*,' laughed Jocelyne and repeated the punchline. '*Hé, c'est qui, ce mec là-haut à côté d'Eric*? I know that joke.' .

'Me too,' said Milou. '*Wie is die gast daar bij Eric*?'

Eric, with an insouciant smile, was glancing up at the window.

'What's wrong with that curtain?' he asked.

I explained that Jean-Louis and I hadn't been able to reach the curtain ring.

'Do you have a ladder?'

'It's in the *grand gîte*.'

'Do you have the key?'

'I don't think it's locked. Jean-Louis has been doing some work there.'

We got the ladder; Eric climbed up and attached the hook to the ring.

'*Merci*, Eric,' I said, putting the canned literature in my makeshift bookcase. 'I'll devour this later.'

LE CHEMIN DE SAINT-JACQUES

The second last week of September was the week of *les journées nationales du patrimoine*, national days of heritage, when all the government-owned historical monuments of France are open and free to the public. All week little groups of people parked their cars on the *place* and wandered through the old cemetery and into Notre-Dame du Val-Paradis, then down the Chemin des Dames and into the *cour* to admire the remnants of the old priory.

'*Oh là là!*' they exclaimed as they rounded the corner. '*Quel joli clocher*, what a pretty bell-tower!'

If Charlie happened to be sunning himself in the *cour* and approached them for a pat, they added, '*Bonjour, le chien. Comment ça va?*'

If I happened to be on the landing, keeping an eye on him, they would say, 'What's your dog's name, *madame?*'

'Charlie. *Shar-lee, en français.*'

'*Bonjour, Shar-lee. Il comprend le français, madame*, does he understand French?'

'*C'est un chien australien, mais il est bilingue*, he's bilingual.'

''Ow are you, Shar-lee? Good dog. Sit down. Give me your foot.'

Mme Dany Senac, Anaïs's grandmother and the nominal guardian of the *gros chien*, Espagnac's wandering Saint Bernard, was a member of the *Association Chemin de Saint-Jacques*. During *les journées nationales du patrimoine*, Dany organised an exhibition in the *salle des fêtes* called *Le Chemin de Saint-Jacques de Compostelle Chemin d'Europe*, which was intended to showcase the European pilgrimage routes to Santiago de Compostela.

There are four different starting points in France of the Chemin de Saint-Jacques: Paris, Vézelay, Arles and Le Puy-en-Velay. The routes converge at Puenta la Reina in the Spanish part of the Basque country, then a single route proceeds west across northern Spain, ending at the Cathedral of Santiago in the town of Compostela on the Iberian Peninsula. The route that starts at Le Puy-en-Velay in the Massif Central traverses the waves of the Margeride and Aubrac mountains, the plateaus of Rouergue and Quercy, the hills of Gascogne and the Pays-Basque and many ancient towns, including Figeac and Cahors. It takes at least four months to walk from Le Puy to Compostela. Pilgrims travelling at night can find their way by following *la voie lactée*, the Milky Way. In the Midi-Pyrénées, *la voie lactée* is also called *le chemin de Saint-Jacques*.

Legend has it that after Saint James was martyred in Jerusalem in AD44, his friends brought his remains to northwest Spain and buried them in a field. Eight centuries later, in the thick of the battle of Clavijo, a warrior on a white horse, brandishing a pennant with a red cross, spurred the Christians on against the Moors. Even though the Christians lost the battle, everyone believed that the red cross warrior was a manifestation of Saint James. A few years afterwards, a hermit noticed a brilliant star over the same field. He dug up the field, and found a marble sarcophagus containing bones that the hermit knew instinctively were those of the saint. The sarcophagus was placed in a cemetery or *compostum*, which later developed into the town of Compostela. When this part of Spain was eventually reconquered by the Christians in the eleventh century, news of the shrine spread, pilgrims came from all over France and Spain and even from England, and miracles were attributed to the relics. The pilgrims carried a scallop shell to collect water in and drink from, and this, the *coquille Saint-Jacques*, became the symbol of the pilgrimage.

The pilgrims became a lucrative source of revenue for the towns and villages along the pilgrimage routes. Souvenirs were manufactured so the pilgrims could show what they'd done and where they'd been. The first guidebook of the pilgrimage routes, the *Codex Calixtinus*, made its appearance in 1140.

Espagnac is not exactly on the official ancient route, but close enough to be on a semi-official variant, which many pilgrims choose to take because of its beauty and interest. This is good for the village because it is a day's walk from Figeac and pilgrims regularly stay the night in the *gîtes d'étape*.

In the spring and now in the autumn, occasionally Charlie and I came across pilgrims on the path to La Source Bleue, coming from the direction of Figeac. Apart from the telltale *coquilles* pinned on their shirts or jackets, the backpack and maybe a staff made from an osier from the riverbank, they were easily distinguishable from hikers and recreational walkers like me. They had a certain ethereal look about them. Unlike most people we passed on our walks, they didn't seem at all interested in having a little chat about the weather, even if it was pelting with rain. They might ask how far it was to the ancient priory at Espagnac, where they would rest that night, and look pleased to hear they were almost there, that was all. They were usually alone, although we did once meet a group of pilgrims which included a labrador dog wearing a *coquille* on his collar and carrying panniers, containing his own food supplies, attached to a harness round his middle. The dog, preoccupied with higher matters, passed by Charlie without a second sniff. Charlie cocked an eye at me. Weird.

One evening, around 5pm, when I was sitting by the window finishing some notes on the legend of Saint James, Nicole called up to me from the Chemin des Dames.

'Maureen, there's an Australian woman staying in the *gîte d'étape* tonight, on her way to Compostelle.'

Charlie and I went up the Chemin des Dames to say hello. The woman, whose name was Carol, was washing a few things in the sink in the utility room of the *gîte d'étape*.

'Is there somewhere I can get a meal tonight?' she asked.

She hadn't booked ahead with Jacotte and Thierry, whom Nicole and I both thought weren't at home. The nearest restaurant, the *Hôtel de la Vallée* at Brengues, which might or might not be open, was 2 kilometres away, so I invited Carol to share my meal that night. She accepted immediately.

'I'm vegetarian,' she added.

'That's lucky,' I said. 'I'm making a chick pea and tofu curry.'

An hour later, having showered in her room in the tower, she came up to our apartment. She pulled off her shoes and threw herself lengthwise on the *canapé-lit*, narrowly missing Charlie, who had to jump out of the way. He jumped back up again and perched precariously on the arm of the sofa, just beyond her head, watching her resentfully.

'Are you going all the way to Compostelle?' I asked. I was interested to find out what it was like to be a modern-day pilgrim.

'Eventually,' she replied. 'I do a section of the Chemin whenever I've saved enough money. I work in London as a live-in carer. I save everything I earn, and I don't pay any rent. It's a twenty-four hour job, and some of my clients are really demanding. I do the Chemin to get sanity back into my life.'

Charlie stared at her over the cushion she was resting on. Without looking at him, she gave him a little nudge and he found himself on the floor again. He wandered into the bedroom and came back out to the living area with his stuffed rabbit dangling by the foot from his mouth.

'I was born again when I was twelve,' said Carol matter-of-factly.

'One day at Sunday School, I knew that Jesus was with me and he's been with me ever since. When I'm walking the Chemin, He's walking with me.'

She had a physical glow and a focus that I found fascinating.

Charlie was throwing the rabbit up in the air and then pouncing on it where it landed on the floor.

'When I left school, I studied music at university. I was a gifted pianist. Then I won a scholarship to do a PhD in America, but I couldn't handle campus life. It was too confronting. I went to pieces and gave up my studies.'

Charlie was growling at his rabbit and knocking it on across the linoleum like a rugby league player. It landed up against his water bowl, so he took a noisy drink, munched a few dry *croquettes* and belched.

'I sometimes sleep under the stars,' Carol said. 'I never worry about where I'm going to stay the night or what I'm going to eat. Some days I only have fruit and cheese. Jesus always provides.'

When the curry was ready, she came over to the table. Charlie immediately picked up his rabbit and jumped back onto the sofa, where he concentrated on biting one of its eyes out while Carol and I ate and talked. Somehow, she got on to the gospels, and she told me about the Magdalene gospel, which I had never heard of. Until that moment, I only knew about Matthew, Mark, Luke and John, but she had a strange new tale to tell.

'After Jesus was crucified, Mary Magdalene came to France and lived in a village in the Pyrenees called Rennes-le-Château. She was the ancestor of the Merovingian kings, including Charlemagne ...'

Charlie had broken off blinding the rabbit and was staring across the room at Carol as she told the story, full of fascinating, if puzzling, detail. I shot him a little cautionary frown.

'Thank you very much,' she said, as soon as her plate was clean. 'I have to get up early in the morning.'

'Shame on you, Charlie,' I said, after she left, and I went round the room picking up the cotton wool rabbit stuffing he'd scattered all over the floor. He padded around after me complacently, wisps of lint hanging out the sides of his mouth. 'What a way to treat a born-again pilgrim.'

He bowed, stretching luxuriantly from his long front legs, then went back to the sofa, grinning.

'If Mary Magdalene was Charlemagne's female ancestor, I wonder who the male ancestor was,' I mused as I washed up the dishes. 'Nah, it'll never catch on.'

Next morning, as Charlie and I made our way up the Chemin des Dames, en route to La Source Bleue, I saw that Dany Senac had put up a notice board outside the *salle des fêtes*, listing everything in the exhibition of *Le Chemin de Saint-Jacques de Compostelle Chemin d'Europe*:

> *des affiches*, posters
> *une bannière XVIII*, an eighteenth century banner
> *un vitrail XVIII*, an eighteenth century stained-glass window
> *des ampoules de pêlerin*, pilgrim's phials
> *un salon lecture documentation*, a research reading room, that is, the *salle des fêtes*
> *et encore de multiples surprises*, numerous additional surprises.

One of the additional surprises for me was to read on one of the posters about the relics to be found in Reading Abbey, which is on the pilgrimage route from England. These included: a hand of Saint James; hair and vestments of the virgin Mary; a tooth of Saint Luke; the head of the apostle Saint Phillip; numerous fingers of lesser known martyrs; another mummified hand (but whose?); and some blood and the foreskin of Christ. I had difficulty swallowing the hand of Saint James, because Carol had told me that his entire remains were definitely in the cathedral at Santiago de Compostela.

HARVEST

The English classes, which had been suspended during the summer, had resumed, after a fashion, on Saturday evenings. As before, Terry Kempley took the beginners and I took the more experienced group. Sometimes up to fifteen people presented themselves, that is if nothing else cropped up, like Jean-Louis and Didier being occupied fixing René's tractor, a late lunch and a long *sieste*, a good film at the cinema in Figeac, or they simply forgot. It was a different combination of people every week and it was impossible to prepare an ongoing program for them. I didn't know how I was going to manage the whole group after Terry and Anne went back to England for the winter.

One Monday, when I went round to the *mairie* to pick Charlie up after my weekly wrangle with the *aspirateur*, Martine beckoned me into the little office under the tower and shut the door.

'The *comité de la commune*,' she began, 'has decided to put everybody's rent up.' She smiled. 'We agreed that your rent will go up by five euros a month. We also decided that Madame Cashman should stay in the *petit gîte* next summer at the same rent if she wants to. But there is a condition. You have to stay till the end of the year. *Et toi, toutou*,' she said to Charlie, who had his paws on her knee and was nuzzling his head under her hand. 'Do you want to go on living here?'

This was something to think about. I really didn't know how long Charlie and I would stay in France. Originally, we were going to stay until I had completed a first draft of *Blue and Brown*, but that no longer seemed likely. I had considered the possibility of our going to live in Ireland for a while before we returned to Australia, but I suspected that the booming Irish economy, the 'Celtic Tiger', put that beyond my means.

Supposing we did stay till the end of next year, did I want to continue living in the nuns' room which, though quintessentially charming, was never intended to be a permanent residence? If not, did I want to start again in another village and turn my back on the acceptance and kindness Charlie and I had experienced and the friendships we had begun during the last seven months? Could we ever find such circumstances anywhere else? Could I bear another year of wrestling with the old *aspirateur*?

'*Merci*, Martine,' I said. 'It's a very generous offer. We both love living here but I don't know yet how long we're going to stay.'

'*Mais ça va*, that's all right. Think about it, *quoi*? You don't have to give an answer now, but we'll need to know by Christmas because people will want to book the *petit gîte* for next summer.'

The long autumn had begun in August with the premature leaf-fall from the parched trees. In September, the *orages* spent themselves in days of steady rain interspersed with golden days of sunshine on ripe crops.

In the meadows along the path to La Source Bleue the Rochefort *brebis* began to drop their lambs. When they saw Charlie and me passing, they moaned and groaned and flocked together to stare us out of sight. A few days later, the lambs, tails shivering with the joy of existence, were chasing one another up and down the meadows as if they knew the fun would end all too soon. One day, a pheasant darted noisily from the undergrowth and through the trees towards the river, its bright tail dragging like the keel of a mythical ship.

On the way to Marcilhac one Saturday, to get bread at the *boulangerie*, passing a vineyard in a meadow between the road and the river, I spotted the whole Cabrignac family – Solange, René,

Jean-Louis, Christiane, Pascale and little Manon – among the rows of vines. I only saw them for an instant as I drove past, but the image was so lively, it was like a snapshot that clicked in my brain. They all wore big hats and carried big baskets, and looked busy and happy as they moved among the vines. Didier was standing on the tractor, looking like a hero-peasant in a Soviet revolutionary poster, feeding the grapes from the baskets the others handed up to him into a press.

Another day, after a few days of rain, there was René filling big buckets with thousands of the little white mushrooms that sprinkled the field which lay beyond the village, in the loop of the Célé. He came over to chat. By this time, I had become reasonably competent at interpreting what René said, without actually understanding most of his words. Solange, I gathered, was going to preserve the mushrooms.

I mentioned that I'd seen the family at their *vendanges* the other day and asked him whether the excessive heat and drought of the summer had damaged their grapes. No, he said, with his wide, gap-toothed grin. Although generally the grape crops in the region had been poor, their crop was a bumper one. The deep roots of the old vines, planted long ago by Solange's father, drew enough moisture from the river. Rather than suffering, they had benefited from the extraordinary heat and sun.

Next day Charlie and I passed him outside Mme Delfour's cottage, filling buckets with windfall plums from her tree.

'Is Solange going to make jam?'

No. René had a friend who had an *alambic*, a still, and the plums would be turned into René's annual supply of *eau de vie*.

One day, our way was blocked by a flock of *brebis* trotting behind Martine Rochefort along the road from Salabio, leaving a trail of pebbled droppings on the bitumen in their wake. The younger of the two border collies, Tam, brought up the rear and kept the sheep more or less in line. When we saw the *brebis* coming towards us, I put Charlie on his lead, and we waited beside the road for the procession to pass by.

While we waited, we watched Alain and Oualou practising with the remaining sheep in the meadow between the road and the river. Alain was working on one side of the meadow, doing something with the electric fence, at the same time calling and whistling orders to Oualou over his shoulder – '*Stop!*', '*Avance!*' – not even looking at her. Oualou was having great fun moving the sheep around. She raced backwards and forwards till she had them huddling together in a corner of the field. Then she crouched on the ground, staring at them, ready to pounce if any dared to stray from the mob. After a while, Alain would quietly give another set of orders and Oualou would spring into action and move them to another corner of the field.

'Oh, good girl!' I breathed.

Charlie looked on dispassionately, stretched and yawned.

That autumn, whenever we met him in the Chemin des Dames, the *gros chien* had a more distracted air than ever. He had clearly suffered from the great heat of the summer. Then, his owners, the Haufrichts, had been in residence in their house at the end of the Chemin des Dames but now they had returned again to the north. He was once more physically in the Senacs' care, but alone, as before, in his mind.

On Mondays when we were out walking, we sometimes met a couple of *chiens courants* which had run too far the previous day. Charlie never made friends with these dogs who behaved as though he wasn't there; I received the same far-away look, but they did at least come over diffidently for a pat, before bounding off again into the undergrowth. The owners would be weaving through the forest tracks in their four-wheel drive vehicles, hallooing for the dogs, and eventually, after a few days, the dogs would be hungry enough to reveal themselves.

'I'd get lost too,' I said to Charlie, as we listened to the mournful howling of Didier Cabrignac's dog, Tenor, echo through the valley, 'if I'd spent the last nine months cooped up in a cage.'

He grinned, as if remembering the weekends when all the humans he knew went hot-air ballooning and left him in the backyard by himself.

One drizzly Sunday afternoon, sitting by my window at the computer, I jumped up at a sudden burst of gunfire and shouting from the *falaise* on the other side of the river, and I looked outside. On the rim of the *falaise*, men with rifles were silhouetted against the stormy sky, while one of them scrambled down the steep slope between the scrubby oaks towards a deer lying halfway down.

Jean-Louis, who was working in the *grand gîte* that afternoon, came across to the *petit*.

'Did you see?' he said excitedly. 'They've killed a beast. *Un chevreuil.*'

'The poor thing,' I remarked.

'*Oui, le pauvre,*' he agreed.

I got out my binoculars and we took turns watching the scene on the *falaise*. The hunter who had shot the deer waited beside it in the rain, shrouded in his yellow hooded jacket. Eventually the other hunters in the group slipped and skidded down the *falaise* and all stood around the slain animal for a few minutes before they lifted it by the legs and bumped the carcass down to the road.

Later that day, Martine knocked at my door.

'Maureen,' she said, apologetically. 'I have a favour to ask. Boris has an English assignment due tomorrow. He's put off doing it for two weeks, and now …'

'Of course I'll help him with it, Martine,' I said. 'Tell him to come round. Did you know the hunters killed a *chevreuil* this afternoon?'

Martine looked embarrassed. '*Oui,*' she said, '*c'était Boris, qui a fait sa première mise à mort.* Boris has made his first kill. *Boris,* my little boy.'

With the autumn, another activity revived, which I hadn't been involved in before the summer because I was occupied with visitors and my excursions to Loir-et-Cher and Languedoc-Roussillon. This was walking on Tuesday afternoons with a group of *villageois* called the *volontaires*, from three *communes*, Espagnac-Sainte-Eulalie, Brengues and Corn. Weather permitting, the group would meet at a prearranged venue and set off on a long, relaxed walking circuit. The regular participants from Espagnac-Sainte-Eulalie were Jean-Claude and Ginette Grosse, André and Jeanine Pelaprat, Jocelyne and Pierre Sommie, Christiane Cabrignac, Eric and Milou, Charlie and me. M. Henri Chanut joined us from Brengues. A couple called André and Thérèse and two elderly ladies whose names I never discovered, though we were on kissing terms, came from Corn.

Jean-Claude Grosse and André Pelaprat normally took the reins. They would have telephoned one another during the morning to decide the important details, such as the state of the weather, the circuit to be followed that day, the meeting place and the transport arrangements. They would be equipped with one of the little brochures available in most of the *mairies* of the local villages, containing sketch maps and describing the walking circuits and the points of interest. If the meeting place was distant from our village, Charlie and I usually went with the Pelaprats in their car.

The group would stroll along, stopping to discuss and admire everything they saw. They surveyed the landscape from the *points de vue* marked on the maps, examined the state of the trees, commented on the architecture of village houses and churches and explored all the *dolmens* and *cazelles* en route. If we came across a friend or relative of anyone, or someone known to the people of our respective *communes*, there would be an exchange of kissing and news. If we came across a farmer or another stroller, we would all stop for a chat to discuss the weather, the season, the particular features of the local environment and architecture. Ginette and Christiane always clucked at the poultry in the farmyards: the chickens with their glossy jewel-coloured feathers, the elegant snowy geese and the neurotic *pintades*, guinea-fowl that strutted around in utter panic, emitting cries of dismay.

Jean-Claude would call to the fat milking cows and the donkeys. '*Hé, ma belle; viens ici, ma belle!*' The donkeys came to the fence for lumps of sugar but the cows just stood, ruminating.

At first, I found the relaxed pace rather frustrating; when it was just Charlie and me, armed with my large-scale IGN – *Institut Géographique National* – maps, we would cover the same territory in half the time. In fact, we had hiked several of these circuits already. But with the *volontaires* I was forced to slow down and stop to look at the details that were the essence of this unique and captivating environment. I began to recognise the subtle changes in the flora that recounted the changing seasons and the particular climatic events of recent years. André would point out how the roots of an old oak tree he had climbed in his childhood had spread like a net over a crumbling stone wall that had been repaired by his grandfather. We would all stand around a *lavoir*, a stone trough beside a stream, with a roof constructed over it, where women in the not too distant past used to meet, armed with ash and stone, to do their households' washing.

'*Oh, là, là,*' laughed the women in our group, shaking their hands from the wrists, '*quelle corvée*, what a chore!'

These walks became one of the highlights of our week, Charlie's and mine. Charlie revelled in the company, the pats and the conversations about himself.

'*Hé Shar-lee Brown*,' said Jocelyne, '*tu t'amuses*, you're having a good time?'

As we rambled along the ancient paths and through the hamlets, both inhabited and ruined, my companions shared with me the legends and traditions of the region, and explained the natural features of the landscape. I heard stories about what had happened here between the two world wars, under the German occupation and during the *âge d'or*, the golden age of the 'fifties. As time went by, I came to appreciate the interconnectedness of all these things, so different from my own experience and culture.

One of these walks followed the *sentier* up to the *causse* from the hamlet of Diège, the same circuit Rolande had guided me on shortly after we arrived in Espagnac, and where Charlie had picked up his first French tick. The *sentier* began where the road ended at the top of the hamlet, at the house of Jacqueline Poulain. I had met her occasionally, but although we were on kissing terms, we had never sat down together or stood around to have a chat. She was the secretary of the *Amis d'Espagnac-Sainte-Eulalie*, and took a major role in the activities they organised, such as the village fête and the clean-up days. She was a close friend of Rolande and Mimi and Sigrid, and I would hear from them that she had gone to Bruniquel or Limoges to look after her grandchildren, or that she had gone to the Pyrenees to *faire de la randonnée*, hiking with her neighbours Jacques and Claudette Nadal.

On the day the *volontaires* passed her house on the way up to the *causse*, Jacqueline happened to be in her garden, raking up the fallen leaves. As usual, we stopped to chat and she asked me if I had seen the program for the winter season of *spectacles*, the shows in Figeac. Yes, I said, I'd gone to the *Centre culturel* at Figeac and they had sent me a program.

'Then come for *un petit café* tomorrow morning and we'll talk about what *spectacles* we might go to together, Maureen, *hé?*'

On the first day of October, although I wasn't an official *amie d'Espagnac-Sainte-Eulalie*, I joined the little team tidying up the village for winter. Lucien Dabout and Jacques Nadal cleaned the *calvaires*, the wayside crucifixes dotted around the two villages and three or four hamlets of the *commune*, with Jacques's petrol-fuelled steam-cleaning machine. Milou and France weeded around the plinths and installed fresh baskets of plastic flowers. Didier Cabrignac and Philippe Bagreaux, the self-confessed religious sceptics of the *commune*, brought ladders and brushes into the church of Notre-Dame du Val-Paradis and dispersed the dust from the top of the baroque altarpiece and cleaned the heads of the gloomy statues. Jacqueline Poulain, Claudette Nadal and Rolande cleaned the apse and nave. Sigrid and I, with borrowed mattocks, chopped out about a hundred and fifty irises from the bank near the bridge and planted them along the wall beside the road leading into the village.

'I hope it's all right,' said Sigrid, as we dug out thick clusters of bulbs. 'These irises were planted by Madame Pelaprat, before old M. Pelaprat died. She's in the nursing home in Figeac but there would be no point asking her. Anyway, the irises have multiplied over the years, enough to go round.'

'Just think, Sigrid,' I said to her. 'Every spring, in the years to come, when we're gone from here, *Espagnacois* and future visitors will enjoy these irises we planted.'

That day, France and Lucien invited Sigrid and Charlie and me to their house for lunch the following Sunday. The three of us walked the little track from Espagnac to Diège. Rolande and Mimi were also there.

Lucien gave me a tour of the house which was on three levels. Unlike Milou and Eric's house, which had already been renovated when they bought it, or Terry and Anne's or Walter and Sigrid's, which they had renovated themselves decades ago, this house was a work in progress. Lucien and France worked on it every time they came down from Paris. What they had done – installed a staircase, built a deck on the back with a view of the valley and the *falaise* on the other side of the river – was impressive. But what they still had to do, to my mind, was daunting.

We sat around the fireplace, while Lucien brought out an array of snacks and the *apéritifs* –Ricard, Dubonnet, Pineau des Charantes, and home-made concoctions of wines flavoured with orange and peach and walnuts.

'*Mon Dieu*!' I exclaimed, with the arrival of each bottle.

'You have to know us,' laughed France, disappearing behind the curtain that screened the kitchen from the rest of the room.

Catching a glimpse of her kitchen, I realised how little I had to complain about mine in the *petit gîte*. Despite the lack of working surfaces, shelves and cupboards, she had prepared soup, roast chicken with lentils, green salad, cheeses. The lunch also featured a chewy fricassee of snails in parsley and cream, prepared by Rolande, as a surprise for me because Nicole had told her I'd never tried them. Rolande also brought a fruit compote laced with rum. We finished with coffee, cake and Calvados.

The following week, France and Lucien departed with a couple of suitcases for their other home in Paris, promising to come back from time to time during the winter. For the Kempleys and Sigrid, vacating for the winter was a more complicated process that reminded me of my own experience preparing my house, Charlie and myself to come to Espagnac. The Kempleys finished draining their pool, took some of the contents of their *cave* upstairs in case of winter floods, drained their water pipes to stop them cracking in the winter freeze and departed for England. Sigrid scrubbed her floors, drained her pipes and packed up the personal belongings and the tapestry she was hoping to finish before she returned to Espagnac the following spring. On the night before she left for Osnabruck, she invited me to her house for a *dinette*, a little picnic dinner with Rolande and Mimi in front of her fire. We sat at the table that had been on the little terrace outside her French windows all summer, and which she had now moved inside. Early next morning, a cold breeze ruffling our hair, I helped her fasten the shutters on her doors and windows. Charlie and I stood in the *place* and watched her car turn out of sight around the corner to the *pont*.

Leaning towards us over the wall of her *potager* one windy morning at the beginning of November, Mme Bonzani said, 'Winter's coming. Now the village is becoming quiet again. You will be lonely again.'

'I won't mind being lonely,' I said. 'Perhaps I'll be able to do some more work on my book.'

'Perhaps,' she replied. *'L'hiver, c'est une saison pas triste, plutôt méditative*, winter isn't depressing, it's contemplative.'

That night, a full moon rode on waves of purple cloud in the sky above the *causse* outside my window. I turned out the light, opened the curtains and put a disc of Schubert piano sonatas in the CD player. The *poêle*, supplemented by a little petrol heater I'd bought in Figeac, and a shawl over my knees, kept me warm enough. *La voie lactée* shimmered palely in the darkness. The moon that had shone on nuns and pilgrims, *seigneurs* and serfs, revolutionaries and farmers, *causse* and *falaise*, river and forest, houses and churches of Espagnac-Sainte-Eulalie, shone on my face. On the bed on the other side of my desk, Charlie emitted a gentle, rhythmic snoring.

LES FÊTES

❀

Cold nights, misty mornings, bright days. The burnished leaves of oaks and poplars cast clear patterns against pure blue skies, dappling the *falaise* in shades of coppery-red. Tiny birds, crimson and grey, black and white, flashed through the woods. On our walks to La Source Bleue, showers of rippling leaves – lime-gold, copper and bronze – rained on us from the long arcade of trees and carpeted the paths and verges of the meadows. Luminous mushrooms, shallow white conical chalices, stood in a row in the leaf litter along the river beneath the thin, moss-covered oaks.

It was time for the annual general meeting of the *Société des Amis d'Espagnac-Sainte-Eulalie*. Didier Cabrignac, president, Jacqueline Poulain, secretary, France Dabout, Milou and other committee members, Charlie and I, all turned up punctually at 5.30pm in the *foyer rural*, the function room next door to the *mairie*. The other interested observers – that is, most of the sixty-seven inhabitants of the *commune* – straggled in over the course of the next hour, with a new round of kissing at each arrival, then stood around chatting. Eventually Martine Bagreaux came in; the conversations stopped, Didier and the *conseil d'Administration*, the office bearers, took their places around the long table, the rest of us sat on benches at the back and the meeting got under way.

Didier made a long speech, then everyone else on the *conseil* made a speech fine-tuning or correcting what Didier had just said. Charlie sat on a bench between Gerard Pelaprat and me but became bored from time to time and jumped down to make his way around the room for pats. Unfortunately, I reflected, as the speeches went on and on, this option was not open to the human participants.

The office bearers resigned and were re-appointed unopposed in the same positions, except for Jean-Claude Grosse. Jean-Claude made a long speech, the gist of which was that the *conseil* needed a young person to represent the youth of the *commune*, so he was willing to give up his place to Philippe Rochefort. Philippe, Alain and Martine's sixteen-year-old son, wasn't actually at the meeting, but his appointment to the *conseil* was applauded by everyone who was.

The meeting was followed by the annual *choucroute*, another *repas* in the *salle des fêtes*, at which the main dish was a bed of sauerkraut, potatoes, different kinds of sausage and ham, and *cornichons*, tiny pickled cucumbers.

With the purchase of my meal ticket, for only two euros extra, I received a card identifying me as an *Ami d'Espagnac-Sainte-Eulalie*. At last I was official.

In December, it rained. The Célé broke its banks. Beside sodden, soup-leafed paths, knobs of pale green moss dappled darker green on trees and rocks. Slender trees, naked but for their corsets of knotted ivy, regarded their reflections in temporary lakes. The meadows and all the little bridges between Espagnac and Figeac were inundated. Doleful cattle huddled on islands in the muddy swirl. The normally dry rivulet running from the *grotte* at La Source Bleue drove a clear blue stream from its subterranean source into the turgid Célé.

Water cascaded from caverns in the *falaise*, ran over the road, glided and mingled in the meadows, swirled round water mills, rushed over walls, folded against arches of bridges, beat trees into frantic jigs. In the mornings, white mist trailed against ghost-white *falaise*; white morning fogs were pierced by liquid sunbeams from a shining leaden sky.

Thierry Dubuisson, raincoat dripping on the linoleum, banged on my door one morning at 5am. 'Maureen! Maureen! The water is coming up the Chemin des Dames. You have to move your car up to the *place* before the *cour* is flooded!'

I shrugged on my tracksuit and raincoat and in the pre-dawn dark Charlie and I felt our way down the steps behind Thierry and paddled across the *cour* to the car.

Thierry, Jacotte and their helper Dani were all on the *place*, Thierry struggling to get his tractor to start. 'Our *cabane à poulets*, our chicken-house, has been swept into the river. We're going to rescue the chickens. You can go back through our *cave*,' said Thierry, shining his torch into their garden where steps led down to the long cellar that ran between the *place* and the *cour*.

So while the others headed for the flooded meadow, Charlie and I made our way through the dimly-lit *cave*, past boxes and bins of eggs, fruit and vegetables and the wine and cheeses for the *repas paysan*, and up the steps to our *gîte*, and went back to bed.

When I woke again, the rain had stopped and I saw from my window the water lapping around the walls of the priory precinct. Beyond the wall opposite, on the other side of the Senacs' inundated meadow, only the top of a goal net broke the surface of the water covering the football field. The empty Haufricht house was cut off. The *gros chien* waited at the water's edge all day until it receded and he could take up his usual post by the door.

The flood had peaked just before dawn. Charlie and I went out to explore the changed landscape. Thierry and Jacotte's raspberry frames lay tangled in the water covering the meadow. The *cabane à poulets* had caught up against a tree about 200 metres downstream, just before the loop around to Brengues. At the other end of the village, the Kempleys' swimming pool and their *cave* were under water. We saw René doing what he could to rescue machinery and other equipment Terry had left in the *cave*. René had phoned him in England and Terry was already on his way back to assess the damage and clean up.

I was going to spend the week before Christmas in Amsterdam with Penny, then we were both going to Paris for Christmas with Judy and David. Penny was then to go to Spain with friends she'd made at the Conservatoire for the rest of her holidays and I would return to Espagnac. Charlie was going to stay with the Bagreaux, *comme d'habitude*.

'But you'll be back for *la Saint-Sylvestre*, New Year's Eve?' asked Martine. 'We're going to have a *repas* in the *foyer*. Just a few friends. *Les jeunes*. Not the whole village.'

I had come to understand that there were a variety of social groupings within the *commune* and that many of them went under descriptive names that seemed arbitrary. Among these were *les jeunes*, the young ones, and *les vieux*, the old ones. *Les jeunes* comprised a core group, some older than the core group that made up *les vieux*. I often did things with *les vieux*: Rolande, Mimi, Jacqueline, France, Lucien. But I also walked on Tuesdays with the nominal *jeunes*, Jocelyne, Pierre, Christiane. For the purposes of the *repas de la Saint-Sylvestre*, apparently, I was *une jeune*.

'I'd love to come,' I said.

Before I left for Amsterdam, there was a *réunion* at Jean-Louis and Christiane's house to plan the *repas de la Saint-Sylvestre*. Apart from Jean-Louis, Christiane, Martine Bagreaux, Milou and me, the rest of the 'planning committee' – Jocelyne and Pierre, Philippe Bagreaux, and Martine and Alain Rochefort – arrived in dribs and drabs over the course of the first hour. With each arrival, after the kissing, it was necessary to explain what had already been discussed and ensure that the newcomers were either in agreement or had an opportunity to put another case.

The discussion ranged over how many varieties of shellfish and how many different sizes of shrimp were required, how many oysters anyone would expect to eat, whether we would have *pâté de foie gras*

– '*Obligatoire*,' everyone murmured, nodding their heads. Then there was the question of the main *plat*: should it be *magret*, duck breast, or *volaille*, poultry. Until that moment, I thought duck breast *was* poultry, but evidently I was wrong. Pierre suggested a side of beef but was completely ignored and didn't mention it again. Martine eyed me across the table and asked which I would prefer. I said Maigret, which of course is the name of a Belgian detective, but it was close enough and I could see by the flourish with which she wrote it down that I had given the correct answer. Then we talked about who would prepare the different parts of the feast.

At last the business was over, Eric arrived with champagne, Jean-Louis found some white wine, Christiane pulled a quiche out of the oven, the sausages Jean-Louis and Philippe had been cooking in the fireplace were ready and everyone started eating, drinking and telling jokes.

Like many of my other trips, the visits to Amsterdam and Paris that Christmas had little to do with Charlie's and my lives in Espagnac, so I must skip the details.

Of how Penny was loving her life in Amsterdam, and how much she was learning. Of the museums and concerts of Amsterdam. Of the museums of Paris. Of the two of us shopping for Christmas presents in Bon Marché. Of midnight Mass in Notre-Dame de Paris with the great organ and the choir in gowns of French racing blue and matching voices, singing excerpts from Masses by Janacek, Mozart, Poulenc and the *credo* in Gregorian chant. Of Penny and me walking back to the seventeenth *arrondissement* in the small hours of the morning under shimmering veils of Christmas lights, past the Louvre, Saint-Roch, Place Vendôme with the floodlit La Colonne piercing the sky, Sainte-Marie-Madeleine and the Palais d'Élysée. Of Christmas dinner with friends of Judy and David, in an apartment full of books and music and beautiful furniture and lamps, overlooking a lovely classic Parisian *boulevard* near Place d'Italie. Of …

Meanwhile, back at Espagnac, Charlie had started out as usual with the Bagreaux. When they went to Martine's sister's family in Toulouse for Christmas, he stayed with Nicole in Figeac. When Nicole went to visit her mother in Saint-Geniez d'Olt, Rolande minded him in Diège. Then Rolande had to look after her grandchildren in Decazeville, and he was passed onto her neighbour Mireille, a teacher who lived in Paris in term-time, whom I had never met.

Charlie's groomer, Sylvie, of *Toutou chic*, gave him a *foulard* for Christmas, a little triangular scarf with rocking horses and ducks and kites and planes and cars all over it.

And now it was freezing. The sun rising over the *falaise* shot glittering shards of light through the ice-blue air. During the day, along the path to La Source Bleue, the mud crackled underfoot. On New Year's Eve, it snowed. After nightfall the low blanket of cloud, like dented pewter, reflected the light from the Christmas tree outside the *mairie*. And on the soft luminosity of the cloud lay the uplit shadow of the spire of Notre-Dame du Val-Paradis.

While the adult *jeunes* and their young children, such as Bastien and Anaïs, celebrated *la Saint-Sylvestre* in the *foyer*, the other *jeunes* comprising Philippe Rochefort and about forty of his teenage friends had another party in the *salle des fêtes*. They had brought sleeping bags, as they were only sixteen years old and were under instructions to stay as long as it took them to sober up the next day.

Jean-Louis turned on the heating in one of the rooms in the tower so that at the end of our party Charlie and I could sleep there without being disturbed by Philippe and his friends.

Martine Bagreaux, Jean-Louis and I went caving in the foundations of the priory to get salt from the sacks stored there, to sprinkle over the stone paths and steps so people wouldn't slip on the ice. The *foyer* was decorated with streamers and balloons and a branch of *gui*, mistletoe, that Martine Rochefort had found on the *causse* and which Eric and Bastien hitched onto a rafter in the *foyer* with ropes. Dishes of figs, muscatel grapes and oranges were scattered over the tables.

For *apéritif* we had champagne and little toasts with caviar, smoked salmon and lemon wedges. Juste Llorden and Alain Rochefort opened the oysters and stacked them on big silver platters. The table was groaning with the gleaming platters of glistening oysters and dishes of *amandes de mer*, big, flat, almond-shaped shells, *escargots de mer*, sea snails, little black *bigorneaux*, winkles, *crevettes grises*, tiny shrimp from the North Sea, *grosses crevettes*, king prawns. It looked like a still life painting by Willem Claesz Heda that I had seen in the Rijksmuseum in Amsterdam.

After the seafood and champagne, there was sweet wine and a *foie gras* prepared by Martine Bagreaux in a *bain marie* with *fleur de sel*, sea-salt from the Camargue. Martine's ability with *foie gras* was legendary, and her secret, which she shared with me, was to seal the lid of the earthenware casserole in which she cooked it with a paste of butter and flour, allowing just enough steam to circulate inside. Philippe Bagreaux and Jean-Louis cooked the *magrets* on the open fire till they were *à point*, just right, that is, singed on the outside and bloody in the middle. We had them sliced with *pommes de terre Duchesse*, potatoes creamed, swirled and toasted, by Christiane, and mushroom sauce and home-made bread by Milou. And a magnum of Mouton Cadet de Rothschild Baron Philippe 1997. After the cheeses we had chocolate mousse cakes by Odette, who wasn't there because she was otherwise engaged with her *agriculteur*, and orange and almond tart and kiwifruit in Cointreau by me.

Pierre had compiled a special disc of jive music. At midnight, without stopping dancing, everyone embraced everyone else and wished one another '*Bonne année*, Happy New Year!' and good health and happiness.

In the early hours, Charlie and I climbed the wooden steps to the room at the top of the silent tower. We slept till late on the morning of *le jour de l'an*, New Year's Day.

And snow fell all around.

WINTER PASTIMES

Instead of being *méditative*, as Mme Bonzani had promised, winter proved full of activity. But despite my best intentions, as the season progressed, *Blue and Brown* remained a collection of notes and papers and a few abortive beginnings, while I continued to enjoy and write about our adventures in Espagnac.

I thought I was beginning to understand what made the village tick, but there were some circumstances that baffled me. For example, there was the matter of the logistics of the English class.

A core group of four turned up consistently: Christiane Cabrignac, Solange Cabrignac, Jeanine Pelaprat and Rolande. They were all complete beginners. Others seemed to bowl up if they remembered or if they didn't have anything else to do. If several people made an appearance, I would ask the group that had studied English at school to prepare little sketches to present to the beginners' group at the end of the lesson. This was a lot of fun because of the lurid imaginations of some of the participants. But it only worked if there was a critical mass of people to start with. Sometimes I would put in hours of preparation and end up having to scrap my plan in view of who did and didn't turn up.

I put the problem to Martine. Saturday evening wasn't such a good time for everyone, I suggested, but Friday, when many were tired from the week's school or work, or Sunday, when they were getting ready for the next week, would be even worse. I proposed that Christiane, Solange, Jeanine and Rolande come to my apartment on an evening during the week and we would work through a program. Then it would be up to the Saturday group to sink or swim.

'*Tu as raison*, you're right, Maureen,' said Martine. 'Most of us work during the week so we don't have so much time for a *séance* every week. Philippe does shift work on weekends sometimes. And Bastien, he's in the junior tennis competition on Saturdays. I have to drive him to the matches all over the Department. But the children can come and see you when they need to revise for school tests or get help with their homework?'

'*Bien sûr*, Martine.'

It finally dawned on me that for most people, the original arrangement was a fun, summertime thing. I'd been taking it too seriously. The Saturday *séances* sank. What a relief.

But for various indefinable reasons, the beginners group persisted on Tuesday evenings, after the walk. It wasn't that anyone would ever actually need English, least of all Solange and Rolande, who were in their seventies, and whose lives revolved around the village, their families and the church. It was just a cosy and disparate group of friends, relatives and neighbours.

My role was made easier after Christiane went with Jocelyne to a book fair at Brive. There they found an English teaching and learning system that Jocelyne was familiar with, and which she said was the best English course she had come across, so Christiane bought it for the class. The course started from scratch, comprising a book of lessons and CDs of the English dialogue involved in each lesson. Each lesson built on the previous ones and focused on imagined situations. They were unlikely scenarios for my students, such as a bloke trying to pick up a girl in a pub, or a group of school teachers going on a holiday to Birmingham. There were revision lessons at certain culminating points throughout the course. It was designed for a lesson a day, but, following the kissing and exchange of news about family members, we tackled it as a lesson a week, and sometimes even more slowly if someone couldn't make a class, or it was a holiday. No one was in a hurry, even though it was clear it would take about five years to come to the end of the course, at the rate we went.

Jeanine made good progress because she had a good ear for the sound of the language, practised during the week and always had questions to ask when she came to the class. She and André had been primary school teachers. At first, nobody could say the word 'the'. Jeanine eventually did pretty well with the 'th' sound and could even distinguish between when it was pronounced as 'thuh' and when it was pronounced as 'thee'. Christiane had left school at fifteen and was diffident about her ability. '*Oh, là, là!*' she cried, flushing with the effort of pronouncing a phrase. '*C'est dur*, that's hard!' And she would try again: 'Hi'm 'oliday, I'm on holiday'.

In French, every syllable is pronounced while in English certain syllables are emphasised and others are subsumed in the rhythm of the language. Christiane didn't pronounce the pronouns because she simply didn't hear them. Solange and Rolande looked and sounded as if they had lost control of a mouthful of chewing gum. 'Wat wedda lik, What's the weather like?,' Solange spluttered. Rolande inhaled her 'h's instead of aspirating them, so she was frequently gasping for breath. When it was her turn to repeat a sentence, she struggled to make the right sounds, and when she finished she looked up under her eyebrows like a child hoping no one noticed she'd just spilled porridge in her lap. But everyone turned up most Tuesdays, and even phoned me or sent a message if they couldn't come. The English class, with these four cheerful, unpretentious women, became as important to me as the Tuesday walks.

As for Charlie, he adored them. He recognised their footsteps in the entry and with each arrival his tail would quiver and he would throw himself at the newcomer with delight. He would beat Christiane and Jeanine to the sofa and wriggle along it, sending the pillows and cushions flying, so that he would be ready to put his head in the lap of whoever sat down first. Everyone sat in the same places every week: Solange and I in the wicker chairs, Rolande on the bed, Jeanine and Christiane on the *canapé-lit* with Charlie snuggled between them.

Sometimes I went to the cinema in Figeac with Jacqueline. It often showed foreign films in *version originale*, that is, not dubbed into French, as foreign films often are, but with French subtitles. This had a double advantage for me, especially if the films were American or British, because I could read the French while I was listening to the English.

We also went to the *spectacles* we'd subscribed to. One was a well-sung but rather bizarre production of Mozart's *Cosi Fan Tutte*, where the set was angled to look a bit like the stateroom of a sinking ship. The *dramatis personae* included a non-singing *Valet en Vert*, a footman in green, evidently Don Alfonso's sex object, in a curly blonde wig and green dress with a corset bodice, heavily made up with red lips and cheeks. Fiordiligi and Dorabella were shocked to discover his gender when they spotted him in the bath. The audience, however, saw this moment coming a mile off. I'd never before been to an opera that featured full-frontal nudity. Jacqueline was so nonchalant about it, I concluded it must happen all the time.

Then there was another *poule farcie*.

I had put a rinse in my hair to hide the grey at my temples.

'*C'est bien, ça,*' Pascale commented. '*C'est joli,* that's pretty.'

'You needn't have gone to all that trouble just for us,' said Didier.

'Would you like to sleep with me?' asked Jean-Louis.

'*Non, non,*' said Christiane smoothly. 'I'll find you someone else.' She pretended to survey the room for possibilities.

I felt rather flattered to be the subject of this repartee. It was a long time since the days when my university friends and teaching colleagues – all except me, it seemed – were becoming involved romantically. I too would have liked to meet someone that I could fall in love with and who would fall in love with me, and to have children. Now, my new friends seemed to be suggesting that at least part of this scenario could still happen.

Over the *salade composée*, Lucien told me a joke: a man goes into a restaurant and says to the waiter, 'Excuse me, do you serve *cornichons* in this restaurant?' The waiter replies, 'Certainly, *monsieur*, we serve anybody.'

A man I'd never met before came by our table and said in an almost impeccable David Niven accent, 'Hello, Maureen, how are you?'

He was apparently an *ami*, because he was helping to serve the *repas*.

'*C'est* Bernard,' said Rolande. 'He and Danielle have a house at Diège. They live in Toulouse.'

Periodically during the evening Bernard returned with another English phrase he had been working on in the meantime.

'Are you satisfied, *madame*? May I be of assistance?'

Laughing, I mentioned that our table didn't have any *cornichons*. After that he returned several times with a few *cornichons* on a dish. Eventually, he brought a napkin rolled into a cylinder. On the outside was written 'Gift for You'. It was packed with *cornichons*. There seemed to be no end to *cornichon* jokes.

The *assemblée générale annuelle*, the annual general meeting of *Les Aînés Ruraux*, the old country folk, was held in the restaurant La Taverna at Beduer. Before the lunchtime *repas*, there were verbal reports of all the activities of the past year and discussion of those planned for the coming one. The office bearers, Jean-Claude Grosse and André Pelaprat from Espagnac, M. Henri Chanut and Rosette from Brengues, were re-elected unopposed. Following the speeches there was *kir*, *soupe de légumes*, vegetable soup, *salade de gésiers de chevreuil et canard fumé bernaise*, deer gizzard and smoked duck salad, *côte de chevreuil*, deer ribs in a rich sauce with baked dumplings, *chevreuil rôti*, roast leg of deer in a lighter sauce with a green salad, cheeses, baked custard tart or nougat ice cream with cream and a raspberry *coulis*. Coffee. *Vin de pays*, local wine.

It was quite a contrast to the soup, cheese and salad I normally ate for lunch.

Throughout the *repas*, the conversation all around me was of *confits* and *pâtés*, for the hunting season was over, and, as our *repas* demonstrated, there was a lot of meat around.

And, as Lucien Dabout informed me, 'When French people sit down at the table, they talk about what they ate yesterday and what they are going to eat tomorrow.'

Rolande said she would order a duck from the butcher and show me how to make *confit de canard* and would lend me the equipment. Meanwhile I was to buy a kilo of *gros sel*, coarse salt, and some *chair à saussice*, sausage meat, when I went to Figeac to do my shopping.

The following Saturday I took delivery of my duck from the butcher's van. It was the first duck I ever bought, and confronting for a temporarily lapsed vegetarian. It seemed enormous, complete with lolling head and stiff feet and the body covered in a thick layer of fat.

Rolande had no qualms about it. She arrived at my apartment with an assortment of sharp knives, a big iron frying pan, a large *cocotte minute*, pressure cooker, two half-litre *bocaux*, preserving jars, and one 750-millilitre *bocal*, rolled up her sleeves and we both set to work. I made an effort to disguise my distaste. First, we scraped off the fluff and pulled out the odd quills remaining in the skin and fat. We jointed the duck and cut the breasts from the carcass. We cut off the fat, leaving a layer about 2 centimetres thick on the breasts. We salted the legs, shoulders and breasts with the *gros sel*. We cut the fat into little pieces and sprinkled it with *gros sel*. We refrigerated the salted meat and the fat overnight.

After Rolande left, Charlie and I went for a cleansing walk. Then, to take my mind off the day's carnage, I prepared some pasta and ratatouille for dinner and listened to Beethoven's Pastoral Symphony on the CD player while I ate.

Next day, Rolande was back and we resumed our labours. We pulled the skin off the duck's neck and stuffed it with the *chair à saussice* and sewed up the ends. We melted the pieces of fat in the frying pan over a low heat and strained it. Then we fried the pieces of duck and the stuffed neck skin in the fat that remained on them and some of the melted fat, with a couple of bay leaves and pepper, at a low temperature for about forty minutes.

'Some people,' Rolande said, 'use additional *herbes aromatiques*, but *à mon avis*, in my opinion, herbs detract from the flavour of the meat.'

After we removed the pieces of duck we continued frying the stuffed neck for another twenty minutes or so. Then we packed a leg, a breast and a shoulder into each of the two half-litre *bocaux* and the stuffed neck into the 750-millilitre *bocal*. We poured the fat into the jars, making sure there weren't any air holes, leaving about 2 centimetres of space at the top of each *bocal*. We sealed the *bocaux* and then Rolande went home. As instructed, I cooked the *confits* in their *bocaux* in the *cocotte minute* on medium heat for one hour after the pressure cooker started to hiss.

Now, all but reconciled to my blood-guilt, with the neck and carcass, I made a thick soup, *La Garbure Landaise*, with kidney beans, potatoes, herbs, pimento, *lardons*, bacon pieces, onion, leeks, turnip, pumpkin and cabbage leaves and a *bouquet garni*. There was enough to feed about ten people and the soup was dense enough to freeze in freezer bags. It was so delicious that afterwards I occasionally bought carcasses at the *marché* in Figeac and *La Garbure Landaise* became a staple in my freezer, to supplement the vegetable and pulse stews, curries and stir-fries I usually made.

Gerard Pelaprat was driving a ride-on mower around the spindly oaks in a field on the high side of the road. He stopped the machine and came down to kiss me and pat Charlie.

'What are you doing?' I asked. The field was like the rest of the fields along the road, a bit overgrown, maybe with fewer of the oaks that grew all over the place.

'I'm cleaning it up. Maybe I'll get some truffles this year.' He didn't sound very hopeful.

'I didn't know this was your field,' I said, 'or that there might be truffles in it.'

'It was my inheritance,' Gerard said, and spread his hands in a helpless gesture.

'Have you ever found truffles here?'

'Fourteen, perhaps fifteen, years ago.'

I smiled sympathetically. '*Bonne chance, alors*, good luck, then. If you need a dog to help you find them ...' I gestured to Charlie, who was sitting on the road between us, looking almost as thoughtful as the *gros chien*.

Gerard smiled sceptically, perhaps at the idea of Charlie as a truffle dog, perhaps at the possibility of ever finding truffles under his oak trees.

Truffles are otherwise known as *l'or noir*, black gold. They are ugly, black pitted lumps of fungus that grow in the soil at the base of oak and birch trees and have a penetrating, earthy smell that is particularly attractive to pigs, dogs and flies. They grow beneath *les chênes du causse*, the small, spindly oaks that are part of the natural forest of Quercy, but there's no point looking for truffles in the forest. They are found in privately-owned fields which the owners keep tidy to make it easier for the pigs, dogs and flies to sniff them out. There is also no point trying to find truffles on private property, because the minute you appear with your poodle and your little *panier*, basket, the farmer will appear with his *berger allemand*, his German shepherd and *fusil*, his shotgun. Nicole told me the story of some truffle-poachers caught by the *fusil*-toting *producteur* who made them hand over the truffles and their wallets and remove their clothes, and sent them shivering on their way.

There are several legends relating to truffles.

In one, a poor orphan-girl yearns for the love of the Prince of Aquitaine, who has fallen ill. One cold winter's day, on the *causse*, she notices an iridescent fly flitting around in the grass. She chases the fly, wondering aloud what it could be looking for. To her astonishment, the fly speaks.

'I seek the black pearl of the *causse*, my child.'

The fly tells the girl to scrape the soil away at the foot of an oak tree and she digs up a hard, knobbly black object. Puzzled, she looks up at the fly, which is zooming around her head, excited by the odour of the thing she is holding.

'It's a truffle!' shrieks the fly. 'Take it home and make an omelette with it, the most delicious omelette you ever tasted.'

Conquering her doubts, the girl obeys the fly and takes the omelette to the Prince, who immediately recovers both his appetite and his health. He asks her to marry him and they live happily ever after and have many children.

In another legend a shivering, toothless old woman leaning on a stick knocks at the door of the thatched cottage of a poor peasant and his family, asking for shelter.

'You are welcome to come in,' the peasant says, 'but we only have chestnuts to eat tonight.'

'You may have only chestnuts,' says the old woman, 'but you have a big heart. I'm going to reward you. Here are some seeds. In springtime, sew them under your oak trees and in the autumn you will reap a fragrant harvest that will make you rich, for I have given the seeds only to you.'

She disappears up the chimney in a shower of sparks.

The following autumn, the peasant digs up big black truffles. He shares his riches with the rest of the village, but after he dies, his children live in luxury while their neighbours languish in poverty. One winter's night, a toothless old woman comes to the door of their mansion.

'Please,' she begs, 'let me come in and sit by your fire for a while. I am perishing with cold.'

'Certainly not!' they reply. 'Go away.'

It's the same old woman as before, who is actually a fairy. She brandishes her stick and makes the fine house disappear and changes the peasant's children into sows. From that day on, sows have been used to collect truffles.

That year, because of the heat and drought of the preceding summer, truffles were as scarce as the teeth of a fairy in disguise. The newspaper of the Midi-Pyrénées, *La Dépêche*, reported that truffles were selling for 3000 euros a kilo at the regional truffle *marché* in Lalbenque. These prices, understandably, kindled a burst of truffle fever.

Gaby and Dany Senac, Anaïs's grandparents, spent a week in February burning the rubbish on a piece of land adjoining their house and planting sixty oak trees in the ashes.

'We won't live to see the truffles,' said Gaby. 'It's for the grandchildren. It takes about fifty years for the fungus to get going.'

I thought of telling the Senacs and Gerard about the fast-track fairy route I'd read about, but something in their eyes – Gaby and Dany's optimism, Gerard's fatalism – held me back.

'*Eh, bien, bonne continuation!*' I said.

'Let's go to Lalbenque,' said Nicole, eyes bright with excitement. 'We'll just look. Or maybe, if they're not too dear ...'

So, on the last very cold Tuesday in February, we drove to the little town about 20 kilometres south of Cahors where truffle *producteurs* trade every Tuesday afternoon from December to February.

We parked in the car park at one end of the town because barricades had been set up at each end of the main street. On the barricades there were notices giving the official code of the truffle *marché*. Among other things, the truffles had to be clean, with all earth brushed away and the exact weight of each lot recorded. One side of the street was lined with five or six trestle tables, on which the *producteurs* displayed their little hoards of treasure. When we arrived, there was a rope barrier about a metre away from the tables. For an hour before 2.30pm, when sales began, an official with a notebook and calculator approached the *producteurs* as they arrived and recorded the quantity they had brought. Each *producteur* displayed his or her *etiquette*, a little card naming the *exploitation*, the farm, the truffles came from.

Nicole and I joined the crowd of potential buyers, mostly restaurant owners, and the gawkers and tourists jockeying for positions against the rope, trying to see and smell the truffles or take photos of them using zoom lenses.

'There are usually more tables than this,' said Nicole. 'Usually from end to end of the street.'

The *producteurs* comprised a few respectable looking elderly women in colourful padded coats, with little baskets of truffles covered by checked napkins, and some scruffy old men, with truffles wrapped in grey handkerchiefs or in plastic bags in lots of 100 grams.

Nicole pushed me to a spot against the rope barrier where I had an unimpeded view. I asked one of the women if I could take a photo and she obligingly lifted a corner of her napkin and posed with an expression of earnest pride in the suspicious-looking pile that lay beneath.

'May I smell them?' I asked.

The woman held out the basket at arm's length and I leaned as far as I could across the rope to sniff them. They had a rich, earthy aroma. I was getting hooked.

Farther down the line, one of the scruffy old men flicked open a corner of his handkerchief to let me see his truffles. I asked if I could smell them too.

'Ten euros,' he said.

Meanwhile, Charlie had got under the rope barrier and was sniffing as much as he wanted for free.

I asked the official with the notebook if the *producteurs* agreed among themselves what the price would be that day and she smiled knowingly and said '*Chaque producteur fait son prix*, everyone sets his own price.'

The scruffy old man in front of us had five plastic bags of 100 grams each for eighty euros a bag. It was 2.30pm. The rope fell away and the crowd surged forward. There was no time to lose. I held out three notes – a fifty, a twenty and a ten. The man had come prepared with a pocketful of twenties, expecting to be handed 100-euro notes. He took my fifty and gave me a twenty. Nonchalantly, I slipped the two twenties and the ten in my pocket. Then there was some kerfuffle about which bag was for Nicole and me. During that fateful moment, a quiet, penetrating voice somewhere near my right elbow said, '*C'est que cinquante*, it's only fifty.' With a light laugh, I withdrew the other two notes and handed them over.

I looked around to see who had spoken, but the truffles were all sold, and the crowd was dispersing. An old woman, bent over a stick, hobbled along in its wake.

Between us, Nicole and I had ten little truffles. We decided to use two for an omelette and the rest we divided into lots of two and froze them in little jars in Nicole's freezer for later use.

For the omelette, we put three eggs and two truffles into a preserving bottle and sealed it so the aroma of the truffles could infuse the eggs for several days. In due course, we made the omelette.

First, break the eggs into a mixing bowl. Shave the truffle skins into the eggs and whisk the mixture. Slice the rest of the truffles finely. Heat some goose fat in a pan until it is very hot and pour the egg mixture in, dropping the sliced truffles on top. Shift the egg mixture a bit with a wooden spoon so that it is cooked through but not hard.

It was aromatic and rich, with a burst of taste on biting the little bits of truffle. We washed it down with another bottle of Nuits Saint-Georges.

Nicole proffered Charlie a tiny shaving of truffle skin on the end of her finger. He smelt it, licked it and let it drop to the floor.

'He doesn't think it tastes as good as it smells, evidently,' I said, laughing. 'But then, he's not an expert.'

Nicole sat back, savouring the aftertaste of the omelette. 'Do truffles grow in Australia, Maureen?'

'I think they've begun to grow white truffles in Tasmania but I've heard they're not as good as these black ones.'

'A good reason for you to stay here, *alors.*'

'Well,' I smiled, 'if we were to do that, we wouldn't be eating truffles every day. But I can think of plenty of other reasons to stay.'

DEUX AMOURS

The beginning of March brought glorious weather and the first of the flowers that multiplied daily in number and variety. For a week the nuns' room was invaded by little orange beetles, *bêtes de Dieu*, God's creatures, so called because they eat greenflies, which are *bêtes du diable*, the Devil's creatures. Charlie ate both species indiscriminately, in his own existentialist way.

The swallows returned too, breast-stroking through the currents of air flowing between the *falaises*, darting in and out of the niches in the limestone.

Over the next two or three weeks a flock of the Rocheforts' pregnant black-eyed *brebis* moved their big round bodies on delicate stick legs along the Célé, field by field, until they had eaten all the winter grass.

One Sunday evening, walking back along the track from the river, I noticed a *brebis* lying on its side among the trees near the riverbank. Back at the village, passing through the *place*, I saw the lights on in the *mairie*. Martine Bagreaux was in her office, having a quiet smoke and catching up on her paperwork. I went in and told her about the *brebis*.

'Maybe it's asleep,' said Martine.

'It was very still,' I said doubtfully. 'Do sheep sleep lying on their sides?'

It was Martine's turn to look doubtful. 'It's Sunday,' she said. 'It would be a shame to disturb the Rocheforts if the *brebis* is just having a little rest.'

'I wasn't close enough to see what the problem was,' I said.

'I didn't want to take Charlie across the field, he would have frightened the flock.'

Martine reached for the phone. Martine Rochefort said she would come down to investigate, and Charlie and I went home.

The next day, I saw Alain and Martine and the two dogs in their van, driving through the *place* on their way to the meadow. They stopped to tell me what had happened.

'There's no grass left in the meadow and the sheep are looking for it on the riverbank,' said Alain. 'The *brebis* got tangled up in the tree branches.'

'She fell over,' said Martine.

It never occurred to me that a sheep might fall over and be unable to get up again.

'*Oh, Dieu merci!*' I exclaimed. 'I thought she might be dead. What did you do?'

'I pushed her back on her feet,' Martine laughed. 'She's carrying twins. We're taking all the *brebis* back up to the *bergerie* now till the grass has time to grow again.'

They drove on down the lane and Martine Bagreaux appeared on the landing outside the *mairie*.

'*Hé*, Maureen,' she said, 'maybe Martine will give you a *côtelette* as a reward for saving the *brebis*.'

I didn't get the chop, but this didn't stop me, on our return from Figeac one Saturday lunchtime, from phoning the Rocheforts myself with what I supposed would be helpful information.

'Martine, there's a flock of sheep on the road, heading towards Figeac. All the cars are stopping to let them pass.'

'They couldn't be our sheep,' said Martine, in a tone of voice that implied, *we look after ours better than that*.

She speculated whose they might be and said she would phone the careless *agriculteur*.

'I am not the Good Shepherdess, obviously,' I remarked to Charlie, ruffling his wool. 'I can't tell one flock of sheep from another.'

The warm spell was followed by the *giboulées de mars*, sudden showers punctuated by brilliant sunshine. Just as suddenly, as if shaken and scattered from the clouds, there appeared grape hyacinths, wood anemones, great drifts of cowslips, crocuses, orchids, buttercups and daisies over the meadows, woods and lanes. By mid-April, the white and gold fairy-skirts of wild narcissi swayed again in the hidden meadow on the *falaise*. The plum trees standing in a row on the way to La Source Bleue were luminous with white blossom.

Then it was cold and raining for days and the river threatened to break its banks again. And then the sun was out and the birches on the *causses* were shrouded in a haze of delicate green. The oaks hadn't yet put on their leaves and everyone was waiting to see how many survived last year's drought. Already it was clear from the sad brown shapes among the green that many of the fir trees and juniper bushes had died.

Driving through the village of Ambeyrac on the southern bank of the Lot a few days later, I noticed an *À vendre*, a For Sale, sign on a gate. Beyond the gate was a two-storey house surrounded by lean-to sheds and a garden full of fruit trees, tulips and daffodils. I wrote down the phone number of the real estate agent.

The cottage, a deceased estate, was in a fairly run-down condition, but it fired my imagination. The lean-to carport could be demolished and the shed at the back could be converted into a workroom. The kitchen and parlour on the ground level could be extended to include a laundry and toilet, and over that you could build a deck running the length of the south side of the house and overlooking the river.

The loft could be made into a large studio; there would need to be a proper staircase to replace the ladder, but the existing floorboards could be patched and polished ...

I had been thinking that, if Charlie and I did stay in France, we would have to quit the nuns' room. It was, after all, a basic holiday apartment, not a proper home. But if we left the priory, we would probably have to leave the community of Espagnac-Sainte-Eulalie and start again somewhere else. We had been so much looked after here, could we stand on our own six feet somewhere else?

'You'd come and visit us if we lived at Ambeyrac, wouldn't you?' I asked Rolande and Mimi.

They said they would, but I knew that their lives, like those of other *villageois*, centred on the activities of the village, the local associations, their close friends and their families. Ambeyrac wasn't even in the Lot Department as it was situated on the Aveyron side of the river.

'Ambeyrac, it's a bit isolated,' said Nicole. 'You'd be better buying something in Figeac.'

'I'll think about it,' I said, 'but if I stay, I'd rather live in a village than a town.'

At Easter that year, I had two groups of visitors. Firstly, John, Fiona and Mary came from Birmingham for a week before the holiday.

I took them to see the house at Ambeyrac.

'This house would be a very good buy,' said John, the second time we untied the rope fastening the two sides of the gate together, 'but I think you shouldn't do anything till you go back and live in your Canberra house again.'

'When in doubt,' said Mary cheerfully, 'wait it out.' She who had lived in the same house in Birmingham since her marriage in 1942.

The week after John, Fiona and Mary went home to Birmingham,

Mary's son Hugh, his partner Gill, and their friends Larraine and Gerard arrived from Australia. The two couples rented a house near Cajarc. They arrived on Easter Sunday. The shops in Cajarc were all closed so I invited them for lunch and afterwards we strolled around the village.

By this time, I no longer felt self-conscious about showing visitors around Espagnac, and now exchanged smiles and waves with anyone we saw in the distance, and switched easily from English into French if our paths happened to cross our neighbours'. The presence of friends from England and Australia made me realise how much I now felt at home here, not just in Espagnac, but the whole region – and that Charlie and I had explored in one year probably as much territory as some of the *Espagnacois* had in their lifetimes.

At the same time, it was satisfying to catch up on personal gossip and news, even if some of the political news, such as the continuation of our involvement in the war in Iraq, the growing anti-refugee sentiments and the new anti-terrorist measures, was depressing.

'You don't give me much incentive to go back,' I said.

'No,' they agreed, laughing, 'you might as well stay here.'

'You're obviously having a great experience here,' said Gill. 'We love reading your emails. Every time we finish reading one, we start looking out for the next.'

'We did wonder what happened to your book,' said Hugh, gently.

I explained the situation. 'I've basically given up on it for the time being,' I said. 'I could make more effort with it, but really what I'm doing, exploring this place, soaking up the atmosphere, reading, talking to people and then writing about it, is so much more interesting. And more fun, too.'

'Well, we're enjoying it,' said Gill. 'Keep it up.'

'There's plenty of time for your book,' added Hugh. 'Some time in the future.'

As with the Birmingham Three, I took them to see the house at Ambeyrac.

We stood outside the gate and I described what I envisaged might be done with it.

'But,' I added, 'everywhere I go, I see English people working like slaves on houses they've bought here. I don't have the skill or desire to do that. I'd have to employ builders, and spend at least another 100,000 euros on top of the purchase price of the house. I'd have to sell up back home and I love my house in Canberra. Besides, I'm not sure I could afford to live here just on my superannuation pension. And I wouldn't want to commit to living here if it meant I couldn't afford to go back every now and then. I love it here but I love Australian landscapes too.'

Into my mind's eye came the image of the house on the New South Wales south coast, which my father built when we were children and my brother and I had inherited. It was in a national park, 50 metres from a pristine beach, a long crescent of golden sand and grassy dunes, washed in changing blues and greens of sea, sky and coastal foliage. Seagulls on the beach, plovers and ibises in the lagoons, sea eagles riding the winds. The banksia trees and casuarinas surrounding the house were inhabited by rosellas and wattle birds, kookaburras and blue wrens. There was the constant sound of waves crashing or rolling on the shore, depending on the weather and tides. It took three and a half hours to get there from Canberra; from Espagnac, it would take the best part of a day to get to the flat, dun-coloured beaches of Languedoc.

The others were still trying to be helpful.

'You might be able to get a mortgage on your Canberra house, to be repaid when you ... um ...' said Hugh.

'I think you have to be very old to do that,' said Gill. 'They'd want some guarantee that you'd ... um ... in the foreseeable future.'

'But, seriously, what if I do get health problems? My arthritis has been playing up.'

'You need to have a house here and something in Canberra,' said Gerard and Larraine. 'We know a financial adviser, she'd give you good advice. You'd probably have to sell the house in Canberra and get a flat there, to have somewhere to go back to if you wanted or needed to. You'd always find other Australians to rent this house.'

'And what about Charlie? I couldn't leave him here for months at a time.'

I realised that the house at Ambeyrac wasn't a realistic proposition but I continued to indulge in the possibility of extending our stay indefinitely.

'I'd like to live in a tower,' I said to Martine, 'a *pigeonnier*.'

'There's one for sale near Livernon,' she said. 'It's fifteenth century.'

I found it eventually in the middle of a wood. There was a cyclone wire fence surrounding the wood and a cast-iron gate in the fence. There was a huge iron lock on the gate. As Charlie and I poked our noses through, admiring the magnificent red brick tower, a car pulled up next to ours on the road. A man and a woman got out. The man had a camera. The woman had a large key. She unlocked the gate and invited us to go in with them.

The woman said that she had inherited the *pigeonnier*. But what would she want with a *pigeonnier* here in the Lot? Her home was in Nice. The man, a real estate agent, was going to take pictures of the *pigeonnier* to advertise it on the internet.

The door was crumbling, but the inside was sound. There was no floor, just bare earth. You would have to build the whole interior – a spiral staircase and three floors of rooms, like Yeats's tower at Gort

– to make it habitable, and arrange for some kind of water and electricity supply.

'We're asking 200,000 euros,' said the woman, 'but it will probably go for more. The English, the Dutch, the Belgians …'

Not long after this some English acquaintances told me about a property near Saint-Simon. It was another deceased estate, a complex of semi-ruined farm buildings, including a *four au pain* like the one at Diège. The family said that if I didn't make an offer, say – 250,000 euros – they would advertise it on the internet and get a lot more.

'It will be bought by Belgians or Dutch people, or English people who will make it into a bed and breakfast,' said the family wistfully.

'If it were fixed up, it would make a great bed and breakfast, with different apartments for the guests,' the English friends said. 'You could put in a pool.'

'But we don't want to run a bed and breakfast,' I said to Charlie, as we drove back home to Espagnac. 'I've got a book to write. Besides, we just want to live here.'

Anyway, we didn't have that kind of money. Also, I thought, if we stayed in France, it would have to be for ten years or so, until, assuming that the conviction of the old man in the church at Saint-Pierre Toirac and my father's unorthodox theory was correct, Charlie exchanged his terrestrial paradise for the celestial one. He was now only seven.

Then there was the financial issue. While in France, I had two sources of income: my superannuation pension and the rent from my house in Canberra. This just covered our living expenses in France and the trips I did from time to time, but it wouldn't cover regular trips back to Australia. On the other hand, living in Australia,

I wouldn't be able to decide on the spur of the moment to go to Greece, England, Ireland, Spain or Italy.

Around this time the teacher at the primary school at Brengues, M. Cardon, asked me if I would read to his class of eight- and nine-year-olds, who had started to learn English.

'My accent isn't very good,' he said. 'We have a book that we read but I want them to hear it read by a native speaker, even if it is in an Australian accent.'

'I'd be delighted,' I said. 'A little boy from my village, Tanguy, is in your class.'

I brought a Steve Parish calendar with pictures of iconic Australian sites to show the children. The teacher set some work for the smaller children to do, and ushered the others to the little desks, where they sat, smiling. I recognised some of them who visited the children at Espagnac, their friends and cousins. Tanguy was beaming, as usual. I showed them the first picture, which was the Sydney Opera House.

'*C'est un dragon*, it's a dragon!' whispered Loïc fearfully.

'It does look like a dragon,' I agreed. 'But it's a big building where people play music and sing.'

'Do they play the accordion?' asked Olivier.

'I think so,' I said. 'Sometimes.'

'Say the name of the month,' said M. Cardon, bringing us all back on task. 'January.'

The children, still staring at the dragon, mouthed, 'Jan-u-ar-y.'

The next picture was the Sydney Harbour Bridge by night, bathed in lurid red light, a sight even more unnerving than the Opera House, judging by the gasps from the children.

'February,' said M. Cardon.

The children sighed with relief when at last we sailed into the calm blue waters of the Whitsundays and the Great Barrier Reef, until little Henri mentioned the *meduses*, the stinging jellyfish, and the *requins*, sharks, they had seen on the Friday night television program 'Thalassa.' The previous two episodes had been on the *Grande Barrière de Corail*, the Great Barrier Reef, so these dangers were fresh in their minds.

'But it's quite safe there,' I reassured them. 'I've swum there, on the *Grande Barrière de Corail*. It's very beautiful. There are thousands of fish in all the colours of the rainbow.'

I wanted to tell them that it wasn't just the Great Barrier Reef that was so beautiful; that there were so many places, and such a variety of different fascinating landscapes: desert, rainforest, plain, mountain, coastal.

'Now Mme Cashman will read our book,' said M. Cardon, gently but firmly. It wasn't a geography lesson.

The Tuesday walks had been abandoned over the harshest weeks of the winter but with the fresh spring sunshine everyone was keen to be out and about again.

Sometimes the chosen circuit would start in one of the neighbouring villages, sometimes in a village more distant. Charlie and I walked round to the Pelaprats' and went to the meeting place with them in their car.

Jeanine and André had both been teachers in some of the villages where we walked or had driven past. I had been a teacher for most of my working life; and for the ten years before I retired, I had worked on national school curriculum policy. I enjoyed hearing about their experiences of teaching in village schools and in the French education system in general. My French was still not good enough for me to participate in a large group conversation, but with our common interests, my interest in the region, and André and Jeanine's patience and willingness to talk, I felt confident in asking questions and sharing ideas with them. By this time, everyone knew that I was writing about the local area.

We had many conversations about the changes in people's lives in rural villages over their lifetimes, André talking from his personal experience, as well as from a more learned point of view that came from his teaching background. The same experience and learning applied to what he said about the geographical features of the landscape we were driving through. Sometimes, when he was explaining or describing something, Jeanine would interrupt with, '*C'est vrai*, is that true?' or '*Ça existe*, is there such a thing?' Jeanine came from the Pays-Basque in the Pyrenees. Both were interested in and knew quite a lot about Australia. André would ask me tricky questions about geology and plant life, while Jeanine would ask about climate and cuisine, subjects that were easier for me to deal with.

When everyone had arrived at the meeting point, André and Jean-Claude would confer at length over the village notice board and their maps and discuss the state of the terrain, how much of the circuit to do, and whether it would be better to follow it clockwise or anti-clockwise. Meanwhile Ginette Grosse and Christiane Cabrignac, itching to be off, would explore the village and admire the houses and sometimes keep going along a track they'd found so the rest of the group could do nothing but follow them. André and Jean-Claude would valiantly try to locate the track on the map and find some point where it connected with the planned circuit, forging ahead of the rest of the group to recover the situation before it got out of hand. The rest of us would catch them up at a crossroads, poring over the map, looking around and each pointing in the direction he thought was the right one. Jeanine would ask with a merry grin, '*Nous sommes perdus*? Are we lost?'

As soon as we were off the village roads and following paths through woods or meadows, I would let Charlie off his lead. Having neither social nor linguistic inhibitions, he would scamper ahead or drop behind, attaching himself temporarily to one or other of the little groups that formed and changed as we went along.

Every walk had its own particular features: the ubiquitous *cazelles* and *dolmens*; the *puits*, wells; the *pigeonniers* and *tours*, dovecotes and towers, that sometimes adjoined the houses and sometimes stood alone in fields; the *moulins*, water mills or windmills; the *lavoirs*, communal laundries. Everything had to be observed and commented on.

'*Hé, ben dis donc*! *Quel joli toit*! Gosh, what a pretty roof!'

Passing a collection of farm buildings, we might glimpse through the door of a ramshackle shed an old lime-green or tomato-red Citroën. Once there was an elegant old sky-blue Versailles covered in dust, still the last word in long-ago motoring opulence, going by the murmurs and whistles of admiration from our companions.

Every farm had capacious roofed wire cages the height of the houses, packed with the coarse cobs of maize that had been harvested the previous autumn and stored to feed the animals over the rest of the year. Next to the maize stacks were often the enclosures that penned the farm dogs and the hunting dogs, which barked and howled as Charlie trotted past at liberty.

Some farms or village houses had special memories for different walkers. Here Pierre came to play with his cousins when he was a child. In the loft of that house, Thérèse's aunt hid to escape the Gestapo reprisals on their retreat north in 1945.

On a track out of Livernon, we stopped to inspect a *dolmen* called *la Pierre Martine*. The massive stone slab on top had split across the centre and concrete blocks supported the two ends which jutted out over the side stones.

'Long ago,' said André, 'the stone on top would rock backwards and forwards under the pressure of a hand. But eventually, after all that rocking, it broke in two.

'But there's a legend that gives another explanation for the slab breaking and also explains why the dolmen is called *la Pierre Martine*, Saint-Martin's stone.

'Saint-Martin lived in the fourth century. He was a Roman soldier who became a Christian monk. One day after he had become a monk, he was traversing the *causse* of Livernon. He met a local man who told him about a stone where devils gathered on nights of the full moon to celebrate black Masses. At the next full moon, Saint-Martin went to the place and saw, as night was falling, a pack of devils dancing on the rocking stone. He prayed to Saint-Eutrope, the patron saint of locks, to deluge the place with holy water. Sure enough, rain came pelting down on the dry limestone. The slab that the devils were dancing on split in two and the devils fell through the gap into the bowels of the earth, howling.'

'And which story do you think is the right one, André?' I asked.

'It's hard to say,' he replied. 'But it would take a considerable number of dancing devils to break a stone like that.'

Typical village houses had a stone staircase on one side leading up to a kind of porch outside the front door.

'The main part of the house is on the first floor and the *cave*, the cellar, is under the house,' André explained. 'The staircase protects the *cave* from the sun and helps to keep it cool so the stored fruit and vegetables don't spoil. In the past, every household had its own vine growing in a little soil beside the house, and the vine climbed in the sun by the staircase. In fine weather the women could sit in the shade of the roofline while they were doing their sewing and knitting. The door to the *cave* was close by, at the bottom of the steps, so it was convenient for the women to get what they needed to prepare a meal.

'*Regarde les épis*,' he said, pointing up to the roof of an imposing *manoir*.

Almost every building had one or more *épis*, decorations in stone, wood or pottery, on the apex of its roof. Sometimes they were very simple, blunt spikes like the cobs of maize they are named after, chipped roughly from stone, similar to the ones that perch at jaunty angles on top of the *cazelles*, like the stems of Basque berets. The ones along the coping of the *manoir* were pottery birds.

'The bird shape,' André said, 'represents the ties between the living and the dead, between the people who live in the houses and their families and neighbours, as well as the land.'

Sometimes we would come upon a fairytale *manoir* set in groomed gardens by a little lake, or a substantial village house, recently restored.

'English,' someone would say. 'Look at the garden.'

The garden would be neat and bright with cultivated flowers in beds with borders, not rough and utilitarian like the French farmyards.

'The English have the means to repair the old houses.'

'The Dutch, too.'

'They drive the prices up so the French can't afford to buy them.'

'At least, that way, the houses don't fall into ruin.'

On occasion, the track sometimes led through a village of lovely old turreted *quercynoise* houses, with maybe a medieval fortified church. André would point out the various architectural features, the roofs of *lauzes*, stone tiles, the round or square *tours* and *pigeonniers* with their steep, pointed roofs, the lintels carved with the dates of completion, the carpenter's or stonemason's initials, or with various emblems, such as hearts and flowers.

I inspected closely any modest-looking houses that were for sale.

'That one would suit you very well, Maureen, ' someone would say. 'A little garden for Charlie. Not too dear.'

I would gaze longingly at the pitched roof with missing *lauzes* and broken *épis*, the crumbling steps running up to the rotting boards under the carved lintel with termite holes in it.

One fascinating walk, near the village of Caniac-du-Causse, was in *L'Espace Naturel Sensible du Massif de la Braunie*, a region classified by the Departmental administration as a sensitive ecological area. The thin earth over the limestone hosted *pelouses sèches*, dry lawns of hardy little creeping plants bearing tiny yellow, blue and white flowers. The *pelouses sèches* teemed with lizards, crickets, grasshoppers and butterflies. In the surrounding woods were the inevitable scrubby oaks, as well as ash, hazel and hornbeam trees and bushes with clusters of berries. Pipits scrabbled about under the bushes; warblers sang in the trees; curlews and crows strutted over the open ground, picking off the insects. High overhead wheeled the magnificent brown and white speckled falcons that inhabit the region.

Our circuit took us over terrain pitted like a gigantic slab of *Gruyère* cheese with caverns, shallow pools and deep vertical holes in the ground, called *igues* or *gouffres*.

'Some of the *lacs*, the pools, are natural formations,' said André. 'But most have been chipped out of the limestone by shepherds, to ensure permanent water for their flocks.'

We stood on the rim of the Igue de Planagrèze and stared down into the blackness.

'It goes down more than 100 metres,' said André. 'A few years ago, they put a dye into the water at the bottom. The dye emerged more than 20 kilometres away to the west, near Rocamadour.'

'There must be hundreds of caves around us where prehistoric people lived,' I said. 'Maybe with more paintings, like the ones at Lascelles in the Dordogne and Pech-Merle here in the Lot.'

'*Sans doute*,' said André, 'probably.'

On the way back to Espagnac, we stopped in the village of Caniac-du-Causse to visit the twelfth century crypt holding the relics of Saint-Namphaise.

Saint-Namphaise was a warrior, a companion of Charlemagne, who, weary of the violence of war, like Saint-Martin before him, became a monk. He came to Quercy in search of solitude and an environment conducive to meditation and prayer. He founded a monastery, but he spent as much time as he could away from it, in order to be alone, away from the company of the other monks and nuns. Immersed in prayer, he didn't notice that some of the nuns had fallen into pagan ways, such as sacrificing children to the Devil.

One day, one of the nuns was busy stoking the kitchen stove with yet another child when the hearth caught on fire. The monastery was consumed and all the monks and nuns were burned to death.

On his return in the evening, Saint-Namphaise was appalled to see the smoking ruins of his monastery, to find all his followers had perished and to discover the cause of the fire. For a while, he stayed at the monastery at Marcilhac, but eventually left there and took up residence in a cave on the *causse* near Caniac-du-Causse. There, eventually, he found a way to make up to his fellow man the dreadful events that had occurred at the monastery he himself had founded. He would, with his mighty hammer and chisel, dig hollows in the rock to collect rainwater for the shepherds and their flocks.

Over many years, Namphaise excavated all the *lacs* and *bassins* on the *causses* of Quercy. But one day, as he was chipping away he noticed over his shoulder a bull, snorting and pawing at the ground, ready to charge. Namphaise only had time to hurl his hammer away with all his strength before the bull fell upon him and gored him to death. The hammer landed in the parish of Caniac, where the people built a church to shelter his remains.

All that is left of the original twelfth century church is the crypt, which lies below the current, nineteenth century church.

'But what happened to Saint-Namphaise's relics between the eighth century, when he died, and the twelfth century, when the church was built?' I asked André.

André stroked his beard. 'That's a mystery,' he said.

For six weeks in May and June of that year, 2004, I went to Ireland, and Charlie went to stay *chez* Bagreaux at Figeac, because it was during the school term.

It wasn't the same for him at Figeac as when he was staying with them in the village, where everyone knew him and he had people to play with and things to do all day, between rests. The only animal smells around the Figeac house came from the cats that haunted the little back garden.

'I was frightened to let him out there on his own in case those cats attacked him,' said Martine. 'He had to stay inside while the boys were at school and Philippe and I were at work. Boris came home at lunchtime and let him out, but sometimes, that was just too long and he had a few little accidents.'

As soon as someone opened the front door, she told me, he tried to make a bid for freedom. A few times he enjoyed brief success, running down the street to the road that might eventually take him back to Espagnac, except they always caught him before he got very far. Once Martine was driving down the street and in the rear vision mirror noticed him in hot pursuit. She stopped and called him. He jumped in the car, elated that his ploy had seemed to work. Then she drove round the block and put him back in the house again.

On Mondays and Thursdays Martine took him to work at Espagnac, where he gave a big welcome to all the visitors to the *mairie*.

'*Tu vas bien, Shar-lee?*' they said.

Sometimes, if nothing much was happening, he slipped out and went for a walk round the village by himself.

People he met said, '*Shar-lee, tu te promènes tout seul*, you're going for a walk all by yourself?' Then they accompanied him back to the *mairie*, where he had a little bed in a corner of Martine's office.

On the *journée communale*, while the humans were busy cleaning up the village, he played all day with Cajou, the *petite chienne* of Marion Rochefort, Alain and Martine's daughter, who was visiting from Cahors. One night he went to a dinner party with Martine and Philippe and met Nina, *une chienne normande*, from Caen.

'They had a *nuit folle, une soirée non stop*,' Martine told me, blushing at the memory. 'Perhaps there will be some babies of Shar-lee and Nina.'

'*Mais, Charlie est castré*, he's desexed,' I said.

Martine's jaw dropped in disbelief. She looked disappointed and squatted down to fondle his ears. '*C'est vrai, mon toutou*? *Tu as perdu ton sexe*, you've lost your genitals?'

Sometimes he went with Martine to visit Mimi.

'*Hé, Shar-lee*,' Mimi would say, 'are you hungry? Would you like some cake?'

'Non, *maman*,' Martine would remonstrate, while Charlie signalled '*Oui*!' with a flurry of his tail. 'It's not good for him!'

'*Il va évacuer*, he'll get rid of it,' Mimi would retort, and down would go another little treat.

I loved Ireland, the home of my ancestors, and thought again about the possibility of our living there for a while before we returned to Australia. But the thought evaporated as my train from Paris pulled in at Figeac, I picked up Charlie at the Bagreaux's and we set off back along the Célé valley to Espagnac. Standing on the back seat, his nose pointed at the windscreen, chubbier than he had been six weeks ago, he gasped with excitement. We were going home again.

CRUSADER DOG

Throughout the spring, there was a steady and growing stream of visitors to the priory. We heard them walking down the Chemin des Dames and if our doors were open to catch a breeze that flowed through the entry and into the nuns' room, Charlie was there to greet them.

Usually there was an exchange of pleasantries but one day he ran out onto the landing to find a contingent of cyclists stationed around the *cour*. Instead of friendly faces, his eyes met only taut little lycra-clad bottoms, as the insurgents discharged their weapons at the wall of M. Bonzani's *potager*, the ruins of the church, Thierry's orchard, and every nook and cranny of the *cour*.

Throughout the operation, most of them still held their bicycles upright using one hand, aiming their pistols with the other. When I went out on the balcony to call Charlie in, I found him still there, staring down at the invaders. One looked up, changed hands and gave me the careless wave of the conqueror. Charlie gave a low growl at the noise of the man's bicycle, momentarily unsupported, falling over. When the squad had stowed their equipment and ridden away, he hurried back down and spent an hour scouting all over the field, re-taking their positions. Eventually, his ammunition spent, he staggered back into the nuns' room, took a long, noisy drink, and jumped up on to his bed.

Charlie made other contributions to the life of the village, according to his capability. For example, he often assisted Mme Bonzani with guided visits to the village and the church. We always knew when the tours were about to begin. We heard voices in the Chemin, followed by a ringing of the cowbell outside the Bonzanis' door. Mme Bonzani emerged and marshalled the visitors onto one side of the lane in the lee of the arch. She began her presentation by drawing their attention to the damaged relief on the keystone, the coat of arms of the Cardaillac-Brengues family.

By the time she got to the story of Aymeric d'Hébrard, Charlie was there, at her disposal. First, he made everyone's acquaintance by discreetly sniffing their shoes. Then he sat in front of the group, paws together, front legs straight, back legs tucked under his haunches, eyes fixed on Mme Bonzani's face, ears twitching at every nuance of her speech, just as if he hadn't heard it all dozens of times before. Then he accompanied them round to the corner of the *cour* for the most picturesque view of the *clocher*, the church steeple, and the fragments of the original monastery.

At this point, while everyone was pointing and clicking their cameras, he was sometimes distracted by the soft grass in this part of the *cour* and rolled on his back and grunted to himself. Sometimes he would mime a sub-commentary on things that Mme Bonzani had evidently missed: the crumbs around the picnic table under the walnut tree; places where the cats hid; the sites of the more important skirmishes in his crusade to retake the *cour* after the blitz of the pissing cyclists. Meanwhile, up in the nuns' room, I listened for when the group chattered their way back up the lane *en route* to the church. I would then lean out of the window and call him in because he wasn't allowed in Notre-Dame du Val-Paradis.

'*Merci, Shar-lee*,' said Mme Bonzani, as he made his departure.

'*Merci, Shar-lee*,' said the visitors, patting his head by way of a *pourboire*.

His relationship with M. Bonzani had mellowed somewhat by now, and even involved little jokes on both sides. One lunchtime, Charlie running ahead of me down the Chemin des Dames, we saw M. Bonzani sitting at the table outside their door. The door was open and a delicious aroma from the lunch *madame* was cooking inside wafted out into the lane. Charlie cocked an eye at *monsieur* and stopped opposite the door. His nose turned towards the doorway, his jaw slackened into a silly grin, and, still keeping an eye on *monsieur*, he took a couple of steps towards the door.

M. Bonzani had resumed reading his paper, pretending not to notice Charlie's cheeky advance. I passed under the Cardaillac-Brengues keystone and called softly to Charlie. He ignored me.

Eventually, M. Bonzani lowered his newspaper, looked at Charlie over his glasses and said to him, in a pleasant tone of voice, '*Entré*, come in.' Then, 'Jacqueline,' he called to Mme Bonzani, '*le chien est venu pour déjeuner*, the dog has arrived for lunch.'

From inside, Mme Bonzani, who hadn't heard precisely, shouted, '*Mais nous avons du porc pour déjeuner*, we're having pork for lunch.'

'*Ça peut changer facilement*, that could easily change,' said M. Bonzani.

Between Charlie's teasing and M. Bonzani's rapier wit, they reached a kind of truce.

One Saturday in June, when we returned from the *marché* in Figeac, the entrance to the *cour* was blocked by a barrier of branches of mistletoe and rocks and pebbles from the river, and there was a crowd of strangers busy transforming the area. I had to drive on down past Jacotte's garden, turn around and go back up the Chemin des Dames and park in the *place*. Then Charlie and I walked back down the Chemin and watched the scene unfolding in the *cour*.

One group dug a hole in each corner and planted a branch of mistletoe in each hole. In the middle of the *cour*, another group arranged river stones to create a semi-circular fireplace. On one side, near the ruins that denoted the extremity of the long nave of Aymeric d'Hébrard's church, another group erected a row of white pavilions which they garlanded with paper flowers. One man was occupied in positioning a table a few metres distant from the fireplace. When he was satisfied that it was in the right spot, he set two stands containing bamboo lanterns on each side and an easel in front of it.

As Charlie and I stood there, we were joined by some of our friends and neighbours, who came down the lane to see and comment on the goings-on.

'It's for a wedding,' said Nicole. 'That man over there is a Druid.'

'It's not the usual kind of wedding we have in our village,' Sigrid remarked.

'The bride is Albert Hériat's niece, I think,' said Jocelyne.

'Perhaps the fire is to sacrifice virgins,' said Pierre. 'They might be hard to find.'

'There aren't a lot of Druids in the Lot, either,' said Jean-Louis. 'This one came all the way from Clermont-Ferrand. Albert's niece found him on the internet.'

'How do they know what to do in a Druid wedding?' scoffed Mme Bonzani. 'The Druids didn't leave any records because they didn't 'ave a system of writing. The Romans suppressed them when they conquered Gaul. All we know about them is they were priests who worshipped in groves and cut mistletoe from oak trees.'

'I'm going to be a marriage celebrant,' said Eric in Flenglish. 'I kiss all d' brides.'

'Maybe dey don' wanna kiss you, Eric,' said Milou.

'Dat's also possible,' said Eric, 'but not likely.'

In spite of the general scepticism, in addition to the official party, there was a little audience of *Espagnacois* scattered around the *cour* to observe the ceremony, partly because of the novelty, and partly because the bride was indeed Albert's niece. First, the bride and groom went to the *mairie*, where Martine, wearing her sash of office, performed the civil ceremony. This ceremony is obligatory in France for a marriage to be valid, whoever the celebrant is, even the Pope himself, or Eric.

Meanwhile, Charlie and I, with Sigrid and Nicole, brought out chairs and a little table from the nuns' room and settled down with a pot of tea on our *perron de l'escalier*, the little landing at the top of our steps, to watch the spectacle taking place below. We had a box seat. While the official party was up at the *mairie*, the Druid, wearing a white robe over his grey slacks, made final preparations for his part of the business. First, he took an oversized folio out of an oversized briefcase, opened it and set it on the easel. Holding a bent stick with coloured streamers attached to the top, he walked around all the installations once and then walked around the fireplace three times, shaking his stick.

Then he fixed a camera on a tripod aimed at the table. He lit a candle that was on the table and it fizzed and he burned his finger and said '*Merde*!' He walked around the table a few times muttering to himself. A musician dressed as a medieval troubadour emerged from under the arcade and blew a medieval instrument like a flugelhorn. At that moment all the guests, who included a little black French bull terrier with a garland of green leaves wound around his collar, came round the corner from the Chemin des Dames. With his stick, the Druid pushed and prodded the guests into a circle, then the bride and groom appeared from the Chemin, crossed the *cour* and stood on either side of the Druid. The Druid disengaged himself to take a photo of the bride and groom. Someone stepped forward from the crowd and said something to the Druid, who went back to his place. The person from the crowd stayed at the tripod and took all the rest of the pictures.

The groom went outside the circle of people and hid behind some of the guests and the bride pretended to look for him. When she found him, the bride and groom and the Druid read the words on the first page of the folio on the easel. Sigrid, Nicole and I, watching from above, agreed that these sounded almost identical to the words used in civil and church wedding ceremonies. Meanwhile, the bride took one of the bamboo lanterns and lit the fire and the Druid turned over the next page of the folio. They read that page and gave one another pieces of bread and apple and drank something from a big glass. Then they both walked round the circle of guests three times and the musicians began to play medieval tunes on their instruments.

And now it was July, full summer and apart from the tourists every day of the week, every weekend there was some new happening in the *cour*.

First was the *marché fermier*, which Thierry Dubuisson organised. Local *producteurs* set up stalls where they sold little pats of *chèvre*, goat's cheese, and *brebis*, ewe's cheese, *saucisse* and *saucisson*, pork sausage, *confits de canard, jambon*, ham, jams, preserved fruit, honey, spice cake, bread, and Jacotte's famous *sorbets* made from fresh fruits.

Then there was the annual *brocante*, the second-hand sale organised by the *Amis d'Espagnac-Sainte-Eulalie*. Many *amis* paid for a space in the *cour* to sell objects they no longer, or perhaps never had, any use for. There were electric woks, waffle irons, vertical grills, broken furniture, shaving sets, canisters, old school books, dusty paperbacks.

Each event was followed in the evening by an impromptu communal *repas* in the courtyard. Once the stalls were dismantled, everyone helped to carry tables and benches out from the *salle des fêtes* and brought their picnics to share with everyone else. Sitting under the stars, sharing our *jambon* and *chèvre*, our *pain de campagne* and *vin de pays* by candlelight, the *amis* decided to have other night picnics now and then for no reason at all.

At one of these picnics, we met Line Bresson, who was staying for a while with Sigrid. Line lived at Saint-Maur des Fosses, a suburb east of Paris. Sigrid, with France and Lucien, had met Line years before on a four-wheel drive safari in the Sahara Desert and they had all been friends ever since. Line had been a physics teacher until her retirement, and had recently separated from her husband, to the great surprise of her friends in Espagnac.

'It was my idea,' she said, matter-of-factly. 'I didn't want to be married anymore, so I asked him for a divorce.' She smiled. 'He didn't say no.'

She had been twice to Australia, where her daughter and son-in-law had met one another and lived for some years, and had been to the Great Barrier Reef, the desert, the rainforest ...

'I understand,' she said, when I told her about my dilemma regarding where I wanted to live. 'You love Australia but you love France, too.'

Jacqueline, Sigrid, Mireille and I subscribed to some of the summer *spectacles* presented under the auspices of the *Festival de Saint-Céré et de Haut-Quercy*. There were eight possibilities, of which I chose four: Verdi's *Rigoletto*; the Brecht/Weill *L'Opéra de Quat'sous, The Threepenny Opera*; Mahler's *Le Chant de la Terre, The Song of the Earth*; and Mozart's *Requiem*. By the time of the last concert, Penny and my brother and sister-in-law would be visiting, so I got tickets for them, too.

Jacqueline wanted to go to the two operas, Mireille to *Rigoletto* and the *Requiem* and Sigrid to *Rigoletto*. Each opera and concert was staged at two or three different venues, over a wide area of Haut-Quercy within a fifty kilometre radius of the village of Saint-Céré. The venues included *châteaux*, churches and *salles polyvalantes*, village multi-purpose rooms. We chose the dates of the performances to coincide with the venues we wanted to visit.

Some of the performers appeared in several different productions, so Gilda in *Rigoletto* might also sing the soprano part in *Le Chant de la Terre*, Macheath in *L'Opéra de Quat'sous* turned up as the captain of the guards in *Rigoletto*. The festival was an impressive logistical undertaking and every performance was stunning in its own way.

The first was *L'Opéra de Quat'sous* in an old factory at Saint-Céré that had been converted into a theatre. The company, Opera Eclate, was the one that presented the *Cosi fan Tutte* that Jacqueline and I saw during the winter season at Figeac, and the production had the same off-beat, *louche* quality. The performance was in the round. Jacqueline and I had seats right beside the stage, which sometimes had us inside the *demi-monde* of Cheapside. Macheath, caged like an animal, and Polly, in a little red fringed dress, coiled round a pole, permeated the atmosphere with dangerous sensuality. A short exchange between Polly and Jenny conveyed multiple meanings and nuances of the word '*madame*', from the distinction between a married woman and a single one, through issues of entitlement and superiority, to insinuations relating to the oldest profession. The singing was superb. The orchestra formed part of the cast and featured some fabulous jazz piano.

It was an hour's drive up the autoroute to the twelfth century Abbatiale Eglise de Sainte-Marie at Souillac for *Le Chant de la Terre*. Charlie came along for the ride. I parked the car in a shady lane so while I was at the concert it wouldn't be too hot for him until sunset around 9pm. The church is in the centre of a lively town with a network of cobbled lanes intersecting in pretty little non-geometric *places*. We did a little tour of the town, then Charlie returned to the car and I went back to the church.

I chose this venue because I had read in my guidebooks about the marvellous bas-reliefs in the church. I had a lot of time to admire them because the paying patrons were kept waiting for nearly half an hour by the non-paying ones. The mayor, town council and their friends, for whom the pews at the front of the church had been reserved, lingered at a reception in another part of the *abbaye*. I was surprised at the apparent forbearance of the other patrons, who sat quietly chatting to one another in the pews while they waited.

Half an hour after the advertised starting time, when at last the official party started to trickle down the long aisle, the rest of the audience took their cue. They hadn't wasted their time complaining to one another, they had been saving it all up. They hooted, jeered and applauded loudly, shouting sarcastically *'Bon SOIR, mesdames et m'sieurs – allez, allez, allez –* let's go!' For their part, the officials, in their dinner jackets and long frocks, made a pretty good pretence of not noticing the clamour all around them, and smiled and nodded to one another as they looked for their places and sat down unhurriedly, the epitome of *sang froid.*

The members of the orchestra, who had also been cooling their heels on the stage most of this time, failed to conceal their amusement as the officials and their friends ran the gauntlet. The mayor was hardly seated when the conductor and the two singers came in from the sacristy, to tumultuous applause, and the concert began. It was worth the wait, not only for the exhibition of collective one-upmanship. The mezzo-soprano, Marie-Therese Keller, was magnificent.

Opera Eclate also presented *Rigoletto*, in a performance that reflected well the moral bankruptcy of the Duke's court, the tragic compromise in Rigoletto's position and Gilda's heart-wrenching innocence. The opera was staged at the best preserved and most romantic *château* of the region, the Château de Castelnau. The massive hilltop *château* overlooks the Dordogne River and the rolling countryside for kilometres around. The action of the opera took place in the courtyard in the centre of the castle. Windows and niches in the walls served as part of the set and gave a suitable fading, echoing quality to the Duke's last reprise of La Donna Mobile, as he disappeared through a window into one of the castle chambers. Isabelle Phillippe's performance, as Gilda, was extraordinarily touching.

Penny arrived at this time, and she and I and a small party of *Espagnacois –* France and Lucien, Mireille, Rolande and Jacqueline –

went to our own local *château*, the Château de Beduer, for a concert on the grassy terrace overlooking the Célé. The concert featured members of the Bartok Quartet, and the local talent, violinist Olivier Pons. On this occasion M. Pons didn't actually play, but he did hold the umbrellas, one in each hand, to protect the other two performers when it started to rain. At interval, the owner of the *château*, an Englishman, decided to move the concert into the baronial hall, under the gallery, painted beams and chandelier. All the *Espagnacois* were grateful for the rain because otherwise they would never have had the opportunity to see the interior of the old *château*.

'I think I saw Gilou's car parked up at Le Mas,' I said to Penny the morning after she arrived. 'Thought I'd better warn you.'

'Is he still … you know …?'

'Depressed, yes. He lost interest in his studies, his work. But Jocelyne says it's nothing to do with you.'

'Oh, right. All I know is, I don't want to bump into him here.'

'Penny, it's been a year. As you said, you only knew one another for a couple of weeks. He must have got over that by now. Jocelyne said his dog died. It fell off the balcony of the flat and had to be put down.'

'Oh, God.'

We were walking back from La Source Bleue when a car passed us and stopped. Jocelyne and Pierre got out and came back to say hello.

'Penny, it's nice to see you.'

'Are you staying for the fête?'

'My brother and sister-in-law arrive tomorrow,' I explained. 'They'll spend a few days here, then we're all going to Paris. Penny will go back to Amsterdam from there, and her parents will go back to Australia. But *I'll* be back in time for the fête.'

The next few days, we were out *en famille* and often away from Espagnac in the car, so there was little risk of Penny running into

Gilou alone. We made a circuit of the village, stopping at each garden gate for introductions and pleasantries.

'Penny, welcome back! *Bonjour, monsieur le frère de Maureen. Bonjour, madame la belle-soeur. Votre fille vous ressemble,* your daughter looks like you, *madame. Très jolie,* very pretty.'

My brother Gavan tried out his school French. '*Elle ne me semble pas*, she doesn't seem to me,' he said. '*Très bonne chose*, very good thing.'

They smiled through their puzzlement. At least he made the effort.

All four of us went to the last *spectacle*, Mozart's *Requiem*, in the Cathédrale Saint-Etienne at Cahors. We picnicked on the banks of the Lot before making our way to the twelfth century cathedral, with its magnificent tympanum featuring a frieze of naked people, possibly cyclists, being stabbed in the backside. But I digress.

'Beautiful,' said Jan, my sister-in-law, afterwards. 'The singing was perfect. The conductor was excellent.'

'The choir was too big for the orchestra,' said Gavan.

'They were authentic eighteenth century instruments,' said Penny. 'Fantastic.'

'Yes, very good,' said Gavan. '*Magnifique.*'

Interspersed with the *spectacles* of the *Festival de Saint-Céré et de Haut-Quercy* were the local shows.

The first of these was at Brengues, in the open-sided shed where the *méchoui* was held the previous year because of the threat of *orages*. Though it was another stifling evening, the shed was packed with people jammed together on the hard benches. There was a strong presence from Espagnac-Sainte-Eulalie because at the last minute our own André Pelaprat had agreed to take a minor role in place of one of the *Brengois* who had suffered a near-fatal attack of stage fright.

It began with the appearance of the Mayor of Brengues, Lucien Olié, dressed in traditional *lotois* costume, gliding to and fro over the stage, raising his broad-brimmed black hat and swishing his red and black cape, and making a long-winded, ceremonial speech of welcome in *patois*. Then a group of school children performed a traditional dance and sang several songs about animals.

The play, entitled '*Les Maris et les Femmes*, Husbands and Wives', was written by Mme Nicole Ricaud, an inhabitant of Brengues. The first part began with two milkmaids in white smocks and caps dancing onto the stage, spreading hay everywhere. This caused a ripple of coughing in the audience. Bastien Bagreaux, who suffered from asthma, had to be taken outside.

While Bastien was being removed, a man and a boy came on, the boy leading a beautiful white goat with an enormous udder and elegant curved horns, the man leading a chocolate-coloured goat with a broad face. The man and the boy had no other role than to sit down and restrain the goats on either side of the stage throughout the first act. Of these four, the brown goat was the most expressive performer, looking fearlessly into the audience from time to time, then soulfully into the eyes of his minder.

The milkmaids sat on stools and got their buckets ready to milk the goats. The confusion of the one trying to milk the brown goat caused much hilarity among the audience, because this goat was, in fact, a *bouc*, a buck. Then an older woman came on singing and dancing and announced that her husband had left her so she didn't have to be a household drudge any more. Then Rosette, the president of the *Aînés Ruraux de Brengues/Espagnac-Sainte-Eulalie*, came on and said that *her* husband was never home anyway: always at the *foot*, football, or René's bistro. The milkmaids and the first woman tricked Rosette into thinking that René was actually a woman called Renée and her husband was spending all his time with her. Then

André Pelaprat, playing the part of René, came in with another man dressed in a frock and the curtain fell with a thud.

In the second act, it turned out that the first act had been a *rêve*, a dream, of Rosette, who in 'real' life was Lucien Oulié, the 'real' mayor's secretary. (The fact that Lucien really was the mayor of Brengues added a further layer of comedy to the play.) Because of the dream, Rosette gets the bright idea of turning the village back in time as a drawcard for the tourists. She asks René from the bistro (André Pelaprat again) what sort of shops and services they would have to have. 'René' tells her there would have been a *café, boulanger, boucher, cordonnier et ainsi de suite*, and she asks him to find out what they have to do to set this up. He comes back with a stack of documents containing the official European Union and French Government regulations for all these services. Rosette looks around to see who she can get to read all this stuff, spies Lucien Oulié in the front row of the audience, and dumps it all in his lap.

The curtain came down and bounced up again so that Lucien could come back onto the stage and name all the players and they could take a bow. The little boy who had held the white goat looked disappointed that he didn't get a mention. Nor did the goat.

The amateur production at Saint-Chels, up on the *causse* between the Célé and the Lot, had been mounted every summer for about fifteen years and was said to be well worth the seven euros, more than twice what we paid at Brengues. For a start, there would be two different plays, as well as singing and dancing by the school children.

The hall had a proper raised stage and chairs with backs. There were two female *animateurs* who explained in tandem everything that was going to happen before each piece, including the *dénouements* of both plays.

The first play was delayed because the curtain stuck, so some of the children were ushered out of their seats and back on stage to sing as many verses of '*Tous les animaux du monde*, all the animals of the world' as necessary till the problem was solved. The play was spoken in *patois* and was called *La lobeta tastabrusques*. There was a lot of stage whispering in the audience by older locals, such as Rolande, who understood the *patois*, translating for others, such as myself, Sigrid and Mireille.

Two peasant couples, Toenou and Ulali, and Bernat and Arsula, are eating a dinner of mushroom stew. They look out the window and discover that the dog, which has also eaten the stew, has died. They embark on a bout of realistic vomiting. Then a doctor, who happens to be in the neighbourhood, comes in, spots the mushroom stew and helps himself to a plateful. The peasants are so convulsed with vomiting that they are unable to stop him from eating the stew. While he's eating, he tells them that he has run over their dog. The peasants are furious because he has eaten all the mushroom stew.

The second play was called *Pyjama pour six*, which was just like one of the bedroom farces I used to perform in in the rural town where I first started teaching in the late sixties, and which are probably still in the repertoire of the dramatic society in that town today. The set fell down twice and the tired children, pressed into service yet again, sang their way to *yack* and *zébre* before they were released.

The evening's entertainment ended well after midnight and we all agreed that it was worth every *centime*.

On my return from Paris, on the evening of the fête, I was standing in the *cour*, chatting to Jacqueline, when a tall, handsome young man approached me and kissed me on both cheeks.

'*Bonsoir*,' was all he said, before moving on to rejoin his friends who had gone ahead.

Then Jocelyne and Pierre came round the corner into the *cour* and I realised that the young man walking coolly into the crowd was Gilou.

'That's his *petite copine*, his girlfriend,' said Jocelyne, as we kissed, gesturing towards the girl at Gilou's side. 'They were at school together.'

'*Génial*, fantastic!' I smiled.

The *repas* proceeded under a miraculously clear sky, with the usual cheerfulness, music and dancing. Charlie shared himself around between France and Lucien (meat), Sigrid and Rolande (cheese) and Mimi (cake). The children asked to take him for walks.

'Eh?' said his eyes as he was led off, but he trotted round gamely beside Bastien or Manon or Anaïs. On a leash. In his own *cour*. Which he had reclaimed single-handedly from rival forces. With every last drop of his strength.

La Table de Chaponnage

❖

By September, the holiday people had left, the children had gone back to school, the few *Espagnacois* who had paid jobs had returned to work and the village dozed and woke intermittently again. Once again, Charlie and I became sometimes the only figures in the landscape, sometimes sharing it with René trundling around on his tractor, Solange in Tenor's run collecting eggs, Thierry fixing a frame for his raspberry canes or Mme Delfour basking in the sun on her little terrace.

The exception to the somnolent ambience was the constant industry of Alain and Martine Rochefort and their dogs, Oualou and Tam. We saw them almost every day, checking the sheep up on the *causse*, driving a flock through the *place* back to the meadow beside the river where the grass was again lush after the summer *orages*.

We'd be walking through the village and see Oualou streak past and hear a clopping, crowding sound around a corner and know that Alain or Martine was coming along the road with a flock. I'd immediately put Charlie on the leash and prepare to pick him up, but Oualou would be too busy to notice him. Seeing us, Alain would stop, the sheep also, Oualou would flatten herself on the road, staring down the sheep in case any of them might think of making a run for it. Charlie would stand stock still staring at the other animals and they would all remain posed like that while Alain came over to us to *ça va* and exchange kisses.

One day I noticed Alain in one of the pastures on the way to La Source Bleue, where there was a flock of *brebis* and their newborn lambs. One of the *brebis* had a little leg protruding from her uterus and Alain was stalking her with a metal crook. With a deft movement, before she had time to panic, he got the crook around her leg and brought her to the ground. Then he grasped the leg in her uterus and pulled a baby lamb out, like a collapsing bundle of sticks. Alain stood aside while the mother got up and immediately began licking the golden amniotic fluid off the lamb, while the bright red bulb of the afterbirth hung on its thin purple cord behind her. Alain, smiling, looked up at Charlie and me watching from the path and said, '*C'est une bonne mère*, she's a good mother.' The lamb began struggling to get to its feet, pushing forward elegant long front legs and collapsing back on its haunches.

By the time we came back, about an hour later, Alain and the dogs had gone. The *brebis* had cleaned the lamb up completely and was now eating the afterbirth.

Another day, towards the end of August, the white van pulled up beside us in the *place*. Over the chugging of the engine, Martine asked casually if I would be interested in watching her chicks being turned into *chapons*. I realised that this meant that the chicks would be deprived, somehow, of their ability to reproduce. 'You don't have to stay long,' Alain put in, possibly detecting my smile freezing slightly. They gave me directions to the *grange* that they leased from Maxim and Antoinette Liauzun on the Causse d'Espagnac, where the great emasculation was to take place the next morning.

Early next morning, Charlie, disbelieving at first that I was going out at that hour without him, returned to his bed and I, equally incredulous at what I was doing, drove up to the *causse*.

Alain greeted me just outside the long, high *grange*. Inside, the light was dim and hazy and the air was relatively cool. Three men in blue overalls, with plastic overshoes and gloves covering their forearms, nodded and smiled at me as they moved purposefully around the area. Their pockets bristled with sharp little instruments.

'*Les chaponeurs*,' Alain explained quietly as we watched them checking their equipment. 'They come from south of Toulouse. This team is highly sought after all over the south-west and in northern Spain. We have to coordinate the age of our chicks with their schedule. The *chaponnage* has to be done before the chicks are four weeks old; after that, the procedure is too dangerous.'

Just in front of us was a metal frame with fixed feet at either end. Three or four arms, attached to a bar running the length of the frame at waist height, protruded from each side. The dim *grange*, early sunlight cutting across motes of straw suspended in the air, reminded me of a torture chamber I had seen in a Ken Russell film.

As if on cue, Alain's whisper brushed my ear, 'It's called *la table de chaponnage*.'

The floor was strewn thickly with hay and grain. Further into the interior, small water troughs were suspended from the roof by chains. To one side of the space near the door were stacked a large number of crates. A tentative chirping issued from the invisible occupants, like a chorus backstage that keeps singing after the conductor has brought his baton down.

'Our neighbours helped us put them in the cages last night,' Alain said, 'when the temperature went down. There are a thousand of them, twenty to a cage.'

The team was ready. They sprang into action, working quickly and efficiently. One man took three little birds at a time from one of the crates, bound their legs with plastic clips, slipped one wing of each chick over one of the arms protruding from one side of the frame and with a sharp little razor, shaved the feathers around its nether orifice. Then he went off to get the next three. Meanwhile, the second man, the *chaponeur*, performed the surgery on each chick in turn, trimming the top and side crops of its head with a sharp blade, making an incision in its body and squeezing under the incision so that the tiny genitals popped out like sesame seeds. Hard on his heels came the third man, who stapled the wound, sprayed disinfectant on it from a can and released the bird into the hay on the floor. The newly castrated *chapon* immediately hopped over to one of the tubs of water, drank, then proceeded to peck greedily at the grain among the hay, as if nothing had happened. I let out a long breath.

'They're hungry. They haven't had anything to eat or drink since they went into the cages. Now they'll eat non-stop till Christmas. *Chapon* flesh is very tender,' Alain added with a smile. 'Very popular for the *fête de Noël.*'

'The chicks aren't chirping anymore,' I remarked.

'That's right,' said Alain, 'after the procedure they never sing again.'

Apart from Thierry and Jacotte, Alain and Martine were the only people I knew who actually earned their living from farming the land around Espagnac-Saint-Eulalie. I was surprised when I first discovered in a casual roadside conversation with them that, like Thierry and Jacotte, neither was *lotois*. Alain's family came originally from Alsace, but he was born in Algeria. His great-grandparents went to Algeria, which France had annexed in 1842, following the Franco-Prussian war of 1870, when Alsace was annexed by Germany.

'When Algeria became independent in 1962, it was too dangerous for the *pieds noirs*, the French settlers, to stay. My father was a farmer but when we came to France he found work as a mechanic in a factory in the Gironde.'

'Alain and I were at the same school,' Martine said. 'I was a boarder. My father's family have been *vignerons*, wine-growers, forever, but my mother's family is Catalan. They left Spain when Franco came to power.'

'We didn't start going out together till after we'd both done the *bac*, the exam at the end of high school. I left school in 1976 and started working in a bank but I always wanted to be a farmer. We got married and started farming in 1981.'

Alain and Martine owned some land in the area, but also used pastures belonging to their neighbours, such as the Liauzuns, the Cabrignacs, the Senacs, Mimi and Rolande. They paid rent for larger parcels of land, but with the others' like Mimi's and Rolande's, they paid in kind with lamb, turkeys, *pintades*.

A few weeks after the *chaponnage* the Rocheforts' van stopped beside us on its way to the meadow beyond the football field.

'*Hé*, Maureen!' Martine called. 'We'd like you to come for a *repas* on Saturday night. We're having *sanglier*, wild boar.'

Back in the spring they had discovered the *sanglier*, a sow and two little ones, up on the *causse* among the *pintades*. Alain phoned Didier Cabrignac to ask him to get some hunters to come up and shoot them. The meat was shared among the hunters and the Rocheforts.

'We put ours in the freezer,' said Alain, 'till we decided what to do with it. Didier is going to cook it for us because he knows best how to do it.'

'And Martine Bagreaux is going to make a *salade quercynoise*.'

'I'll make a dessert,' I offered, having achieved some renown for the orange and almond tart I'd made for the *repas de la Saint-Sylvestre*.

It was quite a big crowd of people to fit into their main room, which was not much bigger than the nuns' room and was furnished with a settee, a large dresser and sideboard, a big wooden table and enough chairs for all the guests. Most of the women crowded into the tiny kitchen alcove while Martine Bagreaux was frying the *gésiers* and the *foie gras* for the *salade quercynoise*, and Martine Rochefort was cooking the pasta for the meat sauce.

'It's like an Australian party,' I said, 'the women in the kitchen and the men in the *salon* drinking and telling jokes.'

'It's French, too,' they assured me.

Didier and Pascale arrived with two cast iron casserole dishes, from which wafted clouds of aromatic steam. Everyone started briskly to take a seat at the table. As so often seemed to happen at decisive moments like this, I couldn't see a space for me.

Alain was pulling out a chair at one end of the table and noticed my predicament.

'Please sit next to me, Maureen,' he said, and grasped the back of the chair next to his before anyone else could commandeer it.

For the rest of the evening, interspersed with his responsibilities as host – serving the wine and the cider, answering questions from around the table, clearing the plates, offering the bread – he attended to me. Even after eighteen months, in situations where there were a lot of people, it was hard for me to follow the banter and to fill in the gaps that come easily to people socialising in their first language with their best friends, so I appreciated his consideration.

It wasn't the kind of conversation you'd have with your neighbour at a dinner party in Canberra. I was interested to learn something about sheep farming in France, and Alain was happy to indulge me.

'Our sheep, our *caussenade du Lot*, are not like your merinos in Australia,' said Alain. 'The wool from our sheep is used for stuffing mattresses. The meat is the important thing.

'In our enterprise, we have four hundred *brebis*, ewes, and ten *béliers*, rams. We buy the *agnelles*, the ewe lambs and the *béliers* from people at Saint-Simon who breed them specially to be parent sheep. We buy fifty *agnelles* per year and keep them for eight years. After that they run out of milk or go lame.

'We put the *brebis* and the *béliers* together at the beginning of May for four weeks so that lambs will be born in October. The *brebis* have an *ecographie*, an ultrasound, at the beginning of July to find out if they are pregnant and if they are bearing twins. The ones not pregnant are put with the *béliers* again and they are examined in September. So each of the four hundred gets pregnant once a year.

'The lambs go to the abattoir a hundred and fifty days after they're born.'

A hundred and fifty days.

Alain's sheep never showed signs of being flyblown, they all had their tails and they were never crutched. The sheep munched quietly all day long and the lambs gambolled in lush meadows throughout their short but carefree lives.

Exercising the limit of my expertise, I replied that I had the impression that farming in Espagnac was more humane, on the whole, than it was in Australia. 'In times of drought,' I said, 'farmers there often have to shoot their sheep and cattle because they can't feed them.'

'There's only one time in the year when we don't have pasture,' said Alain, 'after the winter, before the grass grows again in the spring. We have to hand-feed the sheep then.'

'You and Martine work so hard,' I commented. 'Are you able to take holidays?'

'We can usually go away for two weeks at the end of the summer,' said Alain, 'but we can't afford a holiday this year. The big, industrial farms that are springing up all over France make a profit for their shareholders, but we don't make a profit. But there's no pleasure in farming that way. There's no relationship with the animals. Our life is hard but it's what we want to do.

'Fifty per cent of our income is from our produce and fifty comes from the EU. The poultry – the *chapons*, *pintades* and *dindes* – just put bread on the table. Our main business is sheep. We sign a five-year contract with the EU and have to record what we do to protect the environment, *les mesures agri-environmentale*. All farmers of Europe receive the *PAC*, *politique agricole commune*. That means we get thirty euros for each *brebis* because they clean up the land and help protect the environment. Our farming controls the forest overtaking the *causse*. We also receive money for growing pasture. For instance, we don't use chemicals and we limit our use of fertilisers; we mostly use sheep manure.

'When we retire? That's a long time from now. It depends. Our daughter Marion lives in Cahors. Philippe? He doesn't want to be a farmer. He's doing the *bac* this year. Next year he's going to Toulouse to learn engineering.'

Not long after the *repas* at the Rocheforts', Milou suggested that I go with her to Belgium, where she had business to attend to.

'My house in Mechelen isn't far from the railway station,' she said. 'You'd be able to do day trips to Brussels and Antwerp and Ghent and visit the galleries and churches.'

It was school term time and I was reluctant, after their experience with Charlie when I went to Ireland, to ask the Bagreaux to look after him.

'What about Maxim and Antoinette?' Milou suggested.

Maxim and Antoinette Liauzun, whose pastures and buildings Alain and Martine Rochefort leased, lived up on the Causse d'Espagnac. I didn't know them well. They rarely came down to the village. I knew of them because they were good friends of many of the friends I had made. Maxim had once been the most prominent farmer in the area. I knew that all their children, except the youngest daughter Florence, who, with her husband and children had a house near theirs, lived and worked elsewhere.

Maxim had had a stroke some time before our arrival at Espagnac, which confined him to a wheelchair. I had met him at the *mairie* on polling day, back in March, when Florence brought him down to the village to vote, and between them, Florence and Martine Bagreaux managed to get him behind the curtain in a corner of the *mairie* that served as the polling booth.

Charlie and I passed their sprawling farmhouse, sheds and chicken runs whenever we went for a walk up there. They had once farmed all their land, but since Maxim's stroke, they had ceased sheep and crop farming. Fifty metres or so distant from the house they had built some dog pens, not for their own two dogs, which had the run of the yard, but for boarders, which barked in the chicken wire enclosures whenever we passed by. Antoinette had shouldered all the work around the farm, looking after the chickens and the guest dogs, as well as Maxim.

'It's only for a week,' said Milou, noting my reluctance.

'Well, I suppose it would be good for him to get used to it,' I said. 'He'll have to spend a month in quarantine when we go back to Australia.' It was, I think, the first time I mentioned our going back as a reality. 'Whenever that will be,' I added.

Antoinette showed me the accommodation: a small run, about 3 metres square, and beside it a little hut. 'I'll put him in this one,' said Antoinette. The run we were in adjoined the yard where the chickens pecked around in the grass and where Antoinette hung her washing. 'It used to be a *cabane à poulets*, but now we use it for the dogs.'

I comforted myself that he wouldn't be too bored if he could see the yard. The night before we drove to Mechelen, I took him up to the *causse*.

Antoinette stroked my arm. 'Everything will be fine,' she said, gently.

She took the leash from my hand and Charlie trotted away with her in the direction of the runs, without a backward glance.

The evening Milou and I arrived back from Belgium, Eric had been up to the *causse* and collected Charlie, and they were both standing nonchalantly in front of Eric's garage when we turned into the drive. When I went up to pay Antoinette for his board, she said that she had taken him for little walks on his leash around the yard every day.

A few days later, it occurred to me that some aspect of the village had changed and eventually I worked out what it was. The *gros chien* was no longer there. It had long ceased to roam around the village. In the winter, after the flood, it had been confined to a small run in the Senacs' yard, where we would see it in the morning, a snow-encrusted lump, prone on its corrugated iron bed. In the summer, it had been housed with the chickens, where at least it had more company, and where the corrugated iron now served as a roof, a shelter from the elements, rather than a freezing floor.

'What happened to it?' I asked Nicole.

'It just died,' she said.

Back in the nuns' room, Charlie lying beside me on the *canapé-lit*, his head on my knee, I shed a few tears for the *gros chien*. Someone had to.

ITALIAN INTERLUDE

In the back of my mind, I knew that we would return to Australia to live but there seemed no reason to set a date. The previous year, when Charlie and I had returned to the nuns' room after the summer, I had told Martine Bagreaux that I didn't know whether we would stay till the end of this year, 2004. I still didn't know.

'I love living here in the village,' I said to her, 'but if I'm going to stay longer, I'd like a … a *chez moi*, a place that I can make into a home.'

'*Je comprends*, Maureen,' said Martine, 'our *gîtes* aren't *somptueux*, they're just holiday places of two *épis*.' We were standing by her garden gate. 'What about Mme Delfour's old house?' She was looking at the house in the field opposite, a little further down the road. It was a pretty stone cottage with a typical *quercynoise* pitched roof and handsome *épis*.

'I didn't know that house belonged to Mme Delfour.'

'They normally only let it for the holidays, *mais, bon*, you could ask.'

Mme Delfour seemed to be as taken by the idea as I was. 'It would be good to have a neighbour. There's no-one around when Martine and Philippe are at Figeac.'

She shuffled into her bedroom to find the key to the house and we walked slowly across the road. She showed me through the sunny rooms and the vine-covered terrace and around the little enclosed garden. All the windows looked out onto meadows or across the river to the *falaise*.

It was perfect. If Charlie and I moved here, I could visualise us staying for a long time yet.

'I'll speak to my son about it,' she said.

Her son was a violin maker in Toulouse. In due course, he rang me to discuss the rental and I realised that exchanging my one-bedroom apartment for this lovely little two-bedroom cottage would mean I wouldn't be able to afford many more trips to other parts of Europe. In fact, even with the low rent I was paying for the nuns' room, at times my expenditure exceeded my income.

An email from Australian friends, Kath and Graeme, was a welcome distraction: 'Graeme's giving a paper on rock art at an archaeology conference in northern Italy. Afterwards we're going to Emilia Romagna for a month. We've hired a villa in the hills near Piacenza. Would you be able to join us for a week or two?'

It was a chance not only to see old friends and some of Italy, but also to tour parts of France where I hadn't been before, over the two days it would take to get there.

There was the question of Charlie. It was still term time. Kath contacted the owner of the villa, who lived in Canberra. It would be all right if Charlie came, under certain restrictions.

We headed east, through the honey-doused escarpments of the Gorges du Tarn, its villages of turrets and spires nestling in the bends of the river, then along the northern tip of the Cevennes.

The road meandered, undulating, through vivid green pastures and brown and ochre ploughed fields. A lively wind stirred the trees and grasses. At Pradelles, the junction of l'Allier with la Loire, we continued along the Ardeche River threading through hills patched with ancient fortified farmhouses and villages.

Between Valence and Grenoble, smokestacks and electricity pylons marched on giants' legs along the Rhone and Isère rivers. After Chambery, however, there were only mountains: the Chartreuse Massif, with deep valleys, hillsides covered in dense pine forests, high pastures surmounted by great jagged piles of white rock etched on the sky. One of these, clearly visible over 60 kilometres away, was Mont Blanc.

'Maybe we'll get there,' I said to Charlie. 'But maybe not.'

The autoroute burrowed through the mountains in a chiaroscuro of dim tunnels and bursts of sunlight. Suddenly, on the Italian side, the mountains dropped away into the wide flat industrial belt of the Po River.

At Piacenza we turned south into the foothills of the Appenines, up through fields of ripening crops and resort villages clustered around thermal springs, till at last we arrived at the village of Borla.

Kath and Graeme and their eighteen-month-old granddaughter Lux were on the terrace of the villa. Charlie and I reeled out of the car, dizzy with fatigue.

There was much embracing among the humans and an affectionate reunion between Kath and Graeme and Charlie, who had been their houseguest from time to time in Canberra. He felt immediately *chez lui*. As soon as he had had his dinner, a tin of *ragoût à canard avec sa julienne de légumes et de petits pois*, duck, julienned vegetables and peas, he stretched out beside us on the warm tiles of the terrace and slept. Lux, Kath, Graeme and I indulged in Parma ham and cheese and Graeme opened a bottle of the local *frisante* white wine, called Malvesia.

'Normally he'd be dancing on his hind legs, begging for cheese,' I said, touching Charlie's twitching paw with my toe.

'Poor little fellow,' said Kath. 'He's exhausted.'

'It's only his second long trip since we've been in Europe. It takes it out of him. I can't really feed him properly when we're travelling.'

'We don't have the same problem with Lux,' said Graeme, as the toddler reached across the table, snatched another slice of ham from the plate and crammed it into her mouth.

We talked for a while about mutual friends and they told me about the arrangements for the villa, which had several bedrooms, all of which would be filled with friends and relations in the coming days.

'I haven't been among so many English speakers for nearly two years,' I said. 'I'm a bit out of practice.'

'It's a big crowd,' said Kath, 'but different groups will go off and do different things. We won't be in one another's pockets.'

Inevitably, we got around to the state of Australian politics.

'It's the same as when you left,' said Graeme. 'We're still locking up refugees, including children. The Government will be returned because they've convinced the electorate that the alternative means a general downturn in the economy.'

I sighed. 'All, my life,' I said, 'I seem to have been out of step with popular opinion. In the sixties and seventies, when all my friends were breaking out and experimenting with relationships and drugs and so on, I was still nearly as prudish and scandalised as I'd been at school. In the eighties I developed greater acceptance of other people's and my own frailties, and by the nineties I thought I'd caught up with open and tolerant values. But now it's all changed again, I'm out of step once more but this time I don't want to catch up. I might have to stay in France after all.'

'We wondered if you might decide to do that. You've obviously settled into the life, judging from your emails.'

'I do feel at home in Espagnac,' I admitted, 'even though my French isn't fluent and probably never will be. Despite that, Charlie and I have made a lot of friends. I've even looked at real estate in villages around Espagnac, but if I sold my house and bought a cottage there, I couldn't afford to do all the trips, and that's one of the advantages of living in France. If I couldn't travel, and had to settle down to a more humdrum existence, would that be any different from living in Australia?

'And even with my limited French I've picked up that there are big problems in French politics too. I suppose the difference is that I don't have to feel ashamed of what happens in France.'

'And that's the point, isn't it?' said Kath. 'You feel a kind of responsibility for the Australian situation because Australia is really your home.'

I had to admit that she was right. Over the next fortnight there were many conversations on the terrace about Europe and Australia, friendship, landscape, literature, politics, the limitations of conversing in a foreign language and the comfort of conversing in your own, with friends who understand instinctively what you are talking about and what you mean. In particular, we discussed the differences between old cultures grounded in longstanding traditions and societies like ours that had absorbed multiple cultures in a mere couple of centuries.

I realised that Espagnac couldn't really be my home, as it was for the Cabrignacs, Pelaprats, Bagreaux and the other natives of the village. They were *Espagnacois*, *lotois*; the countryside, their family stories, the houses they lived in, the local, regional and national politics and history belonged indisputably to them, were their identity. *My* identity, even while I was living in France, was still rooted in my relationships with friends and family in Australia and a very different cultural history and landscape. The same applied more or less to other migrants to the village like Terry and Anne, Sigrid, and Milou and Eric, who spent the winters elsewhere, and whose other lives were just as complex and just as irrelevant to the real *Espagnacois*, as mine was.

The villa was in a hamlet overlooking Borla, with a view of a patchwork green and brown hillside on the opposite side of the valley and other hamlets and the odd castle perched on other hills, as beautiful, in its own way, as the countryside of the Lot. Unruly hedges of cotoneaster, thick with clusters of luminous orange and yellow berries, sprouted beside the quiet lanes. The hillsides were covered with vines laden with tight, cornucopia bunches of black grapes. Baskets, ready to receive them, sat at intervals along the rows of vines. Further up were oak woods riddled with dusty hunters' tracks, and overgrown with wild daisies, sweet peas, scabiosa, vetches, St John's Wort, cow parsley.

The mellow ring of the steeple bell down in the village punctuated the warm nights, interspersed with the fractious crying of pheasants in the woods. In the evenings we ate on the terrace – long, leisurely meals of grilled vegetables and meats, fruits and cheeses – and sampled the local wines. Lux grazed widely, climbing from one lap to another according to its proximity to whichever food she fancied eating next. Charlie soon learned to scout under the table for signs of her whereabouts, whence fragments of meat, cheese and other succulent scraps rained down like manna from heaven.

Various combinations of the party made excursions to villages, towns and cities near and far. Charlie came on some of these when it was feasible – and even sometimes when it was inconvenient for the humans and not a lot of fun for him. In Verona, there were too many frescoed churches and chapels that he had to wait outside, and too much walking between them. In Parma, a crowd gathered in the Piazza Duomo to watch a medieval procession, including drum bands beating time for teams of flag throwers. The bright flags fluttered wildly in their trajectories overhead. The crowd cheered the exuberant noise, colour and movement. Only Charlie, lost in a forest of legs, was a bit doubtful.

He came to Bologna, a city of leaning towers and gleaming cupolas, monumental piazzas, magnificent palazzos and beguiling statues and fountains, connected by narrow cobbled streets of maroon Roman window blinds and deep green shutters. He enjoyed the cool marble of the colonnades where he met several other dogs and found many places to pee. Passers-by said, '*Ciao, bello!*' and patted him, and little girls crumbled potato chips for him to forage out of the cobblestones. He refreshed himself at the fountain of

Neptune, where arcs of water spurted from the nipples of buxom ladies and splashed refreshingly upon passing poodles.

When he couldn't come with me, he stayed at the villa with whoever didn't go, waiting all day on the terrace, they told me, his gaze fixed on the road.

I went to Padua by myself on the early train from Piacenza, forty minutes' drive from the villa. The train journey, with a change at Bologna, took an hour and a half, across the rich, flat, alluvial plain, lines of poplars and pencil pines in the middle distance, misty mountains behind. I calculated that I could allow myself three hours to spend in the city before catching the train that would connect with the last Bologna-Piacenza train.

The city of Donatello, Mantegna and Giotto is scattered over a wide area. Seduced by the beauties I found everywhere, I minimised in my mind the time it would take me to get back to the station, and the short cut I devised, zigzagging across town, was longer than it looked on the map. With the station in sight, but still a long way away, I began to run, and as I ran, my knees locked and jarred at each step.

It was clear that I wouldn't make the station in time for the train but I kept stumbling along, hoping that Mussolini's successors weren't as punctilious about the timetables as he was. My hopes were realised. The train was late. The station platform was packed with commuters to Bologna, and from there, there were several possible trains back to Piacenza.

For our return to the Lot, by a different route, I allowed three days. The first day, we descended the hills to the coast at La Spezia, then headed north-west past Genoa, then to the border with France at San Remo. At lunchtime, we came off the autoroute and dropped down through the sheer, white, pine-smudged foothills of the Alps into Menton for a stroll along the promenade. From there, we took the Route Napoleon north into the Gorge du Verdon through spectacular rock formations with vertiginous effects from the road. At the end of the gorge, a beautiful view of the silver-blue ribbon of river far below opening into the Lac de Sainte-Croix. On arriving at our *chambre d'hôte* at Chasteuil, we were both nauseous from the long day of winding roads. Charlie jumped out of the car and threw up.

Next day, we stopped for lunch under a tree in a grassy field by a stream at the village of Riez. On the other side of the stream stood four columns, vestiges of a Roman temple. While I was looking at the Roman columns, Charlie scoffed all the ham I had brought from Parma.

'Oh, Charlie,' I said, as he stood placidly over the fluttering paper that had contained the ham. 'I suppose you think that's only fair, after what I've put you through.'

Then across the Luberon, waves of hills scattered with perched villages. We spent the second night a few kilometres west of Avignon. And home, via Florac, at the eastern extremity of the Gorges du Tarn, a pretty village full of the sound of rushing water and the sight of window boxes and little bridges bedecked with geraniums, and a mist-shrouded mountain behind.

The limp and the pain around my left knee, which I had acquired running for the train in Padua, persisted.

'Why don't you go to Michel,' Milou suggested. 'Everyone goes to him for their pills and their check-ups.'

Docteur Michel Liauzun, whom I had met briefly at one of the village *repas*, was the eldest and the only male child of Maxim and Antoinette. He had a clinic in Livernon. The waiting room was crowded with old people and mothers with pale, sniffling children. There was no receptionist and no appointments except on Wednesday mornings. You simply had to wait your turn and hope the doctor wasn't called away to an emergency while you were there. My turn came at about one in the afternoon, four hours after I arrived.

Michel looked tired and rather distracted. I described the pains in my left thigh and shin, the way my knee joint sometimes seemed to pop painfully apart, how my knee wouldn't bend and how I could no longer walk easily. I, who was used to walking many kilometres every day. I explained that I had from time to time suffered from arthritis in my neck and in my right knee, but this pain was new.

He prescribed an anti-inflammatory drug, took blood for a cholesterol test and made an appointment for me to see an *angiologue*, a specialist in blood and lymph vessels, who practised in Figeac.

The *angiologue* used a scanner to examine the arteries and veins below my heart. While I watched a screen showing images of my blood flowing in lively swirls of lurid red and blue, the specialist asked me what I was doing in the Lot. I told her about coming here with my dog, how I had planned to write a book set in Australia, but that I ended up writing about our lives in the village of Espagnac, which I hoped would also become a book one day.

'*Formidable!*' she exclaimed repeatedly, perhaps in reference to my story and perhaps to the impeccable state of my arteries and veins as well.

When I went back to Michel to discuss the results of the tests, he prescribed various homeopathic remedies and suggested I buy a walking stick and limit the distances I walked every day.

'And, *madame*,' he advised, 'avoid dairy products, lamb and pork, *charcuterie*, coffee, tea, alcohol. Eat lean meat, fresh fruit and vegetables, nuts and seeds, and drink green tea.'

'He says that to everyone,' said Milou. 'He knows us all too well.'

It was true that I had adopted the degustatory habits of the region. In two years my borderline vegetarianism had given way to heedless indulgence in the *confits* and *pâtés*, *fromages* and *jambons* arrayed in the *marchés* and served at all the *repas*. I felt a certain conscientious relief at the prospect of reverting to a healthier and more ethical diet. But to limit our walks would be a real sacrifice for both Charlie and me, and would change the nature of our life in Espagnac.

A few weeks later an email came from the real estate agency that was managing the rental of my house in Canberra. The tenants, who'd signed a lease for two years, now had a posting to Washington the following June. They would like to continue for another six months.

And so, the decision on the timeframe for our return was made.

In case they had changed since I left, I searched for the current requirements for Charlie's trip back to Australia on the Australian Quarantine and Inspection Service (AQIS) website. First, I had to apply for a permit to import him. The documents, when they arrived, included a fourteen-page form listing all the required treatments and tests that must be performed and validated by the vet in Figeac. Twenty-four hours before Charlie left France, the form had to be signed by the Official Veterinarian of the Lot Department, whose office was at Cahors.

Charlie's rabies vaccinations were up to date, but he would also need vaccinations for distemper, infectious hepatitis, canine parvovirus and parinfluenza, and blood tests for ehrlichiosis, brucellosis and leptospirosis. The blood tests had to be synchronised with treatments for internal and external parasites. When he arrived in Sydney, someone from AQIS would collect him from the airport and take him to the quarantine station at Eastern Creek, where he would stay for a month.

Reading all the documentation made me very anxious. Getting him back to Australia was going to be a lot more complicated than getting him into France had been. The incident of his arrival seemed a mere inconvenience in comparison with what pitfalls might lie ahead.

I made a timetable covering the following six months, noting the dates for each treatment and test AQIS required, and tried to find on the internet details of agents specialising in live animal exports from France. There were several British companies that provided such services for the multitude of British people and their pets living in or travelling between France and the United Kingdom. Services involving other countries were offered at very expensive rates and involved exporting the animal first to England, and then on to the final destination. I couldn't find any similar French providers on the internet. I contacted Qantas Freight and was dismayed to find that they no longer flew directly between Paris and Sydney. I remembered my brother John's comment when I first talked about taking Charlie to France.

'You'll never get him back,' he had said.

With the help of Alan and Ros Macdonald, my friends in Albi, I tracked down an export agent based near Montmartre. I said I would be in Paris over Christmas, and he said to contact him then, when he would be able to quote me a price for Charlie's export.

PAST AND FUTURE

And so I told Martine that we would remain in the *petit gîte* till the following June.

'*Genial*! But you'll come back to see us sometimes, in the future?'

'Of course, Martine, Espagnac is part of my life now.'

'And when you come back, it will be easier for you to get around without Charlie.'

'Yes,' I said. 'But being here wouldn't have been the same for me without him. I wouldn't have made so many friends.

'And,' I said, 'in the time that's left, I'd like to ask a few of the older inhabitants about their lives here in the past. I think it would be good to include that in what I'm writing about the village. I'm not interested in personal and private things that aren't anyone else's business, Martine. I'm trying to give a general impression of what life was like here in the past and how things have changed over people's lifetimes.'

Months before, it had occurred to me to interview some of the *Espagnacois*. I wanted to flesh out some of the stories I'd heard and what I'd read, and I had been compiling a list of topics I wanted to ask about and questions for individuals. I had put off doing the interviews because I always seemed to be too busy with the here and now. Now that the time of our departure was decided, I needed to act. I felt that Martine, with her knowledge and instincts regarding the village, would give me good advice and would also prepare the way for my project.

'Mme Delfour's husband wrote a history of the village,' Martine said.

'Do you think she'd lend it to me?

'Ask her.'

When Charlie and I called at her house on our way back from La Source Bleue, Mme Delfour had the document ready on her kitchen table.

M. Delfour's 'history', compiled from records of meetings of the *conseil municipal* from 1839 to 1975, was written in meticulous longhand and bound between covers of thick green plastic. Some of it was difficult for me to follow because it assumed contextual knowledge that I didn't possess, but it helped me appreciate some of the changes that occurred over that period. I also reviewed the notes I'd taken from Mme Pernet-Lauzur's book shortly after our arrival.

Briefly, after the nuns left the priory in the last months of 1792, the buildings were sold to residents of Sainte-Eulalie. The combined population of the new *commune* was around 300. It increased to 450 by the middle of the nineteenth century, and declined steadily thereafter, with a few fluctuations. In the 2004 census, when I was staying there, the population was sixty-seven. In 2008 it had grown again, to ninety-two.

The records of the *conseil municipal* painted a picture of struggle and hardship for the families of Espagnac-Sainte-Eulalie over much of the period. From time to time, it voted for assistance for the poor and free medicines for the destitute, aid for schooling and bursaries for some of the children, and exemptions from military service for fathers of destitute families.

In 1905, the *conseil* voted 50 francs for a wood stove for the classroom, asking for the balance of the cost from the Department. It described how the temperature in the classroom remained freezing, even with a big fire in the existing fireplace. In 1911, 180 francs were allocated for privies for the school. In 1933 the *conseil* voted to provide a bursary for an apprenticeship in rural crafts. In 1937 it approved the installation of a water tank at the school so the teacher wouldn't have to find drinking water for the pupils, and called for voluntary contributions to get it. In 1948 it voted for repairs to the school because the school inspector threatened to close it and move pupils to the school at Corn unless work started immediately. In 1967, when the population of the *commune* had fallen to ninety-seven, the *Inspecteur d'académie* closed the school.

The state of the church and the old priory buildings was a continual problem for the *conseil*. In 1884 it appealed to the *Ministre des Beaux Arts* to classify the church as an historical monument because the *commune* didn't have the means to restore it. The church was classed as an historical monument in 1912, but the *commune* seemed to have retained some responsibility, because the *conseil* voted funding for repairs in 1920–21 and for some restoration work in 1923. As for the rest of the priory buildings, in 1959 the *conseil* noted that M. Pierre Bonzani of Vincennes, near Paris, had purchased from the various owners the old house on the west wing, the school garden and the garden between the house and the *grange*. Over the next twenty years, the *commune*, with the aid of the *Ministre des Beaux Arts*, acquired and restored the rest of the priory buildings and established the *foyer rural*, the *salle des fêtes*, the *grand gîte* and the *petit*, the old nuns' room, where Charlie and I were living.

The villages weathered the frequent changes in the national political scene. The members of the *conseil municipal* swore oaths of installation to a succession of political regimes. At Christmas 1942, under the German Occupation, instructions came from Figeac to celebrate the feast with '*une ferveur exceptionelle*', and the *conseil* gave twenty francs to the teacher to decorate a Christmas tree.

By 1912, a bus ran three days a week between Figeac and Conduché, the village at the confluence of the Célé and Lot rivers.

In 1922 a letterbox was installed at the bridge at Espagnac, with the mail picked up twice a day by the bus driver. In 1927, Sainte-Eulalie got its own letterbox. In 1930, Espagnac got a phone box. In 1937, some remote parts of the *commune* were electrified. The *mairie* was electrified ten years later. During the 1950s, various households hosted a public phone. In the 1960s, through the agency of a new alliance, the *Syndicat d'Initiative des Communes de la Vallée du Célé*, which aimed to promote agriculture and develop tourism throughout the valley, roads and communications improved. In 1975 public lighting was installed in the village and in 1976 Espagnac had a television transmitter.

M. Delfour's manuscript fired my curiosity and provided me with a broader context for my interviews. I showed Martine the list of *Espagnacois* I had become quite friendly with, like André Pelaprat, Mimi and Rolande, Solange and Georgette, and Martine herself, all of whom, I was sure, wouldn't object to my asking them questions.

'You should also talk to Roger Sudres,' said Martine. 'And Gaby Senac, you know, he has some very interesting ideas. It would be good if you could talk to Maxim and Antoinette, too, *mais bon*, Maxim isn't well and Antoinette has so much to do.'

Over the following winter and spring, whenever I asked anyone if I could interview them for the book I was writing about Espagnac-Sainte-Eulalie, they appeared to be unsurprised, quite pleased, in fact.

Rolande and Mimi, Solange and Georgette Delfour, arrived together at the nuns' room one freezing night, exclaiming about the weather.

'It's the season of the *grippe*,' said Solange cheerfully. '*Mais, heureusement*, fortunately, a hard winter kills the microbes, so we will survive.'

Georgette was puffing with the effort of getting up the stairs, but when she was seated at the table in one of the cane chairs, she looked around the room with evident satisfaction.

'It was my husband who had that fresco restored,' she said, 'when he was the mayor. And he had the *poêle* put in.'

Mimi was the eldest, born in 1922. Georgette was born in 1926, Rolande in 1931, Solange in 1932. The family of Mimi and Rolande came to live at Diège when Rolande was nine. Georgette and Solange had lived at Espagnac all their lives.

Georgette had brought some photos to show me. One was taken in the 1920s of her parents, grandparents, aunts and uncles, all dressed in black.

'Married women always dressed in black for photos because there was always a *deuil*, a bereavement, among her own or her husband's relatives.'

Another was a blurry school photo taken in 1935, of about ten solemn-looking boys and girls in black uniforms, with black aprons, long blouses, woollen stockings and boots.

'This is me,' said Georgette, pointing out a blank-faced little girl from the drab line of children. 'I was eleven. That's Georges Benet, who married Mimi, and his brother. There's a Roumegoux, a Sommie, a Carbonel and a Liauzun.'

In the front of the group was a little girl of four or five in a print dress, suppressing a smile. 'That's me,' Solange chuckled. 'I was too young to go to school at the time but I wanted to be in the photo. We lived in the house where Didier and Pascale live now and I came over the road.'

Georgette and Solange had received all their schooling in the room that Thierry and Jacotte now used as the dining room of Les Jardins du Célé, and Rolande had had her primary schooling there.

They assured me it was always freezing in winter, even with the *pôele* the *conseil municipal* had installed in 1905. The privy the *conseil* had voted for in 1911 was in the little storeroom tucked around the corner under the *Presbytère*, where Martine and Jean-Louis and I found the salt to spread on the steps of the foyer at Christmas.

'The pan had to be emptied with a bucket,' said Solange.

The *curé*'s privy was in a cavity in the ruins of the ancient *clocher*, where Christophe, the *commune* handyman, now kept his rakes and brooms.

Mimi left school at fourteen and Rolande continued at a convent near Cahors where she boarded till she was seventeen.

'It cost so much to send me there in the first place, I had to stay till my parents thought they'd got their money's worth,' she said.

'And did they get their money's worth?' I asked.

'*C'est discutable*,' she grinned, 'that's debatable. And I had to stay there and work for another year to pay off the rest of my fees.'

Georgette left school when she was twelve or thirteen, Solange at fourteen, to work on the family farm. Every family had at least two cows, a goat, a *four au pain*, ducks, rabbits, pigs, everything they needed to live. In summer the family ate fresh food, in winter they ate lentils, dried beans and other vegetables and fruit: carrots, potatoes, apples and chestnuts that were stored in the *cave*. They sold the cows' milk to neighbours, or drank or made cheese from it. They grew their own maize for the animals and wheat for themselves, which they carted to the *moulin* at Brengues to be milled. Their parents also supplemented their income by running an *auberge* and a bar in the village.

During the Occupation, farmers were required to turn their harvest over to the Germans, so the farmers along the valley took their wheat to the mill secretly at night. The Germans also requisitioned the *alambics*, the little stills that people used to make their own *eau de vie*. The metal was melted down to make armaments.

'Every little corner of the land was cultivated,' said Solange. 'Everyone had vines, instead of fields overgrown with *chênes des causses*, as now. Everyone worked really hard. You had to work hard to live. We didn't use chemicals in cultivation, only animal manure. The first time we used pesticides was for the doryphores in the potatoes.'

'The vines were fertilised with goat manure,' said Rolande. 'There was an argument in the village: one man wanted compensation from another man because his goat had got in among the vines and damaged them; the other man wanted compensation for the manure the goat had dropped among the vines.'

'Everyone had dogs, including a hunting dog, and cats in the *grange* to catch the mice. The animals never came inside the house,' said Georgette, casting a lenient glance at Charlie, dozing on the *canapé-lit*. 'They weren't pets, they were useful.'

'We didn't have bathrooms or toilets or laundries,' said Rolande. 'We washed ourselves in a basin. We washed our clothes with soap in the Célé in the summer and at the *source* at Diège in winter because the water wasn't as cold there. There were no taps. We got water for the house from the *citerne*, the tank, or carried it up from the Célé.'

'Where did you go to the toilet?' I asked.

'Behind the cow, in the cornfield.'

'We got electric lighting in 1936,' said Georgette. 'It was absolutely black outside at night. You had to take an oil lamp. We kept the cows in our *grange*, which is now Jean-Louis' house. Our *papa* always went out with the lantern to see how the cows were before he went to bed.

'A lot of people left between the wars, to find work. But many who stayed, as well as farming their land, worked at different trades. M. Carbonel travelled round the district mending shoes. M. Lacan from Brengues was a stonemason, and his wife was a dressmaker. Our *papa* was a carpenter. There was another dressmaker at Sainte-Eulalie. Mme

Pelaprat kept a little *épicerie*, a grocer's, and a *café-tabac*. The *boulangers* came from Brengues and Beduer; the *boucher* came on Saturdays from Marcilhac: he'd buy a calf from someone, butcher it and sell it the next day. There was the restaurant Marty at Brengues, where the Hôtel de la Vallée is now; and there was a doctor who was also the pharmacist at Marcilhac. The postman came on his bicycle from Livernon.

'Many more people left after the war. But people who had enough land to live on, or who had some other useful capability like carpentry and masonry, stayed. When I was eighteen, there were only two cars in the village, the Sommies' and the Pelaprats'. All that changed after the war. Around 1948, things started getting better. Our parents got the old age pension. Our *maman* spent her first pension on getting her hair cut at a salon at Figeac. People started getting fridges, pressure cookers, cars. We got the first public phone cabin in our house. The *commune* paid 50 per cent of the cost and someone had to be at home between 8am and 6pm to look after it. That's how you got a phone.

'Tractors appeared here in the 1950s. Until then, the wheat was cut by machine, loaded onto wagons and piled up beside the house. Then the *batteuse* would come, the threshing machine. It was driven by a wood-fired boiler.'

'It needed two pairs of oxen to pull each machine,' said Solange. 'Everyone helped one another with the animals and with the work. The tractors made that work much easier, as long as they didn't break down.'

'We got our first washing machine in 1958, but it only washed the clothes, you still had to wring them out by hand,' said Georgette. 'I got my first bathroom when our house was built in the 1960s. The village got running water in 1967.'

I had put together some snacks, biscuits, *saucisson* and *cornichons*, but they remained on the table untouched until the end of our long conversation, when at last my visitors politely accepted the offer of a little *apéritif*.

It was largely through the succession of interviews that I came to appreciate the protocol of the *apéritif*, which I had experienced often enough, but never really thought about: it comes at the conclusion of, and not during, the serious business. And after a serious discussion it is practically *de rigueur*.

The interview with Roger Sudres took place at his house at Pailles. I asked Milou to come with me to interpret Roger's *patois*. We sat in his *salon* at a wooden table barred with shafts of winter sunlight streaming through the lattice windows. Roger's dogs, Rita and Isis, their mangled ears drooping, their scarred faces resting on their paws, snoozed under the table. The ginger cat, Lucky, observed us from his post on a dresser against the wall.

Charlie stayed at home in the nuns' room because whenever they saw him, Rita and Isis snarled and hurled themselves at us. With the Rochefort dogs at one side of the hamlet of Pailles and Roger's dogs at the other, Charlie and I had always made our way gingerly down the lane to the road when we descended the *falaise* at the end of the Espagnac-Brengues circuit.

Roger talked about the farming practices of the past and showed us a collection of old photographs he had put together of himself and his mother with their herd of cows.

'All the land around here used to belong to the convent,' said Roger. 'The nuns brought it as their dowries. My ancestors moved here when the nuns left. My ancestors were always farmers. Five generations of my mother's family lived at Pailles. Fourteen generations of my father's family lived at Le Mas down in Espagnac where my niece, Odette, lives now. I was born in this house in 1922. My mother was born in the house where Alain and Martine live.'

He got up and pulled open a drawer of a dresser and lifted out a bolt of thick white linen. 'Forty metres,' he said, handling it reverently. 'It was my grandmother's *dot*, her dowry. It was woven in a factory and hemmed by hand. It's never been used.'

I asked him about his experience during the war.

In 1943, he told us, all the twenty-two-year-old men in the Lot Department were ordered to be at the railway station in Cahors on a certain day. 'Each of us was given a paper to present to the German officers. Each paper had a number written on it in pencil. When I got to the railway station I saw a friend of mine who was working for the Germans, sorting us all out into groups. He told me the number on my paper meant that I was going to go to Auschwitz and he told me to change it to another number. Other people changed their numbers too so that when their original number was called, they didn't step forward and the train left without them. In the end, all of us who changed our numbers were sent to a Volkswagen factory, 8 kilometres from Hanover on the railroad to Berlin. We were given a uniform and made into a *groupement de travailleurs en cadre*, protected workers.

'The factory made cars, planes and bombs. There were 2000 to 3000 French and 20,000 Russians, Ukranians and Polish. We worked twelve hours per day, men and women together. But the work wasn't as arduous as on the farm. Sometimes there were long periods when we had nothing to do; then we slept and played cards.

'We all wore uniforms. We hung a sign outside our barracks that said *Privés d'amour et de pinard*, starved of love and plonk.

'But it was quite comfortable. We were fifteen per room. We had showers and toilet blocks and a cinema. I saw *Premier Rendezvous* at the cinema. Danielle Darrieux was in it.'

At the end of the conversation he swept the photographs and other memorabilia to one end of the table and carefully put his grandmother's dowry back into its drawer, returning with a tray containing a bottle of Ricard, a jug of water, a bottle of port and three glasses.

'*Un apéritif?*'

'Our family has lived in this house for many generations,' said André. He and I were sitting at the dining table in their salon; Jeanine was preparing something in the adjacent kitchen. 'My grandfather was a carpenter, and my father was a farmer. We grew our own wheat, fruit and vegetables. We had two or three cows to draw the wagon and plough the fields. The cows produced a calf each year, which we sold.

'My mother's parents lived at Vazac, 7 kilometres the other side of Figeac. When I was a child, my mother would take the bus into Figeac, and walk from there to Vazac carrying butter and cheese from our farm for them.

'Our cash income was from tobacco. At the end of the nineteenth century, when the phylloxera epidemic killed all the vines, the powers that be proposed that the farmers grow tobacco. It was a state monopoly and the tobacco money was guaranteed as long as the crop didn't fail. Fifty years ago everyone grew it. It was the only sure resource; the rest was subsistence farming.

'The tobacco-growing process took the whole year and involved the whole family. We sowed the seeds in February and March. When the seedlings were 10 centimetres high, we planted and staked them in the fields. All the farmers helped each other. Everyone had a certain amount they were allowed to grow. When the plants were big enough, government inspectors came to count how many plants each farmer had, to stop him keeping any for himself or for contraband. The farmers also had to cut the plants to the permitted number of leaves. Until the 1950s, when we got mechanical watering, each plant had to be watered individually.

'When the leaves became yellow in autumn, we cut through the stumps with shears. The tobacco leaves were hung in old *greniers* and under the ceilings of the houses. From August to December we had lines of iron wire running under the ceilings of all the rooms in the house with tobacco leaves hung from them in rows. We had to keep all the doors open so the leaves would dry out.

'In December and January, we prepared the tobacco for sale. The prettier the colour and form of the leaves, the more valuable the crop. Everyone in the family worked day and night grading it for different kinds of cigarettes and cigars according to colour – dark or light. We pulled the leaves apart, counted them, tied them in bundles, packed them into boxes, pressed them, tied the boxes with ropes of osier, and marked the boxes with labels.

'Then the boxes were loaded onto wagons or trucks and taken to Cajarc, to a building called the *cité de tabac*. I used to go with my father. Every farmer stood in the hall next to his boxes and an inspector opened them to see that the tobacco was of good quality. Afterwards everyone went to the bar.

'My parents also had a little *épicerie*, right down there by the road. My father had a licence from the state to sell tobacco. Our parents encouraged us to study hard. Poor families like ours wanted their children to become *fonctionnaires*, civil servants, teachers, post office workers, railway workers, to ensure they had greater job security, a steady income and good working conditions. There were lots of examinations to enter these ways of life. In those days, you were assured of an appropriate job if you passed the exams.

'There was great economic change over *les trente glorieuses*, the thirty years from the 1950s to the 1980s. Greater wealth brought us tractors, gas stoves, cars, washing machines, bathrooms, showers. We got our first bathroom when I was fourteen.

'The state still controls tobacco growing, but they've reduced the amount grown. Now people smoke less and prefer mild American cigarettes. Farmers are more interested in growing other crops like maize for animal feed and they need lots more land to make a living from farming. Now, with globalisation, farmers aren't protected and there's a lot of unemployment in rural areas.'

Eventually, Jeanine emerged from the kitchen. '*C'est terminé*, you've finished? *Est-ce que vous voulez un apéritif?*'

Despite Maxim's illness and Antoinette's responsibilities around the farm and looking after him, they agreed courteously, *avec plaisir*, to talk to me one morning before the district nurse was due to visit. On the appointed day I drove up to the *causse* to their farm where Charlie had stayed when Milou and I went to Belgium. This time, as with my interview with Roger Sudres, Charlie stayed in the nuns' room. Maxim had a little pet dog of his own.

Maxim's speech was impaired by his stroke but he seemed eager to talk. Antoinette sat beside him at their table, listening and watching him intently while he spoke, then turning to me and repeating what he said if she saw or thought that I didn't understand. The little dog also watched until her head sank onto her paws and she dozed on the floor on the other side of Maxim's wheelchair.

Maxim's ancestors had farmed land on the *causse* for eight generations, since the Revolution. His father was a prisoner of war in the 1914–18 conflict.

'In the Second World War,' he said, 'during the Occupation, a Resistance member lived in a disused farmhouse in the woods and came to our house at night for meals, even though it was dangerous. On Christmas night he came with the whole family down to Espagnac to sing the midnight Mass. Everyone knew he wasn't from here but we weren't denounced.'

The house they lived in now was built in 1912. Maxim was born in 1928. Then, there were only two rooms, the kitchen and the bedroom, where Maxim, his parents and his two sisters slept.

Antoinette came from an old family of Brengues. After Maxim and Antoinette married in 1951, Maxim's parents, Maxim and Antoinette and four of their children, as they came along, all slept in the same room until they built the second storey in 1965.

'We raised tobacco, hay and cereals, beef and lamb. The whole family worked together from dawn to dusk. We took the little children with us to the fields while we worked.'

'It was quieter in winter,' Antoinette added mildly. 'It was a good life. It was hard, but we didn't think about that.'

'We worked the hay by hand,' said Maxim proudly. 'But now it's all done by machines and put in plastic bales. All the charm has gone.'

'We got our first tractor in 1956 and after that we'd all go down to the village to Mass on the tractor, the kids in a trailer behind,' Antoinette explained. 'We had running water much later than the rest of Espagnac. Maxim used to take the tractor down to the river to load up water for washing and for the animals.'

'The work was easier with the tractor,' said Maxim, 'but we had more money worries, buying and maintaining new equipment. The kids had bursaries for schooling, but not enough.'

Their five children all went to school down in the village on foot or to Brengues after the Espagnac school closed. The three eldest boarded at Cajarc for college, the others went to Figeac or Cahors to study nursing. Michel went to the Lycée Agricole at Albi, then to Toulouse for medical training.

Over the years, by dint of their hard work and as the other small farmers gave up the life on the land, Maxim and Antoinette bought six additional little farms.

'We wanted more space for sheep,' Antoinette explained, 'and for each of our children to have a little house, but all our children have left, except Flo. She and José and their children live in her house. Michel is at Livernon, Arlette is in Figeac, Chantal is married to a doctor in Cantal, Joelle is in Toulouse. Maybe when they retire they'll take over the property for recreation, but not to live. The grandchildren are studying anything but agriculture. Now the farmland is rented by Alain and Martine Rochefort for their sheep.'

After an hour or so, I could see that the effort of expressing his thoughts and memories had exhausted Maxim's emotions as well as his diminished strength. His big frame leaned heavily on one arm of his wheelchair as tears ran down his face and splashed on the floor. He began to talk rapidly, bitterly.

'Now there's no future in farming on the *causse*. It could be profitable but the young don't want to exploit it.'

Not wanting to excite his distress any further, I made to leave not long afterwards.

Antoinette smiled at me reassuringly, as if to say, *it isn't you, he's often like this.*

'Would you like something, *un apéritif?*' she asked, although the nurse, who had arrived quietly, was busy in the bathroom next to the kitchen where we sat. I could hear water running into a basin. I declined the invitation, thanking them sincerely.

I kept Martine up-to-date with the progress of my interviews and one evening during the Easter holidays of 2005 asked her when we could make a time to talk about her job as mayor.

'Come up to the house this evening,' said Martine, 'a little before *l'heure de l'apéritif.*'

She and I settled down at the table in the kitchen. Philippe and the boys disappeared behind the curtain into the sitting room to watch *le foot* on the television. Charlie dozed in a corner. A *pot au feu* simmered on the stove. In answer to my questions, Martine described the processes of her work and the levels of scrutiny of the activities of the *mairie*.

'I have two budgets: water and communal. The communal budget forecasts various things that need to be done. I prepare a budget of projections with the *percepteur*, the tax officer from the *sous-préfecture* at Figeac. He holds the funds and controls finances, makes sure they meet the *Directives financiers*, the financial requirements. Once the budget is drafted, I present it to the *conseil municipal*. All proposals must be approved by the *conseil municipal* and then go to the *sous-préfecture* which approves them or asks for more documentation if there is a concern.

'The income comes from the state, the local habitation tax, rental of the *gîtes* and the other properties owned by the *commune*, such as the pine forests on the *causse*.

'Apart from those sources of income, we can ask for funding for particular projects from the EU, the State, the Department, the Region and the *Parc Naturel*. For example, we got money from the EU and the Region for the *étangs*, the pools, that we bought this year between Espagnac and Corn.

'Some examples of projections? The purchase of the *étangs*. The *assainissement*, the installation of mains sewage, and underground electricity – these are projected for the second half of next year. Public lighting, painting the buildings, rewiring the kitchen under the *foyer*, repairing the roof of the church, installing ADSL broadband. In the long term, we expect to convert the *grenier* in the roof over the two *gîtes* into more accommodation but that will be after my time …

'The whole village is now classed as a *monument historique* and all external work on buildings must be approved by *Bâtiments de France*, which is part of the *Ministre de la culture et du patrimoine*.

'Some of our projections are common projects with the *Communauté des Communes de la Vallée du Célé-Causse*. In 1998, the *communes* were grouped for common projects. We are grouped with Boussac, Corn, Brengues, Grèzes, Saint-Simon, Livernon and Assier.

'I'm responsible for entering the births, deaths and marriages in the village registers. If someone died, I'd have to seal the coffin with an official tool. I can't remember the name of the tool. I've never had to do it. I have police powers of verbal process. If something happened, say, a graffitist in the village or an assault, I would have to negotiate with the offenders and call the appropriate services. But I've never had to use these powers, either.'

In my observation, her civic involvement went beyond the official responsibilities. Like many other *Espagnacois*, she was there for all the pulses of the life of the village, the communal *repas*, the meetings of the *amis*, the *brocante*, the *marché fermier*, as well as many of the private celebrations. She also negotiated the line between her personal friendships and her official responsibilities. She was sensitive to other people's needs and feelings, and the events in their lives – and she could keep secrets, others' as well as her own. She could also make sure that people got to know the 'right' information. She had the ability to get to the heart of problems, whether they were public or personal, and devise solutions for them. Would she stand for *maire* at the next election?

'It depends,' she said. 'Sometimes I think, definitely not, because it's too much responsibility and it takes up so much of my time, but other times, because my projects aren't finished yet and because there are other projects I'd like to start, and because I love the village ...'

Philippe was hovering in the doorway. I put my notes into my bag and stood up.

'*Désolée*, I've stayed too long,' I said.

'*À table!*' he called to the boys.

He threw a cloth over the table and poured wine for Martine and me.

'Oh, but,' I said.

'*Reste là,*' he said. 'Stay there, Maureen, we're going to eat now.'

Martine brought a terrine and bread to the table. The boys pulled out their chairs and sat down.

'*Bon appétit.*'

I wasn't as well acquainted with Gaby Senac as I was with most of the other people I had interviewed, and perhaps that was why I left him till the end, only weeks before Charlie and I vacated the nuns' room at the end of May 2005. Afterwards, when I was back home in Australia writing up the information I had gleaned from these conversations, I was pleased it turned out that way because some of what he said helped me put everything into perspective.

'Before the last war,' he told me, 'several generations of the same family lived together. That was how it was. There were many marriages of convenience. The *curé* had a lot of influence over this. The rich married the rich. A lot of the men remained bachelors because girls didn't want to go and live with another family with only a lifetime of hard work to look forward to. They wanted to marry someone from town. And the boys couldn't compete with men from town. With nothing but a bicycle to get around on, their social circle was narrow.

'After the war, people's expectations changed. The smart ones went to Paris or got jobs with the *SNCF*, the railways, *EDF*, the electricity. The ones who stayed had to look after the parents. And many stayed because they couldn't sell the land.

'I went away when I was twenty and I stayed away for twenty-three years. For ten years I was a sporting presenter for boxing events, exhibitions, bicycle races *et ainsi de suite* and, after that, I did demonstrations in shops, especially garden shops. Presenting, it's my passion.

'At the time, the big shops were directed from Paris. But after the *choc petrolier*, the oil crisis in 1974, the management devolved to the regions, so I went into management. I came back to Espagnac in 1981 because my father died and my mother was alone.

'Then I organised a group of local artists to exhibit their work in our little workshop on the *place* in the summers. We had a sculptor, a cooper, a paper maker, a silk painter, a stained glass maker, a cartoonist, a jewellery enameller. They sold their work here in summer and we all went on the road in the off-season. I wanted to promote ecological development, to produce things locally. Now everyone is doing it.

'Everything has changed. The old ones weren't as educated but they were smart. They knew the flora and fauna, they could judge weights instinctively, they understood what needed to be done. Now the young ones don't know geography, the ecology, elementary things about the country, what's good for their health.

'Now Espagnac is a façade, a leisure culture. In the past, there were no machines to do the work; people helped one another. There were goats, cows, sheep all around the village. Nobody used lawn mowers, the animals kept the grass down. We didn't have recreations, like *pétanque* and all the other diversions, only one big fête. The fêtes now aren't as elaborate as they were. The place is now antiseptic; there are no flies.

'There are some places here where foreigners have come and have changed everything. But Espagnac has benefited from the different nationalities of the people who've come because of new knowledge and the spirit they've brought with them.

'The future? The Lot will become the retirement home of Europe. That won't be so bad if they preserve the patrimony and the quality of the area and if we remain free of factories and pollution and we gain good services. We already have the autoroute nearby, and good restaurants; we don't have to live in a town to get the good things of life. It could be worse, for instance, it could be designated as a dump for nuclear waste.

'For the time being you can't build anything new in the village, but eventually people will be building on the *causse*. At the moment the *Beaux-Arts* prevents this, but Figeac is expanding. The land all around the *rond-point* at Livernon is already sold. In the future the little *communes* will be joined with bigger ones. Maybe the Figeac-Livernon airport will become like Rodez with international flights.'

This last interview took place in the nuns' room. At the end,

Gaby smilingly declined my offer of an *apéritif*. Perhaps it isn't *comme il faut* for a married man to accept an *apéritif* from a woman of a certain age in her apartment with only a poodle as a chaperone.

Maybe Gaby was right and the Espagnac I had come to love was a veneer, a shell of what once had been, the possible 'retirement home' for Europeans who want sunshine and tranquility, and fêtes and *repas* that recall life in times past, but also gloss the harsh realities of that life with nostalgic myth. It was clear that the life for the *Espagnacois* now was different and more comfortable than it had been for them and their ancestors, and in the past there would probably not have been any place for Charlie and me here.

And yet, despite the modern conveniences they were now used to, including satellite dishes on roofs and the internet, and soon to include the mains sewage and underground electricity that Martine had mentioned, the past was still entwined in the present lives of the *Espagnacois*. They might work as public servants or school teachers, salespeople or tradespeople, or have retired from such jobs, but they still valued and engaged in the practices of the past, as hobbies mainly, but also sometimes as a chosen part of their subsistence.

René, Didier and young Boris still hunted *gibier* in the woods, albeit under regulations dictated in Brussels and Paris and toting their *portables* as well as their guns. René still collected and prepared firewood and supplied it to people like me. Didier and Jean-Louis knew that fixing René's tractor had priority over a recreational English class. Everyone keenly watched the signs of the seasons that presaged wild foods to eat and wildflowers to admire. Nearly every family tended a *potager* that supplied them with vegetables, fruit, herbs and flowers for a large part of the year. Solange stored potatoes and onions, fruit and root vegetables, eggs and preserves in her *cave*, as her ancestors had done. The whole Cabrignac family and all the other families who owned vineyards organised their lives around the annual *vendanges*. Gerard Pelaprat and Gaby Senac still held hopes of producing truffles.

Of all the members of the old families who lived permanently at Espagnac, only André Pelaprat had eschewed the labours of his childhood. He had with pleasure turned over his potager to his *voisin anglais*, his grateful English neighbour, Terry Kempley. So Terry laboured throughout the spring and summer, as many *villageois* did still, to produce an autumn harvest of fruit and vegetables to eat or preserve before he and Anne went back to England for the winter. André instead devoted his time to illustrating publications of the regional and local *associations* and committees he belonged to, including the newsletters of the *mairie* of Espagnac-Sainte-Eulalie and the regional branch of Amnesty International. Through his sketches, reading and observations he provided images of the past and reminders of how the past still resides in the old houses and remains in the overgrown walls and ruins in the valleys and *causses*. He kept alive traditional stories, in which humans communicated with other species and saints confronted devils, and balanced them with the scientific explanations for those stories that modern people require. And he and Jeanine bought their food at the *supermarché* and the Saturday *marché* in Figeac.

And, as Gaby observed, the foreigners who had come here had not affected the essential features of the place; rather, in my observation, they were keen to preserve it and to become part of it, as I had done.

But Gaby was wrong about one thing: there were still lots of flies, and I found this thought pleasing.

Many months later, I was walking with Charlie along our beach on the south coast of New South Wales and thinking about how to manage the material from the interviews I'd done within the narrative of this book. I reflected on the similarities between the experiences of the *Espagnacois* and those of the folk at Wentworth and Corowa I had interviewed for my novel. I dwelt on the similarities regarding concerns about the future – particularly the effects of globalisation on old village communities – and also on the differences in the experiences of the real *Espagnacois* and the fictional inhabitants of *Blue and Brown*, stemming from the different physical, cultural and historical contexts in which they had 'lived'. I realised that, ultimately, I'd been able to deal technically with the *Espagnacois* stories because I had simply recorded them: which I felt was all I had the right to do; and because they went no deeper than the external circumstances of the people: all I had the right to know or reveal.

But I had a more complex involvement with the population of *Blue and Brown* and a different purpose in telling their story, which of course was really a part of my own story, before I had even come into existence. In coming to France, I had removed myself physically from the setting of the story, but not emotionally. I thought, when I returned to *Blue and Brown*, I would begin at the beginning and let my characters say what they had to say and do what they had to do. As I had done with this story, I would observe rather than direct them.

'And then we'll see,' I said to Charlie, as he trotted along beside me on the sand. He looked up to ascertain whether I actually had anything important to communicate, then bounded down to the shore to rout a flock of raucous seagulls scrapping over some discarded bait.

THE VIEW FROM MONT BLANC

At the end of October 2004, Line Bresson, Sigrid's friend whom we had met in the summer, invited Charlie and me to her holiday apartment in Haute Savoie, for a week.

I accepted readily; I wanted to see as much of the rest of France as I could before Charlie and I went back to Australia. And this trip, like the interviews with the *Espagnacois*, contributed much to my later reflections on our lives in Val-Paradis.

It rained all the first day of the journey till in the late afternoon we approached Le Puy-en-Velay, situated on the slopes of one of several volcanic cones that can be seen from a great distance rising abruptly from a high valley in the Massif Central. Surmounting other cones are a gigantic statue of Notre-Dame-de-France and the tenth century chapel of Saint-Michel. This extraordinary landscape was where the pilgrimage route of Saint-Jacques de Compostelle began.

In the morning, the rain lifted long enough for us to climb the steep, twisting cobbled lanes and steps to the Cathedral of Notre-Dame-du-Puy. I leaning on my walking stick, Charlie as usual prepared to do anything I wanted, even if it turned out sometimes to be boring or uncomfortable for him.

He waited, tethered to a water pipe in a cold corner near the northern door, while I went inside. The interior of the Cathedral was dark. I stopped just inside the door to let my eyes adjust enough to make out the columns defining the space between the nave and the ambulatory. A few pilgrims were kneeling in a chapel before the image of the Virgin, the statue stained black from incense and candle flame. The ambulatory led around the nave to the portal from which a monumental staircase, on which pilgrims took their first steps on the Chemin de Saint-Jacques, descended to the town. I stood there for a few moments, gazing across the blue waves of the mountains of the Margeride.

'One day, maybe,' I told myself.

I retraced my steps, brushing past some pilgrims coming the other way. They had finished their prayers before the black Virgin and, with backpacks in place, out-thrust chins, and eyes fixed on the light beyond the portal, were setting out on their journey. I turned and watched them till they disappeared behind the colonnade.

When I returned to the corner of the building where I had left Charlie, he reared on his hind legs, straining at the lead and emitting anxious whimpers.

I untied his lead from the water pipe. 'It's OK, little man. We're going the other way.'

The rain continued. We took the *Route Nationale* to Saint-Etienne, then the autoroute, skirting Lyon to the south, and on to Chambery and Albertville. From there, up through a series of vertiginous gorges and passes into the *massif* of Les Aravis. We arrived in the late afternoon in dense fog.

Line's apartment was in one of several buildings of a ski resort on a mountainside overlooking the village of Combloux. In the brilliant sunshine of the following morning, the view from my bedroom window was of the Aguilles de Varens, jagged granite peaks gouged with deep snow-filled depressions. It was somewhat lost on Charlie, exhausted as he usually was after the long days of travel, and between checks on what Line and I were doing – having a long breakfast in the sun-drenched living room – he kept returning to his bed.

'He's having *une grasse matinée*, a lazy morning,' said Line.

Later, we set out on the track leading down the mountain to the village, to the music of running water and the clink of cowbells. The *savoyard* animals – fat cows, chunky mountain horses and long-haired goats – were coloured like confectionery: chocolate, caramel, cream, lemon. All around, the granite peaks were scored with snow and the mountain slopes dappled with myriad tones of autumn leaves. The valley was submerged beneath a lake of mist and the village of Combloux was in shadow, till suddenly the pale sunlight broke through and glinted on the green steel tiles of the slim, onion-shaped bell tower of the church.

'It's called a *clocher à bulbe*,' said Line. 'They are typical of the churches here, but this one at Combloux is my favourite, so fine and delicate.'

Line was determined to show me as much of Haute Savoie as possible in the week we were there. We made day trips to handsome rain-drenched towns full of flower-decked bridges and the sounds of rushing streams, each with its special character and long history. As she commented on the town and village structures, artefacts and designs and explained the architectural style of the farmhouses we passed, it was clear how these features reflected the long social, cultural and religious history of the people of that lush, sparkling region. In contrast, Australia's history before the arrival of Europeans had been expressed over millennia in traditional forms of rock art and cultural practices of the indigenous peoples, and reflected parched brown-red-ochre desert scapes, low mountains and dry-barked blue-green forests that might have belonged to a different world.

I tried to explain to Line how aspects of Australia's history, following occupation by people like my Irish ancestors, were partly what I was trying to grapple with in *Blue and Brown*.

'I understand,' she replied. 'But still the people everywhere have their experience and memories that belong to them, even when they are in a different place, as you are here in France, and I was when I travelled in Australia.'

Line and I spent one day exploring the old town of Annecy. We wandered through the park bordering Lac Lacan, where she told me the names of the trees lining our path, grand old forest specimens that had been planted there long ago. A tree-clad islet and a blue and yellow fishing boat that was tethered to it loomed out of the mist on the lake. On the way back to where she had parked the car, we traversed the 'newer' part of town, zigzagging though streets and across parks she evidently knew well.

'My grandparents lived in an apartment in that building,' she said, at one point. 'I always came here for holidays, but when they died, the apartment was sold. I'd like to live in Annecy, it's my spiritual home, like your house on the coast in Australia is yours. But it would be hard to leave Paris, and then, the children need me. They work such long hours, so I look after the grandchildren two or three days a week.'

In Megève, the nearest town to Combloux, the rushing streams competed with the sound of pneumatic drills chopping up the streets.

'Megève normally has 5000 inhabitants,' Line told me. 'But the population increases to 40,000 in the winter and summer holidays. The ski slopes here were once owned by a handful of rich families like the Rothschilds. Now the *commune* has bought all the ski facilities and can run them more efficiently than the private owners did. The profits go into improving and maintaining the infrastructure for the tourist industry.'

'That explains all the drilling,' I said. 'Thank goodness that sort of thing isn't happening in the Lot.'

'The *savoyards* don't mind,' said Line. 'The tourists aren't here for long, and meanwhile, the towns and villages get rich. If things must change, it's best the changes work for you.'

On other days we tramped in the mountains, through wisps of cloud, to the clinking bells of invisible cattle and the rush of invisible streams; or over rich pastures where Charlie sent the earth flying as he scrabbled in the mole holes. His head periodically reappeared above the surface, like a chocolate-coated ice-cream.

One day, with Line's friend Françoise, we took a steep track up through thick pine forest over ground networked with sinuous tree roots. Some way up, we passed a derelict farmhouse that Françoise said had last functioned as such in 1941, after which the members of the local French Resistance groups used it as a safe house.

Eventually we came to a track deep in mud like a river of mousse, which Charlie negotiated bravely, his legs plopping and squelching in and out of the sludge. Sometimes we were able to climb up the bank beside the track and find other little paths beside the main one, through meadows of dwarf rhododendrons bristling with new tight buds, and blueberry bushes, laden with ripe fruit, on which Line, Françoise and I grazed as we went along.

At last we arrived at a spot on the ridge that Françoise wanted to show us: an ancient Roman stone marker with a Latin inscription, dividing the territory between the local Gallic tribes. On this ridge, among Gallic ghosts, encircled by other mountains, we stood, unable to tear our gaze from the most majestic: Mont Blanc, with its rivers of granite scree and basin of gleaming snow.

One night we had dinner with Françoise and her husband Roger at their house just outside Megève and Roger talked about when he was a little boy growing up during the Second World War.

'My uncle Joseph,' he said, 'had joined up at the beginning of the war, but when Maréchal Pétain signed the armistice with Germany in 1940 he was demobilised and his regiment dissolved. However, Pétain set up youth training camps. In Megève there was a school run by two Marist brothers. Twice a week, they were obliged to take the young boys into the mountains to do physical exercises, to prepare them to go to work in Germany. As well, men like my uncle Joseph, who had truck-driving licences, had to go to Germany to work to replace German men who had been called up. The French police had to deliver the requisition orders.

'Of course, nobody wanted to go to Germany and many took to the mountains to avoid being taken by force. That was how the *maquis* began. They were called *maquis*, jungle, because in the beginning there were many different groups and their networks were so entangled. By 1942 they had become organised. At Megève, they came together in an alpine chalet above Praz-sur-Arly.

'Uncle Joseph was attending his sister's wedding when the police brought his requisition order. They said, "We've brought the order, but we haven't seen you."

'Joseph left immediately for the mountains. At that time the occupying soldiers were Italians, who were then German allies. Joseph found himself with a group of young men as well as older men, like himself. The older men tried to persuade the younger ones to be more careful and to keep out of sight, but their advice was ignored, so the older men left the group. A few days later, the Italians surrounded the chalet, the young men were taken prisoner and the chalet set on fire.

'When the alliance between Hitler and Mussolini ended, the Italians left and were replaced by Austrians, who were nicer to the local people than the Italians had been. Whenever there was a surveillance patrol, one of the officers would always go on ahead to warn the people they were coming.

'One day, when I was eight or nine years old, my mother and I and our dog were looking after the cows in the mountain pasture near our farm when we saw an Austrian patrol approaching. Our dog, who was very strong, ran and jumped up on one of the soldiers. I ran and caught the dog and hung onto him so that he wouldn't be killed. But the officer said, "*Pas méchant, pas méchant*," and asked to go into our house. The patrol just wanted a rooster for their soup. My mother only had cockerels. She told them to come back in a fortnight, when the cockerels would be bigger and she promised to lock the dog in the shed when they came.

'Everything was going well between the soldiers and the inhabitants. But one day in 1944, some *maquisards* from another region attacked the Austrians on the way into Megève at the Arbon Bridge, killing the officer whom everybody had liked. He was the father of two children. The village was filled with dismay.

'After that, the Austrians left, but a column of fifty Germans arrived. The commanding officer said that he was going to take hostages and burn all the houses. The mayor of Megève offered himself as a single hostage. The soldiers saw that the dead officer had been placed in a coffin in the church and been prepared for the funeral service as if he were an inhabitant of the village. This is what saved Megève from disaster.'

Roger also spoke about *faux maquis*.

'There were men who joined the Resistance at the last minute when they saw that the Germans were going to be defeated. They went around the villages requisitioning food and shelter from people who could ill afford to help them, and who ran the risk of terrible reprisals if they did.

'Then, as soon as France was liberated, there was score-settling and instances of personal vengeance. One of our relatives, a man who had actually been wounded in the previous war, had denounced his Jewish tenants to the Germans for money. The Jewish family had been deported to the concentration camps and only the father came back. He wanted to kill their denouncer, but because the man had three daughters, he didn't have the will to do it.'

Back in Line's apartment, I lay looking out the window where the sharp points of the Aiguilles de Varens were edged with moonlight, listening to Charlie's breathing at the end of the bed. I thought about how circumstances, events, experiences, affections and cultural memories both influence the range and kinds of choices available to us, and limit the way we deal with them. That was what I still had to explore through *Blue and Brown* and why I was going back home. But whenever I returned to Europe, I would always go back to Espagnac-Sainte-Eulalie, because, as I had told Martine, it had become part of my life too.

BEDUER

Back in Espagnac, it felt strange to go on behaving as if I wasn't going to leave the village in a few months. I spent many hours thinking about what might have happened if I had made a different choice. I thought about the aspects of the lives of the *Espagnacois* that I knew very little about, and the kinds of skills and attitudes required for several generations and in-laws – indeed, for an entire village – to live in close proximity and apparent harmony. If I had chosen to stay, would I, in a changed role in the village, have wanted or been able to learn and develop those skills and attitudes?

I was sitting at my desk one day, thinking about this and how it also applied to the characters in the novel I told myself I would get back to one day, when I heard a voice calling my name from the Chemin des Dames. I leaned out the window to see, standing in the angle made by the Bonzanis' *pont* and the wall on the other side of the Chemin, a tall, elegant woman in jodhpurs and boots, smiling up at me. Wandering nearby, sniffing at the wall which bore the bouquet of hundreds of Charlie's efforts, were two other dogs, a chubby blonde labrador and a lithe-looking border collie.

'My name is Suzanne,' said the woman in English, in a cultivated accent. 'I've been looking for you everywhere. May we come up?'

'Of course,' I said, though mystified.

Charlie and I went out to the landing. Suzanne and the dogs came round the corner, and Suzanne strode and the dogs hurtled up the steps. The dogs ignored Charlie's sharp bark of greeting and proceeded straight through the entry into the nuns' room so that by the time Suzanne, Charlie and I were there, the labrador had, like a guided missile, found and demolished all Charlie's *croquettes*.

'Oh, naughty girl, Tara,' Suzanne said, sitting down on the end of one of the benches at the table. 'She was a rescue dog, she was starving when we got her, so I'm afraid she's always hungry.'

Charlie stood by the door, watching suspiciously the two intruders bounding around his domain, until he concluded, correctly, that they had come to play and joined in the fray.

Suzanne looked around the room, pausing for a few moments to inspect the fresco, then turned to me with a wide smile. 'So, Maureen, this is where you live!'

Though completely in the dark, I smiled back. 'Would you like a cup of tea?'

As I was filling the kettle, Suzanne said, 'I came to see you last week, but you weren't here.'

An explanation was called for, evidently. 'I was in Haute Savoie.'

'Oh, so that was it. You know, I've left messages in villages along the valley and at all the grocers and butchers in Figeac and Cajarc, asking the Australian lady with the little white dog to contact me. Now I've tracked you down.'

'How ...?' I ventured. The conversation was so well-advanced, it seemed rude now to ask her who she was.

'Stella and Bruce told me about you.'

'Ah!'

Stella and Bruce were an Australian couple who had bought a *château* near Figeac some months before and were turning part of the estate into a rose garden. I had read about their project in *La Dépêche du Midi* and contacted them because I needed an Australian citizen to witness my application for a postal vote in the upcoming Australian elections.

Suzanne had met Stella and Bruce through a club of *château* owners she and her husband had joined. 'We don't own a *château*,' she explained with a droll smile, 'but Peter was an ambassador, that counts for something.' Peter, her husband, had recently retired from the Dutch diplomatic service and they had come to live at a *mas*, a farmstead, they had bought some years before, just outside the village of Beduer. 'We would like you to look after our house and our dogs from time to time, and of course, we'll look after your little doggy when you want to go away too. You'll love our house,' she added, looking around the room again, 'even if it isn't a *château.*'

Her proposal sounded like a good arrangement. Suzanne and Peter would mind Charlie when I went to Paris again for Christmas; and now it would be easier for me to do more travelling in Europe before Charlie and I went back to Australia. England, to farewell my friends there. Barcelona, with Jacqueline and Line. Eastern Europe, with an Australian friend, the following spring. And Milou and I had started to talk about going to Russia for the last two weeks in May, after Charlie had departed to spend a month in quarantine in Australia.

A few days later we went over to Beduer to see the *mas* and meet Peter. Suzanne and I drank coffee on the terrace outside the big wooden front door of the house. Charlie and Tara played together nearby, while Jessie, the border collie, lay in wait behind the wall below the road that wound down from the village of Beduer into the valley. Whenever Jessie heard a car coming, she bolted up the steps onto the road and raced along beside the cars, snapping at their tyres.

'That's her job,' remarked Suzanne, equably, seeing the look of alarm on my face.

Charlie eventually tired of playing with Tara and started watching what Jessie was doing. The next time Jessie shot up the steps to the road, Charlie dashed along the driveway, so that by the time the car had reached the hidden entry from the road, the driver had two barking, snapping dogs to contend with.

Suzanne and I raced up the driveway calling them back.

'It's all right for Jessie,' said Suzanne. 'She knows what she's doing. When you come to stay here, you'll just have to keep Charlie inside most of the time or put him on the chain. That's what I do with Jessie sometimes.'

There was a long chain attached to a ring in a stone by the door. As far as I knew, Charlie had never been on a chain in his life!

'They can't both be on the chain at the same time,' I said.

'Charlie can have the chain,' Suzanne said sanguinely. 'Jessie's more experienced at road work than he is.'

'But what about the drivers?' I said. 'They must get annoyed when Jessie chases the cars.'

'Oh, everybody knows her around here,' said Suzanne.

The first time we took the dogs for a walk together on the river flat below the house at Beduer, all three took off after a flock of sheep. Suzanne and I clumped around in the mud calling them.

'This never happens,' she said.

Charlie came back after a while, but we had to trudge back up the hill to the house and get Suzanne's car to entice the other two out of the woods into which they had disappeared.

'They'll come as soon as they hear the car,' said Suzanne confidently, as she drove backwards and forwards in the gathering dusk along the lane.

Despite my gammy knee, Suzanne and I arranged to walk with the dogs once or twice a week, sometimes on the tracks around Beduer and sometimes around Espagnac and other villages.

'You should reconsider going back to Australia,' said Suzanne.

'What could be nicer than living here? And there are plenty of English-speaking people around. I'll introduce you to them.'

I didn't want to meet people just because they spoke English. I already knew people who spoke English. I really didn't come to France to speak English. But if I changed my mind, and moved to another village, maybe this is what it would come to, the life of an expatriate anglophone person, just another member of the leisure culture. I hadn't yet seen how much effort Suzanne and Peter put into their lives here.

One evening Charlie and I were walking back down the road from the *causse* when a car passed us. It stopped further along the road and waited for us to catch up.

'Maureen?'

I had met Hilary and Steve Corless at a village *repas* shortly after I arrived in 2003. We promised to contact one another when they were in residence at their house in the hamlet of Autejac, near Brengues, during the English school holidays, but we never did. At that time, they were still working in England, but now Hilary had retired from teaching, and Steve was about to retire, and they now lived in Autejac. Steve commuted weekly to England from the airport at Rodez. They had driven up on the Causse d'Espagnac to pick up their two dogs from Antoinette Liauzun, who had boarded them while Hilary and Steve were both in England for a week.

The Corlesses were keen walkers, and they and their dogs, and Charlie and I, showed one another our favourite circuits. They had been coming to the municipal camping ground at Brengues every summer for the last fifteen years before buying the house in Autejac.

About the same time, at a meeting of *Les Aînés Ruraux*, I renewed the acquaintance of another woman I had met a year or so earlier.

Sue Wilson had also recently retired from her job in England, and had bought a house in Marcilhac-sur-Célé. Sue had found her house when she was walking part of the Chemin de Saint-Jacques. Entering the village from the road from the *causse*, she saw the house for sale and decided to buy it. Charlie and I showed her our favourite walks and introduced her to Hilary and Steve. The four of us quickly became friends.

'Where else,' asked Hilary and Steve, 'could you find such richness of bird, animal and plant life, bright starry nights, extraordinary geological formations, ravishing landscapes, attractive architecture and friendly people?'

'Every morning,' said Sue, 'I look out my window across the valley at those beautiful cliffs. I couldn't be happier.'

I sighed. Even though Hilary, Steve and Sue had come to live permanently in the Lot, they could also commute from Rodez to England easily. Like many of my other friends here, Milou and Eric, Sigrid and the Kempleys, they could dash back for emergencies and have their families and friends visit regularly. My situation was more complicated.

'I've made the choice,' I said.

'We know we'll see you here again,' they said.

'Of course.'

Suzanne and Peter went to The Hague for two weeks before Christmas. Their program included various cocktail parties and a reception at the Palace.

I packed a suitcase, my computer and books I'd need and Charlie's nominal bed, which I'd bought in Paris two years previously and which he never used, and we drove over to Beduer.

The *mas* where they lived was a complex of buildings comprising the house, two *granges*, a woodshed, garage, studio where Suzanne sculpted and painted, and a *four au pain*. They had preserved the traditional features of the house and filled it with attractive furniture, antiques and paintings. They were gradually landscaping the grounds and converting the *granges* into *gîtes*. Unlike many of the immigrants I'd met who were restoring big complexes like this, Suzanne and Peter, as well as working hard themselves, employed French builders and gardeners and an Englishwoman to clean the house.

'I could do it myself,' said Suzanne, 'but …'

'She has more interesting things to do with her time,' said Peter.

The house was built on a hillside and had four storeys. The front door, which was on the second level, opened into a spacious hallway flanked by a kitchen and dining area on one side and a formal *salon*, separated from the hall by glass doors, on the other. At the end of the hallway, a staircase led down to the vast cold *cave*, which served as a laundry as well as to store food, wine and crockery that didn't fit into the dresser and cupboards in the kitchen. Opposite the front door, another, wider staircase led up to the third level which comprised their bedroom, a luxurious bathroom, Peter's study and an open area that was Suzanne's study. This was where I would work. From the corner of the open area, narrow steps went up to what was formerly the loft, which they had converted into two bedrooms and a drying space.

The wardrobe of clothes Suzanne had accumulated from the fashion houses of Paris occupied several cupboards on the third and fourth levels of the house. When Charlie and I arrived, she was rummaging in a built-in wardrobe in the loft, where I was going to sleep, deciding which of several cocktail outfits to take to wear to the Palace.

'What do you think?' she asked, draping against her elegant body a little dress that fell in folds of glittering gunmetal. 'Or this?' It was a soft, red wool princess-line.

'Oh,' I said, just as if my own wardrobe had more than a couple of T-shirts, jeans and a tracksuit in it, 'the red. Definitely.'

'I think I'll take them both,' she said. 'Then I can choose, when the time comes.' From the pile of clothes she had draped over the banister she plucked an electric-blue Chanel suit and a long black lace cheongsam. 'These too. I never get the chance to wear these clothes here. Now, shall we go downstairs and have *un café*?'

Suzanne and Peter's trip to The Hague coincided with the first big freeze of the northern winter. While the view from the kitchen window – of the rolling hills covered in snow and the early morning sun shining on the spire of the church at Camboulit on the other side of the valley – was beautiful, the house, despite central heating, was very cold. The fire in the *poêle* in the kitchen never lasted all night and in the mornings I had to reset it several times before I could get it to stay alight. The only way the dogs and I could keep warm was to huddle round the *poêle*, I in a chair with a blanket wrapped round my legs, and the dogs playing musical chairs in Jessie and Tara's beds in the hearth on either side of the *poêle*. Charlie's Paris bed was on the floorboards outside the hearth but he soon learned a way of getting into one of the other ones, by cavorting in front of the occupant till she jumped out, thinking he wanted to play. As soon as she was out of the bed, Charlie jumped in. The farmstead was also quite isolated, sitting below a narrow road that wound down the hill from the village, and for a few days it was too dangerous to drive anywhere because of the sheets of ice across the road above and below the house.

On the other hand, going for walks with my walking stick and the dogs through the snowy lanes was delightful. Once off their leads, the dogs rolled in the snow, ate mouthfuls of it and romped off across the fields after the *cheveuil* which, happily, always got away. Sometimes they all disappeared into the woods and I heard the swish and crackle of their progress through the snow-crusted undergrowth till eventually they reappeared from an unexpected direction, panting and grinning and covered in leaves and twigs.

It occurred to me one afternoon, while trudging up to the woodshed, loading the wood and wheeling it in the wheelbarrow over the rough, icy ground, that, if I had bought or rented somewhere else than the nuns' room, this was the sort of thing I would have to do. There would be no René to stack wood for me, no Jean-Louis to call on if something went wrong with the electricity, no Christophe to change the light bulbs, possibly no one to look after Charlie in emergencies. Suzanne and Peter might have a beautiful house and an Englishwoman to clean it, but I had come to appreciate that they themselves worked hard, chopping wood, potting plants, moving rocks, painting and decorating, in addition to their hobbies. In comparison, the *petit gîte* in the priory of Notre-Dame du Val-Paradis, with its two rooms and bathroom, where the winter sun streamed through the windows all day long, and the *poêle* stayed warm all night, seemed all that was necessary for a pleasant life.

BECKETT, BRECHT, KAFKA, ETC

While I was staying at Beduer, my English group usually drove over from Espagnac for our *séances*. We sat at the little kitchen table by the window that looked over the valley to the Camboulit steeple. Rolande knew the house, which once belonged to her cousin.

'It's different now,' she grinned, as she inspected the paintings and sculptures, the chandeliers and other antiques and *objets d'art* that Suzanne and Peter had filled it with.

Boris came one night too, for a separate English session.

'He's had a month to do this assignment,' said Martine over the phone. 'But he only started it last night. Could you help him?'

Martine dropped him off on her way from Figeac to a meeting in Espagnac. The assignment was based on an extract from Frank McCourt's memoir *'Tis*, describing one of Frank's early experiences in America. Boris wasn't interested in Frank's early experiences in America and the assignment question smacked to me of one of those questions where you had to interpret what the examiner really wants. Boris didn't have a clue what the examiner really wanted and cared less. My only direct experience of the French education system was the day I read to the children at the *maternelle* at Brengues. We did our best. Weeks later, when I asked Martine about the result, she couldn't bring herself to tell me.

The last English class before Christmas took place at the Pelaprats'. Charlie and I drove to Espagnac and parked, as usual, in the *cour*, then walked around to Jeanine and André's. I was the first to arrive.

Jeanine was beaming. From her window overlooking the road I saw Rolande parking her car, Christiane coming down the lane from her house and Solange descending her steps. They arrived at Jeanine's door all together, smiling bashfully.

'We've got a surprise for you,' said Jeanine.

Jeanine, with André's help, had composed a script over several nights, using what the class had learned over the previous eighteen months. Jeanine and André also provided a phonetic version and everyone had practised their parts. The script tells its own story:

> Hey! Friends! Maureen is leaving some weeks!
>
> Oh! Dear! And where is she going to?
>
> She goes to in Beduer, to look after dogs, during a week.
>
> Dogs?
>
> Yes, she loves them, very much.
>
> Then, one week near Béziers, and then one week in Paris; she will be for Christmas.
>
> She's always much busy!
>
> She's very active woman.
>
> But, it's holidays!
>
> She's really lucky to go in Paris.
>
> Charlie's also lucky! It will have got friends, this week.
>
> Oh! We miss her!
>
> She will even forget us!
>
> I have got an idea! We could give her a present for she'll think of us.
>
> And what? Chocolates! Good Christmas chocolates!
>
> No! There is too much sugar!
>
> And too much fat!
>
> There are too many calories!
>
> She has got some cholesterol! She's on a diet!
>
> Poor Maureen! She eats only salads without dressing.
>
> Not any chips! Not any crisps!
>
> Not any lamb, our good lamb of Quercy.

Not any pork! She went even Charlie on a diet!

She will starve to death! It's big problem for her!

Oh! No! She loves fruits, vegetables and pastas.

She doesn't take any exercise?

Yes, she does! Her favourite sport is running behind Charlie.

We can't find anywhere, for present?

I have an idea. Tell me! Does she like to look nice?

Yes! She's! Why do you ask that?

How about a pretty cloth?

I saw in shops nice tunics, a little stylish, a little modern.

She's still young!

How old is she?

I don't know. We don't ask her; that's a very personal question!

Let's buy her a tunic!

You're right, that's a good idea.

So, all right?

All right! That's a very nice present.

We like Maureen very much.

When she's not here, we miss her.

Maureen, comes again quickly. We like working with you!

Happy Christmas, Maureen! And long live English!

It wasn't Beckett, though it had an Absurd quality. It wasn't Brecht, or it would have had an edge of irony. I was deeply moved, not just by the words, the card and the tunic – a lee-tul stylish, a lee-tul mo-derne. Solange and Rolande would never use any of the English phrases they'd learned. Jeanine would, and Christiane might.

'Thank you,' I said, smiling through my tears.

'We got a colour that matches what you usually wear,' said Rolande, 'but you can change it, if you'd prefer another colour.'

'I won't change it. It's beautiful.'

As the script anticipated, Charlie and I spent a few days with Judy and David in the village near Béziers in Languedoc-Roussillon, where we had stayed with Florence the previous year. Then, on our return to Espagnac, he went to stay at Beduer while I went by train to Paris, as last year, to join the Wilsons for Christmas. Penny, craving sunshine and the beach, family and friends, had gone back to Australia for the holidays. Nicole took me to the station at Figeac and said she would park my car there on the day of my return.

On Boxing Day, which in France is treated as any working day, I phoned the export agent in Montmartre but, it seemed, he was unavailable all day. When at last I was able to speak to him in person, he said that his agency didn't actually manage the transportation of live animals and he didn't know any agency that did. I phoned Air France at Charles de Gaulle and after we had spoken at cross-purposes for a while, the person I spoke to said that it would be easier if I came to the airport.

I took the train to the airport and got directions from an information counter to the Air France office – another train, another bus. The office only dealt with human passengers. They gave me directions to another office that might provide services for animals. I took the same bus and train back to where I started from, then another bus to the address I'd been given. It wasn't actually Air France freight, but a call centre of an agency that dealt with several airline companies. A young man spent a long time poring over a list of airlines and flights and rejecting them for one reason and another. Some of the flights went to Sydney and some of them went to Melbourne but, frankly, for reasons he couldn't explain, it wouldn't be a good idea to send a dog on any of them. Then he gave me another address in the great labyrinth of freight terminals and I took another bus there. The bus drivers were starting to recognise me; maybe they thought I was an airport employee; anyway, they didn't ask me to pay a fare. I found a couple of people smoking outside the building I ended up at and they pointed to a lift and a staircase and

I went up into a deserted corridor. I made my way along the corridor, knocking on doors, opening them and, finding nobody, closing them again. Right at the end of the corridor was a man in an overcoat who looked as if he might have got there the same way I did. I told him why I was there and he said to wait. Then a woman and child came out of a nearby toilet, and he said something to her and she asked me to follow her. She led me to an office with a sign on the door: 'Vopak Logistics Management France'.

Of course, if Kafka had been writing this part of the story, there would have been no resolution, only endless frustration and angst.

'Stephanie Daum,' said the woman, shaking my hand. 'I'm in the *Département Alimentaire et Animaux Vivants*, the Food and Live Animals Department. This is my daughter. She's sick today. How can I help you?'

I gave Mme Daum an edited version of my quest. 'I'm so happy to have found you,' I concluded.

We looked at dates and the flight times. 'I loved working with Qantas because they knew all the Australian quarantine requirements,' she said. 'It's a shame they've stopped flying to Paris. Now it's either Singapore Airlines or Emirates.'

I opted for an Emirates flight because it was scheduled to arrive in Sydney during the quarantine station business hours, which would reduce the risk of Charlie having to stay in his cage for another night after the flight landed. The cost of his journey would be roughly double the cost of mine.

Charlie and I were back at the priory in time for the *repas de la Saint-Sylvestre*. Milou and Eric had already left Espagnac for the winter, and I wouldn't see them again till the following spring.

Alain and Bastien slung the *guy*, the mistletoe, on a rope over a roof beam. The walls were decorated with branches of holly and ivy and the tables in white and orange paper, with candles floating in bowls of water or sprouting from nests of holly and pine cones. There were masks and hats for the children.

The party began with the *apéritif*, champagne or whisky. The menu, each course accompanied by a suitable wine, retained the obligatory elements, the crustaceans, the *foie gras*, the *cabécou* and *Roquefort* cheeses. The *viande*, the meat, comprised two Rochefort *chapons*, now grown from the chicks whose emascualtion I had witnessed back in August to plump Christmas fare. The dessert comprised a *vacherin* - a rainbow of vanilla, raspberry, cream and meringue - and a cake that seemed to consist entirely of chocolate and honeycomb. The chocolate cake was another of Odette's creations, but again she was occupied with her *agriculteur*, and wasn't there to partake of it.

Between courses, as usual, everyone danced to music provided by Pierre Sommie in their own special styles: Christiane's angular twist, Martine Bagreaux and Pierre Sommie's reckless rock, Jocelyne Sommie's exotic freestyle, Martine and Alain Rochefort's sexy jig, Christiane's cousin Claude's solid, confident, sure rhythm and little Anaïs Soret's beaming shimmy. I danced too, as if I'd never had any inhibitions about it.

At midnight everyone danced around kissing everyone else and wishing *bonne année* and *plein de bonnes choses*, then it was back to the table to sing the New Year song:

Ceux qui sont nés au mois de janvier, fevrier, mars
Debout, debout, debout
Prenez votre verre à la main et buvez-le jusqu'à la fin
Prenez votre verre à la main et buvez-le jusqu'à la fin.

(Those born in January, February, March stand up. Pick up your glass and drain it.)

We were all back again the following evening to clear up, rocking and swinging to a compilation tape Pierre had made. Then we sat down to finish off the left-over oysters, prawns, *foie gras*, *chapon*, salad, cheese and *vacherin*, supplemented with pasta and sausages grilled over the fire. The children played circus in the labyrinth of furniture in the back room.

Charlie was uneasy in his role as a lion sitting on a stool; he didn't really understand the concept, and the sight and sound of the other 'animals' hissing and snarling and feinting unnerved him. He preferred to stay near the fire where he could keep an eye on the sausages.

BAL MASQUÉ

'We're going to have a *carnivale*,' said Martine, 'a *bal masqué* on the nineteenth of February.'

The date presented me with a problem. The week following the planned date of the *bal*, Charlie and I were going to Beduer to stay for a month, while Suzanne and Peter were in Africa. I was going to turn sixty on the sixteenth of February and I wanted to celebrate it by giving a lunch for all my friends in Espagnac on Saturday the nineteenth. I intended to ask Martine if I could borrow the *grand gîte* for my lunch. Now I would have to postpone it for at least two weeks, because the following Saturday, the twenty-sixth, there was the annual *repas chasse* at Espagnac. I asked Suzanne if she would mind if I gave a lunch for my *espagnacois* friends at Beduer on Saturday 5 March.

'Of course,' she said. 'But I'm sorry we'll miss your party.'

The *carnivale* created much excitement in the community, with everyone discussing or refusing to discuss how they were going to disguise themselves for the *bal*. Solange tried to find some of her mother's old clothes, so she could go as a *paysanne*, a peasant woman from the past.

'We must have thrown them away,' she said. '*Dommage.*'

Martine said she and Philippe might go as Adam and Eve.

'After all, we live in Val-Paradis,' she said. 'But it might be a bit cold in just fig leaves.'

'Then I could be a *serpent*,' I said. 'And Charlie could be a *pomme*.'

Suzanne went through her vast wardrobe and found me a black skirt and lace top, red shawl, red beads and a red half-mask and black lace doily to cover the lower half of my face. She also found some tarot cards, and I went to the *carnivale* as a fortune teller. Charlie would wear the *foulard* with the little aeroplanes and trains and trucks on it, that Sylvie at *Toutou chic* had given him the Christmas before last.

The morning of the *bal masqué*, Line came down on the early train from Paris, a big effort, because she was suffering from a heavy cold. She, Jacqueline and I had lunch together at Jacqueline's and spent the rest of the afternoon planning our trip to Barcelona in March.

I had only time to get back to my apartment and change into my gypsy costume before Maurice Chevalier (Jacqueline), an officer wearing a *casque colonial* (Jacqueline's grandson Joseph), a sick person in a beanie (Line) and Mireille (herself) arrived at the nuns' room. We went down to the *salle des fêtes* together.

The whole village was there, in more or less transparent disguise. France and Lucien wore red satin pyjamas and big conical hats, and Lucien had a painted-on Fu Manchu moustache. Mme and M. Bonzani and several others were dressed as *paysans*, in various combinations of overalls, bonnets, aprons and hats. Martine Rochefort was an *agriculteur* and Alain a milkmaid with a long blonde horsehair wig and a calf-length skirt and lisle stockings with socks over them. Pierre Sommie was Pierrot in a spotted blouse, striped pantaloons and a hat with a pompom. Pascale and Didier Cabrignac were in traditional dramatic *lotois* festival clothes: black trousers, black cape, black hat and red scarf. Natalie and Pierre Soret were clowns. Jeanine Pelaprat came as a kitten, her face having been painted by André, himself a sinister-looking Ali Baba figure. André had also done the make-up for a completely unrecognisable Bastien Bagreaux, a red-nosed clown in a spotted shirt and red pants over a potbelly. The other children were all disguised as *'Arry Potteur*, with cardboard swords wrapped in tinfoil. Jean-Claude Grosse was a court jester, and Ginette a medieval lady. René Cabrignac was a cardinal in a long purple raincoat with a red sash and black hat. Philippe and Martine Bagreaux were both *religieux*, he a priest with a *monseigneur's* hat and she a nun.

During the *apéritif* everyone played up their role. Alain Rochefort giggled and blushed and chewed his tough golden locks. 'Pierrot' Sommie greeted everyone in a high-pitched voice and waggled his bottom. Martine Rochefort went round the room slapping all the 'other' men on the back. Martine Bagreaux lowered her eyes modestly and spoke in a whisper. Philippe adopted the persona he kept up all night, of a drunken *curé*, lounging in the wall-niches and threatening to fart, especially after the *cassoulet*. I read palms and tarot cards and predicted long life and happiness for everyone.

After the *apéritif*, Jocelyne Sommie summoned everyone to gather round the table where Pierre's music system was set up. She took the microphone in one hand and my arm in the other.

'I'm afraid you aren't a very good fortune teller, Maureen,' she said, 'otherwise, you would have known that our *bal masqué* was itself a disguise for your birthday party. We've been planning it since last October.'

I didn't register most of what she said because I was so astonished. My face ached from smiling. Charlie, standing between us, looked up at the faces of his friends who all seemed to be looking back at him. His pompom fluttered contentedly.

'We've made up a song for you,' Jocelyne concluded. 'The tune is 'L'Auvergne', by Georges Brassens.'

While she was speaking, sheets of paper were passed around with the words, and then she conducted the assembly as they sang:

Elle est à toi, cette chanson,
Toi l'Australienne qui, sans façon,
Un beau matin de fevrier,
Dans la vallée est arrivée.

Avec ton grand copain, Charlie,
Venus tout droit de l'Australie,
Ton beau jardin fleuri quitta,
Très loin la-bas à Canberra.

A Espagnac-Sainte-Eulalie,
Tu t'es fait de nombreux amis,
A qui tu as appris l'anglais,
En échange de bon mots francais.

Tu as partagé leurs festins,
Leurs joies, leurs peines et leurs chagrins,
Tu as écrit leurs tranches de vie,
Le jour et la nuit.

Et si nous chantons aujourd'hui,
C'est pour toi et pour ton Charlie,
Ton fidele ami de huit ans,
Que tu aimes passionnément.

Et oui, c'est votre anniversaire,
Vous, deux amis célibataires,
Alors nous chantons tous en choer,
Ce p'tit refrain plein de bonheur ...

(This song is for you, the Australian who, without pretension, one fine February morning, came to the valley with your great companion, Charlie, leaving your lovely garden so far away in Canberra. At Espagnac-Sainte-Eulalie you've made many friends and taught them English in exchange for French. You've taken part in their feasts, joys and sorrows and day and night written snippets of their lives. And if we sing today, it's for you and Charlie, your beloved friend of eight years. Yes, it's your birthday, you two unmarried friends, and so we all sing this happy song … They then sang ''Appy birthday to you' in English.)

Somebody gave me some tissues to wipe away my tears, then we sat down for a *repas*: *potage, cassoulet, salade, fromage*, with the customary dancing between courses. Between the *cassoulet* and the *salade*, trying to swallow the lump in my throat, I made a little speech.

I said that my stay at Espagnac-Sainte-Eulalie had been one of the most important times of my life, which I would remember forever. Also that Charlie had had the best time here but he probably wouldn't remember it for as long as I would. I said that Espagnac-Sainte-Eulalie was like Brigadoon, but *heureusement*, fortunately, it was there every day, not just once every hundred years. I said that my French wasn't good enough to express how much I appreciated everything that people had done for us and how much I had learned from living among them. And, for that matter, my English wasn't good enough, *non plus*. At least, that's what I thought I said, but, really, the words didn't matter so much.

After more dancing and the *fromage*, the lights in the *salle des fêtes* were turned out and the children, under the guidance of gentle *Soeur Martine*, emerged from the door near the kitchen. They carried a board bearing an enormous *pièce montée*, a pyramid of profiteroles covered in toffee and nougat and pink and green plastic flowers and leaves and blue candles and a nougat plaque saying *Bon Anniversaire, Maureen et Charlie*. Then they gave me a painting of a view of the courtyard, arcade and *clocher* of Notre-Dame du Val-Paradis and Charlie an enormous bone. There was also a card, made by Eva Dubuisson, with loving messages on the inside and on the cover:

JOYEUX ANNIVERSAIRE

QUE CETTE SOIRÉE SOIT LE SOUVENIR DE VOTRE PASSAGE, AVEC
CHARLIE, A ESPAGNAC
QUE CELA SOIT LE TÉMOIGNAGE DE NOTRE AMITIÉ ET
DU GRAND BONHEUR QUE NOUS AURONS A NOUS RAPPELER
VOTRE PRÉSENCE PARMI NOUS

(May this evening mark your stay with Charlie in Espagnac, our friendship and our great happiness when we think of your presence among us.)

Two weeks later, at Beduer, I gave my lunch, with some help from my friends. When they came for the Tuesday morning *séance*, my English group sized up the seating situation and said that they would ask Martine if they could borrow tables and benches from the *commune*. They would also bring rolls of paper to cover the tables. Were there enough *couverts* in the house? An hour or so after they left, Rolande phoned to say the group had decided to take care of the desserts. I spent the two days before the party cooking the main dishes and the morning of the party preparing the food for the *apéritif* and the salads.

On the day, in the middle of a heavy fall of snow, twenty-five people arrived on the stroke of 12.30pm. The men swung into action with the tables they had brought, setting them out in the L-shaped foyer of the baronial house and covering them with white paper. The children played in the lounge room. The dogs dozed in the hearth. Pierre Sommie took over the program of music. Christiane Cabrignac started serving the *apéritifs*, which included the last of the bottles of Malvesia, the *frisante* white wine I'd brought back from Italy.

The first *plat* consisted of two lasagnas, one vegetarian, the other not, with a broccoli, feta and cherry tomato salad. Then the second *plat*, beef in orange sauce and a spinach, pine nut and pasta salad. Then a *salade verte* and *fromage*. Then the *petits fours* organised by my English group. At the end of the *repas*, everyone clapped and sang '*Elle a bien travaillé*, she's done a good job.'

A LITTLE FAX

May was a critical time in preparing Charlie for his flight back to Australia as that was the month various vaccinations and treatments had to be timed in relation to the day of his departure. Over the preceding months, I had versed and rehearsed Docteur Delmas, our vet in Figeac, on what had to be done. At first he was sanguine.

'We have many English clients, *madame*,' he said reassuringly.

'But this is Australia,' I said, 'it's different.'

I obtained a copy of the AQIS form that had a French translation interspersed with the requirements in English from the office of the Official Veterinarian of the Department at Cahors. Docteur Delmas seemed to be a bit daunted by the size of it. Together, we plotted the dates for each action and marked them on a working copy of the form. As time went on, whenever Charlie and I appeared at the glass door of the *Clinique Vétérinaire*, Docteur Delmas's confident air transformed to one of concern and, eventually, to an anxiety that almost matched mine.

My angst was complicated by the fact that the timing for the final blood tests for leptospirosis and ehrlichiosis coincided with a trip I had planned with an Australian friend to Eastern Europe. Not only did Charlie have no inkling of my plans for him, he didn't know that I was going to desert him at this crucial moment, either. He would be staying with Suzanne and Peter. Suzanne assured me she would take him to Docteur Delmas on the day his blood samples needed to be drawn. She marked the date in her diary.

'Don't worry,' she said. 'We'll make sure poor Charlie gets his blood tested.'

There seemed to be no reason to keep the nuns' room during the trip to Eastern Europe. When I returned, there would be just enough time to get the last AQIS document signed at Cahors and drive Charlie to Paris for his flight. Sue Wilson, my English friend from Marcilhac, was going to buy the little Ford and, because she would be doing another leg of the Chemin de Saint-Jacques when I got back from Eastern Europe, would lend it back to me for the trip to Paris. After Charlie's departure, I would return to the Lot with the car, say goodbye to all my friends there and leave the car with Hilary and Steve at Autejac for Sue to collect when she returned to Marcilhac.

'You must stay with us when you get back,' said Suzanne.

And so I spent a week in the nuns' room packing up all my memorabilia, books, CDs and papers, including the notes and research for *Blue and Brown*. I dispatched twenty post boxes to Canberra and set about cleaning the apartment. On the last day, which Charlie spent in the *mairie* until Martine went home, I vacuumed and scrubbed, not even trying to hold back my tears. All that day, rain battered the newly-cleaned windows and infused the air inside with a raw chill. We left the priory, as we had arrived, in the dark.

Two weeks later, I phoned Suzanne from Vienna to check if everything had gone to plan with Charlie's preparations.

'We had to take him to Docteur Delmas twice,' she said. 'He didn't take enough blood the first time. He had to get enough to go to two different laboratories. The one that does the *leptospirose* is in Nantes, but the one that does the *ehrlichiose* is in the Alpes-Maritimes. Charlie didn't like it at all.'

'I could imagine,' I said. 'I'm so sorry, Suzanne.'

'Yes,' she said, 'he put up a good fight. He was very strong.'

In another two weeks, when I arrived back at Suzanne and Peter's house in Beduer an email from Stephanie Daum was waiting for me: 'Emirates have just told me they won't send your dog via Dubai. They had a problem last week with a dog going to Australia and now they've got an embargo. So we'll have to send him by Singapore Airlines.'

She had made a booking with Singapore Airlines for the day following the original date. She also sent directions for getting to the Vopak office at the airport by car and instructed me to deliver Charlie at 8am on the day of departure. There the Official Government Veterinarian would complete the export requirements. Charlie's plane would leave at 12.25pm.

And so, in the little silver Ford that now belonged to Sue Wilson, Charlie made his second and last trip to Paris, where we stayed for two nights with Line at Saint-Maur. Line organised a program of outings, to distract the attention of at least one of her visitors from what was about to happen. The first evening she took us to a cliff above the river, a kind of natural belvedere, where we sat, Charlie between Line and me, gazing across the Marne to the City of Light in the distance, the twinkling frame of the *Tour Eiffel* clearly visible.

'And will you be pleased to see all your old friends in Australia, Charlie?' said Line, ruffling his wool.

I had timed his last visit to *Toutou chic* so that he would have enough coat to weather the mild Sydney winter. When we had left the *salon* for the last time, Sylvie was still crying in the doorway as I turned to wave a last goodbye from the car.

'And your own house, and your beautiful garden, and the beach at the coast?' Line went on.

'I wish I had two lives,' I said, 'one here in France and one there.'

Line put her hand on mine. 'You know, Maureen, what impresses me? That you dared to leave the life you were used to and come here, not knowing what would happen.'

'That was partly why I did it, to experience something completely new. And I have learned so much, not just about the village and the country but also about myself. It hasn't all been easy or simple but it has been the most fulfilling time, the *point culminant*, the highlight, of my life.'

The second evening, Charlie's last in France, after dinner the three of us walked under the trees along the Marne, listening to the lapping of the water, our way lit by the moonbeams skipping among the ripples.

Before going to bed, dry-eyed, I checked the export documents, to make sure they were all in order, because we were leaving for the airport early in the morning, and there would be no time to do it then. Certificate A – the fourteen-page document that Docteur Delmas had, with a sigh of relief, completed and the Official Veterinarian of the Department at Cahors had endorsed – identified Charlie by his microchip number, attested his residency in France, detailed his rabies and other vaccinations, the treatments for internal and external parasites, and the blood tests; the laboratory reports on the blood tests from Haute-Garonne (rabies), the Ecole Nationale Vétérinaire at Nantes (leptospirosis), and the Laboratoire Vétérinaire Départmentale des Alpes-Maritimes (ehrlichiosis). The dates of the blood samples were also recorded on Certificate A. The dates of the blood samples on the laboratory reports …

'Line …' I said quietly.

Driving across Paris at 7am is not as nerve-racking as it would be at most other times of the day or night, especially when your navigator is a *Parisienne* and you have clear directions to where you are going. But when your little dog is standing on the back seat, excited to be going on another adventure, oblivious to the implications of the blue-and-white cage next to him, and to the disquieting contents of the envelope lying on the navigator's lap, there is a certain tension.

The Vopak office was locked. Line, Charlie and I floated around the corridors and staircases like wraiths until a young man burst into view around 8.30am. We followed him into the office and I asked if Mme Daum would be in soon.

'*Sans doute*,' he replied, 'probably.'

'My dog is leaving for Australia at midday,' I said. 'At least …'

I started to explain the problem with the documents, speaking slowly and feigning calmness. 'The vet had to take two samples of blood on different days and that's what he's recorded on the certificate that the Departmental vet certified, but the certificates from the laboratories say that all the blood was taken on the same day, and I'm worried that the Australian authorities won't accept that and they might keep my dog in quarantine and do all the blood tests again.'

The young man made an effort to listen, but it was clear he was preoccupied with other matters. I had to keep suspending my long explanation because his mobile phone kept ringing. Evidently he was responsible for a shipment of some birds to somewhere in the Middle East.

Stephanie Daum, her voice buried under a blanket of flu, arrived at last. I showed her the documents. She grimaced, blew her nose, made a husky phone call and told us to go with 'Bertrand'.

'Should I pay you now?' I asked.

'Afterwards,' she croaked.

Bertrand, a young man with red curls and a wide smile, came into the office clutching a bottle of water in one hand. He picked up Charlie's cage and led us along a corridor, down some steps and into a van that smelled of burning rubber and spent fuel. He drove us at breakneck speed, Charlie bracing himself between Line and me, to another building about 500 metres from the Vopac building where we followed him up a concrete stairwell into a large room with a fish tank at one end. The room, furnished with a vast table and several chairs, smelled strongly of animals. Posters on the walls depicted birds and animals and gave warnings about what might go wrong with them.

Bertrand disappeared. Line and I sat on chairs on one side of the table, watching the fish swimming slowly around the tank and pursing their mouths on the glass, waiting for something to happen. Charlie stood stiffly beside my chair, sniffing the air tentatively. Perhaps he sensed something in the atmosphere, or perhaps he picked up something from me, consumed as I was with anxiety and guilt.

At last a door on the other side of the room opened and a young woman in a lab coat entered, extending her hand with a smile. This was the Official Government Veterinarian. I passed the envelope containing the documents over the table to her. While she was checking Charlie's microchip number I told her about the discrepancies in the dates on the certificates.

'I believe the blood was taken on the dates Docteur Delmas wrote on the Certificate. I don't know how important it is.'

'*C'est l'Australie*,' she said seriously. '*Qu'est-ce qu'on peut faire*, what can we do?'

'Perhaps you could telephone Docteur Delmas,' I suggested. It would be too complicated to track down the staff at the laboratories at Nantes and in the Alpes-Maritimes.

She put the phone on speaker mode.

'*Qu'est-ce qu'on peut faire?*' came the familiar, troubled voice over the line.

I was too upset to follow the conversation closely, as they worked their way, with Gallic determination, towards a solution. I felt sorry for Docteur Delmas, whose satisfaction I'd shared two days ago as, smiling, he placed the *point* after his signature on the Certificate.

'Could you then send me *un petit fax, Docteur?*' the OGV concluded.

'*Bien sûr, Docteur,*' replied Docteur Delmas.

The OGV suggested that we take Charlie outside to relieve himself, while she completed her documentation. There was a weedy tract of ground across the road from the building and Charlie knew immediately what it was for and took full advantage.

'Good boy,' I said because, as well as everything else, I'd been worrying about that aspect of his comfort during the journey.

When we went back upstairs, all that was left for the OGV to do was to see Charlie into his cage, tape a copy of the documents to it and seal it with a special tool she had for the purpose. I had a vision of Martine and the tool she couldn't remember the name of, for sealing dead people in their coffins.

Bertrand reappeared, still holding the bottle of water. He also now had a sheet of paper in his other hand. He took a roll of tape from the table and taped the paper to the cage. It said, in English:

MY NAME IS CHARLIE. I AM A GOOD DOG.

Bertrand picked up the cage and we followed him downstairs to the van again, where he put the cage in the back. Line and I got into the cabin and we shot off once more, this time arriving at the loading dock where Bertrand deposited Charlie's cage on a wooden palette. Tears began to well in my eyes. I squatted precariously on my wonky knees and spoke to Charlie through the grille.

'It won't be long, little darling. Only a month. Be brave. I'll pick you up at the quarantine station and we'll go straight to the beach.'

He looked happy and confident, the way Docteur Delmas used to look before we started this business.

While I was saying goodbye to Charlie, Bertrand took the water bottle I had already attached to the cage and filled it from the bottle he had been carrying around all morning. Then, as I straightened up, he stroked my shoulder, while a small forklift vehicle emerged from the back of the loading dock and lifted the palette off the concrete. I saw Charlie's little body lurch and his head move distractedly from side to side. The vehicle disappeared into the recesses of the dock. My tears, dammed for so long, spilled out. I turned around into Line's waiting arms and we both began sobbing.

GLOSSARY

Letters in brackets show feminine form of word
Words divided by a '/' show masculine and feminine forms of word

à point
medium (cooking term)

À ta santé!
To your health!

Aînés Ruraux
association for rural senior citizens

ancien(ne)
former

animateur/animatrice
compere, master of ceremonies

auberge
inn

bal masqué
masked ball

bar-tabac
bar that also sells tobacco products

bassin
small lake

Bâtiments de France
government department responsible for
the maintenance of historic monuments

Beaux-Arts
a style of architecture, euphemism for the
Bâtiments de France

belle-soeur
sister-in-law

bien sûr
certainly, of course

blason
coat-of-arms

Bon anniversaire!
Happy birthday!

Bonne soirée!
Enjoy your evening!

brebis
ewe; cheese made from ewe's milk

brocante
second-hand market

Ça va?/Comment ça va?/Ça va
question meaning 'How are things?'
and answer meaning 'OK' or 'Fine'

cabane à poulets
henhouse

cabécou
small round cheese made from
goat's milk

canapé-lit
sofa bed

caniche
poodle

casque colonial
helmet worn in the past by French
colonists in tropical climates

causse
limestone plateau

caussenade du Lot
type of sheep farmed in the
Lot Department

cave
cellar

cazelle
shepherd's shelter constructed of stone

célibataire
single or unmarried person

c'est tout!
that's all!

C'est vrai?
Is that true?

chapon
capon, desexed cock

chaponnage
surgical process for desexing a cock

charcuterie
processed meat, including pork, ham, paté and sausage; a shop that sells these products

chasse en battue
form of hunting where dogs are used

chasseur
hunter

cheminée
fireplace

chênes des causses
oak trees of the limestone plateaus

chevreuil
deer, venison

chez moi/toi/vous/eux
my/your/their place

choucroute
sauerkraut served with different kinds of sausage, ham and bacon

clocher
bell-tower, steeple

comme d'habitude
as usual

comme il faut
properly or done as it should be

Comment dire...?
How do you say...?

composter
to have one's train ticket stamped

conseil municipal
local council

copin(e)
friend, boyfriend/girlfriend

côtelette
lamb or pork chop

coup
successful attempt

cour
courtyard

croquette
dry dog or cat food in pellet form

cuisinier(ère)
cook, chef

curé
parish priest

de trop
too much

déjeuner
lunch

demi-monde
class of women supported by wealthy lovers in the nineteenth century

Desolé(e)
I'm sorry

digérer
to digest

dolmen
prehistoric communal tomb

Dommage!
What a pity!

eau de vie
plum brandy

écrivain
writer

EDF (Électricité de France)
French electricity company

église
church

en fait
actually, as a matter of fact

en forme
fit, healthy

épi
ear of grain; a symbol of quality; a roof decoration

épicerie
grocer's shop

et ainsi de suite
and so forth

falaise
cliff

festin
feast, banquet

fonctionnaire
government employee

Formidable!
Fantastic!

four au pain
bread oven

fromage
cheese

Génial!
Great!

gésiers
giblets

gibier
animal being hunted, carcass of
animal after being hunted

giboulées de mars
April showers (in France are in March)

gîte
holiday accommodation, such as
a cottage or apartment

gîte d'étape
overnight accommodation

gouffre
sinkhole

grand(e)
large

grange
shed, barn

grenier
loft, originally for storing grain

grippe
influenza

gros(se)
fat, big

Hé!
Hey!

igue
local term for a sinkhole

il va geler
it's going to freeze

jamais
never

jambon
ham

jardinière de legumes
mixed vegetables

je m'appelle...
my name is...

je vous présente...
let me introduce...

jeune
young

journée communale
day when the community works on
common projects around the village

l'heure de l'apéritif
cocktail hour

La Saint-Sylvestre
New Year's Eve

la voie lactée
the Milky Way

lauzes
roof tiles cut from stone

lavoir
communal laundry

lotois
person or thing from the Lot Department

lycée
senior high school

magret
fillet of duck breast

maire
mayor

mairie
local council which provides many
administrative and community functions

mais
but

maman
mum

marché fermier
farmers' market

maternelle
preschool

merci beaucoup
many thanks

Merde!
Shit!

Ministre de la culture et du patrimoine
Ministry of Culture and Heritage

monument historique
historic monument

non plus
either, as in 'I don't like it, either'

normand(e)
person or thing from Normandy

nuit folle
wild night

oeuvre
body of work, usually used for a writer

orage
storm

pain de campagne
country-style bread

parce que
because

parc naturel
nature reserve

Pas de problème!
No problem!

paso doblé
flamenco-style dance imitating a bullfight

pauvre
poor, unfortunate

paysan(ne)
peasant, farmer

pelouses sèches
dry grasses

pétanque
game, similar to lawn bowls, played
with steel balls

petit pain
bread roll

pied noir
French people who settled in Algeria
during the colonial period

pigeonnier
dovecote

place
village or town square

plat
course (in a meal)

poêle
fuel-burning stove for heating
and cooking

point
full stop

Politique agricole commune (PAC)
European Union's common
agricultural policy

portable
mobile phone

pot au feu
stew of beef and vegetables

potage
hearty soup

potager
kitchen garden

pourboire
tip for service rendered

Préfecture
administrative centre of a Department

primaire
primary school

producteur/productrice
producer of commodities

professe
a nun who has taken final vows

prune
plum, also a liqueur made from plums

putain
a very strong expletive

relais
inn where coaches would stop
for refreshment

repas
meal

repas de chasse
dinner that features meat from the hunt

réunion
meeting of an association

roman
novel, book

rond-point
roundabout (on a road)

rue du Circle
Circle Street

salade composée
mixed salad

salade verte
green salad

salle
room

salle des fêtes
function room

salon
living room

sanglier
wild boar

sans doute
no doubt, probably

saucisse
thin pork sausage (cooked)

saucisson
thick pork sausage (cooked)

savoyard(e)
person or thing from the Savoie or
Haute Savoie Departments

séance
session, meeting

seigneur
member of the nobility

sensible
sensitive (describing a person or animal)

sentier
path

Si!
Oh yes!, used to affirm something
that has been doubted or denied

soirée non stop
very busy romantic evening

somptueux/somptueuse
luxurious

source
natural spring

sous-préfecture
secondary administrative centre
of a Department

toilettage
grooming (of a dog)

tour
tower

toutou
doggie

villageois(e)
villager, villagers

vin à discretion
as much wine as you want

vin de pays
local wine

Voilà!
There! There you are!

volets
window shutters

vrai
true